COLLINS GEM
BASIC FACTS

BRITISH AND INTERNATIONAL
HISTORY
1900—1985

J.R. Thackrah MA

C O L L I N S
London and Glasgow

First published 1985
New edition 1988

© Wm. Collins Sons & Co. Ltd. 1985, 1988

ISBN 0 00 459107 0

Printed in Great Britain by Collins, Glasgow

INTRODUCTION

Basic Facts is a new generation of Gem dictionaries in important school subjects. They cover all the important ideas and topics in these subjects up to the level of first examinations.

British and International History 1900–1985 includes, as the title implies, all significant events from the beginning of 1900 to the end of 1985. After 1985, generally the only dates included are where somone has died or has ceased to hold office. Population statistics are given for 1980 unless otherwise stated.

Where a word appears in SMALL CAPITALS, that word is developed further in a separate entry. This cross-referencing system enables the reader to make connections between related entries, and to find further relevant information where required.

ABBREVIATIONS USED IN THE TEXT

Note: abbreviations of organizations, countries, etc. (e.g. EEC, USA) appear as entries in the text, and are cross-referred to the entries for which they are abbreviations (e.g. European Economic Community, United States of America).

c.	circa, about, approximately
C	central
Cap	capital
cent.	century, centuries
C-in-C	commander-in-chief
Con.	Conservative
Dem.	Democrat, Democratic (Party)
E	east
esp.	especially
Fr.	French (language)
Ger.	German (language)
incl.	including, include, included
km	kilometres
Lab.	Labour
Lib.	Liberal
MP	member of parliament
N	north
orig.	originally
PM	prime minister
Pop	population
RC	Roman Catholic
Rep.	Republican (Party)
Russ.	Russian (language)
S	south
Span.	Spanish (language)
sq km	square kilometres
W	west
WWI	World War One
WWII	World War Two

A

Abdication Crisis, constitutional crisis that arose in 1936 when Edward VIII wished to marry Wallis Simpson, an American divorcee, and chose to renounce the throne (abdicate) in favour of his brother, George VI. The British and Dominion Governments considered his intention of marrying the lady incompatible with his position as monarch and head of the Church of England.

Abyssinia, *see* ETHIOPIA.

Accession, Treaty of, treaty signed in Brussels in 1972 by the 6 members of the EEC, plus Denmark, the Irish Republic, Norway and the UK. The Treaty concerned the accession of these 4 new members to the EEC and the European Atomic Energy Community. The countries were obliged to hold referendums, as a result of which Norway refused to join.

Acheson, Dean (1893–1971), US Secretary of State (1949–53). An advocate of the Western alliance, he assisted in the formulation of UNRRA (1945), the TRUMAN DOCTRINE (1947), and the MARSHALL PLAN (1948). He also secured ratification of the North Atlantic Treaty (1949) and the commitment of US troops to NATO (1951).

Action Française, right-wing political, royalist, Catholic, anti-Semitic, and later, Fascist movement founded in 1898 by the poet and political journalist, Charles Maurras (1868–1952). During WWII it supported the VICHY GOVERNMENT and was dissolved in 1944, Maurras being imprisoned for collaboration.

Act of Parliament, a formally codified result of deliberation by a legislative body. In the UK, an Act of Parliament results from a bill (a proposed piece of legislation) being approved by both Houses of Parliament; it becomes statute law when it receives the royal assent.

Aden, capital of the People's Democratic Republic of Yemen. It was a British possession (1839–1967), but with a decline in importance after WWII became (1963) part of the South Arabian Federation of Arab Emirates. It was overrun by the National Liberation Front (NLF) in 1967. The NLF was the victor in a civil war with the Front for the Liberation of South Yemen (FLOSY), and took over the country coincidentally with the departure of the British from Aden.

Adenauer, Konrad (1876–1967), German statesman, first Chancellor of the Federal German Republic (1949–63), Foreign Minister (1951–55), and founder (1945) and leader of the CDU party (*see* CHRISTIAN DEMOCRATS). He dominated West German politics and was responsible for the integration of his country into strong Atlantic and European alliances, as a partner and not a former enemy. He was also responsible for reconciliation with France, and for recognition of Nazi crimes against the Jews.

Afghanistan, republic of SC Asia. Area: 636,000 sq km. Pop: 15,500,000. Languages: Pushtu, Persian. Religion: Islam. Cap: Kabul.

The country has long been a prey to foreign intrigue owing to its geo-strategic importance, standing as it does between Russia and India and the oil-rich Gulf states. The country's history in the

20th cent. has been turbulent, with the tribes violently resisting any form of centralized government as foreign domination.

The monarchy was overthrown in 1973, and since then government has been unstable. Fighting developed between the Moslem fundamentalist tribal groups and the pro-Soviet regime, and in 1979 the USSR invaded Afghanistan in order to consolidate its tenuous position. Since then the Soviets have been fighting a massive guerrilla war against the rebels. The Soviet invasion was one of the principal factors in the breakdown of DÉTENTE.

African, Caribbean and Pacific States (ACP), *see* LOMÉ CONVENTIONS.

African National Congress (ANC), founded (1912) in South Africa to unify African opinion and to draw white attention to the problems of blacks by demonstrations, deputations and overseas delegations. The leaders were mainly Christian, middle-class, and Western-educated, and believed constitutional advance could be made by argument and passive resistance rather than violence.

After WWII the movement became more violent in response to the repressive measures adopted by successive governments and in 1960 it was banned. Guerrilla activity associated with the movement is now common in South Africa.

African nationalism, a prime force in the political awakening of Africa, and in the rebellion of its peoples against colonial rule. An important element was the development among the native populations of a sense of identity as black Africans rather than as subjects of colonial powers, and this was combined with a determination to achieve independence.

As Africans came into contact with Europeans they realized the gap between colonial policies and Western political ideas such as democracy and freedom. The European policy of racial discrimination and separation, as evidenced in land apportionment, politics and education, naturally exasperated native Africans. Conditions of life did not necessarily improve for the natives and in some cases deteriorated as a result of European colonialism. Isolated rebellions took place against European colonization and rule. Notwithstanding their political differences, the African nations conceived of themselves as united in the struggle against 'white colonialism' and sought a distinctive third alternative, influenced by socialism, between East and West.

Forty nations in Africa became independent between 1956 and 1975. The adjustment of pre-industrial living conditions to the modern world became a major task — but hindrances incl. tribal factions, political instability and grave socio-economic problems, which led to demands for development aid.

Agadir, port in SW Morocco which became the centre of an international crisis (1911) with the arrival of the German gunboat *Panther*, ostensibly to protect German nationals and commercial interests, but in fact intended to counteract what Germany thought was French expansionist policy in Morocco in contravention of the Conference of ALGECIRAS. In the end Germany recognized French rights in Morocco in exchange for territory in the Congo, and the *Panther* was withdrawn. The incident alarmed Britain, which feared the establishment of a German base close to Gibraltar and vital trade routes, and a strong warning was issued to Germany.

Aitken, William Maxwell, 1st Baron Beaverbrook (1879–1964), Canadian newspaper magnate and champion of British imperialism. He emigrated to England in 1910, became a Conservative MP and helped to bring Lloyd George to power as PM in 1916. He was noted for his individualism and dynamism in the interwar years, which impressed Churchill during WWII. He served as Minister of Aircraft Production (1940–41), Minister of Supply (1941–42) and Lord Privy Seal (1943–45).

Alamein, *see* NORTH AFRICAN CAMPAIGNS.

Albania, republic of SE Europe. Area: 28,748 sq km. Pop: 2,750,000 (est.). Language: Albanian. Religions: Islam, Eastern Orthodox (prior to 1967), now atheist. Cap: Tirana.

Albania became an Islamic independent principality (1912) after more than 4 cents. of Turkish rule. A republic was established (1925) and Ahmed Bey Zogu became President with the anomalous title of King Zog I. The country was economically dependent on Italy, which occupied it in 1939, deposing Zog.

After Italy's defeat in WWII a Communist republican government was established (1946). Albania was a member of the COUNCIL FOR MUTUAL ECONOMIC ASSISTANCE and the WARSAW PACT but was expelled from the former (1961) because it sided with China in the SINO-SOVIET SPLIT and for what the USSR considered to be its deviationist policies. Albania withdrew from the Warsaw Pact (1968) because it disagreed with the policy of interference in CZECHOSLOVAKIA. It was economically and ideologically linked with China from 1968 to 1978, when the association was terminated by China.

Al Fatah, the Palestine National Liberation Movement. Fatah (Arabic for 'conquest') was the first Palestinian guerrilla organization set up to liberate Palestine from Israeli occupation. Syria has provided arms, money and training facilities. Its leader is Yasser ARAFAT. *See also* PALESTINE LIBERATION ORGANIZATION.

Algeciras, Conference of (1906), international meeting called to discuss the internal government of Morocco. The resulting Algeciras Act pledged Franco-Spanish respect for Morocco's independence but permitted both nations jointly to police the country under a Swiss inspector-general.

During the last decade of the 19th cent. the nominally independent empire of Morocco was in decay and France and Spain wished to open it for economic development and participate in the internal running of the country.

The ENTENTE CORDIALE (1904) was strengthened by British support of the settlement, which also had the backing of Italy and Russia against Germany's opposition.

Algeria, republic of NW Africa. Area: 2,381,745 sq km. Pop: 20,200,000 (1983). Language: Arabic. Religion: Islam. Cap: Algiers.

The country was colonized by the French during the 19th cent. While settlers enjoyed most of the privileges of citizens of France, the indigenous population had practically none, and it was not until after WWII that promises were made of political and social equality. These were slow to materialize and provided reason for a rising tide of nationalism among the native population which culminated in a revolution (1954—62) waged by the National Liberation Front (NLF) in the form of guerrilla warfare.

During the independence struggle a factor intervened that ultimately led to the destruction of the Fourth Republic in France (1958). The French officers fighting in Algeria suspected that the French Government would negotiate a settlement with the FLN, and by their insistence on keeping Algeria French they and the settlers brought down the Government. They also went some way to repeating matters with the Fifth Republic when the Secret Army Organization (OAS) under General Salan (1899—1984) on several occasions attempted to assassinate DE GAULLE. The OAS ceased to function when its leaders either dispersed or were captured.

Eventually the way was clear for independence, and this was achieved in 1962. The first President was BEN BELLA who was deposed in 1965 by Colonel Boumédienne (1925—78), a left-wing socialist whose repressive regime and intransigence towards Algeria's neighbours only ceased with his death. His successor, Bendjedid Chadli, restored better relations with neighbouring states and France.

Allende, Salvador (1908—73), Chilean statesman. A co-founder of the Chilean Socialist Party, in 1970 he became the world's first democratically elected Marxist head of state. Allende tried to establish a socialist society while maintaining parliamentary government, but was increasingly opposed by business interests supported by the CIA. Industrial unrest, followed by strike action and violence in 1972—73, prompted a right-wing military coup, during which he died.

Alliance, the, *see* SOCIAL DEMOCRATIC PARTY, LIBERAL PARTY.

Alsace-Lorraine, region of NE France. Area: 14,522 sq km. Ceded to Germany by the Treaty of Frankfurt (1871) after the French defeat in the Franco-Prussian War (1870—71), it was restored to France after WWI by the Treaty of VERSAILLES (1919). From 1871 to 1914 it was the major source of embittered Franco-German relations, largely due to the prosperity engendered by rapid industrial expansion, esp. steel manufacture. During WWII it was under German occupation (1940—45).

Amin, Idi (1926—), Ugandan political leader. In 1971 he led a military coup while President Obote was abroad, proclaimed himself head of state, and dissolved parliament. His tyrannical regime led to the extermination of numerous opponents. Most Asians and many British were expelled in 1972 and their business interests confiscated. He was Chairman of the OAU (1975—76). In 1979 President Obote regained power in a military coup supported by Tanzanian forces, and Amin went into exile.

Amritsar, city of NW Punjab, India, centre of the Sikh religion. In 1919, 379 people were killed and over 1,200 wounded when British troops opened fire on unarmed supporters of Indian self-government. The Indian nationalist movement was strengthened by the subsequent outrage.

In 1984, Sikh separatist extremists took refuge in the Sikh Golden Temple and were defeated after heavy fighting with government troops. Shortly afterwards, Indira GHANDI was assassinated by 2 of her Sikh bodyguards.

anarchism, a political doctrine that all forms of authority interfere with individual freedom and that government and the state should be replaced by freely associating communities.

Modern anarchist theories developed in the 19th cent. Anarchists have proposed differing strategies for achieving their ends, varying from violent direct action to passive resistance or civil disobedience. Although Lenin believed the state must ultimately wither away, leaving a voluntary regime without class or government, anarchists have generally opposed all state systems, whether capitalist or Communist.

Anarchist movements were politically significant in Russia, France, Italy and Spain at various times in the late 19th and early 20th cents., and were particularly prominent on the Republican side in the SPANISH CIVIL WAR. Anarchist ideas were revived by student activists in the 1960s, but have failed to gain widespread support.

ANC, see AFRICAN NATIONAL CONGRESS.

Andropov, Yuri Vladimirovich (1914−84), Soviet statesman. Head of the KGB (1967−82), then General Secretary of the Communist Party (1982−84) and President of the USSR (1983−84).

Anglo-French Entente, see ENTENTE COR-DIALE.

Anglo-German Naval Agreement (1935), permitted Germany to construct a fleet to 35% of the Commonwealth's strength, except for submarines, which could be up to equal tonnage but should not exceed 45% of the Commonwealth total without prior notice to the UK. The agreement effectively encouraged Germany to infringe the Treaty of VERSAILLES.

Anglo-Irish Agreement (1985), agreement that provides for consultation between the British and Irish governments over Northern Ireland. It has been bitterly opposed by ULSTER LOYALISTS.

Anglo-Russian Entente (1907), an agreement designed to forestall German influence in the Middle East and attempts to undermine Anglo-Russian friendship. It also provided for the division of Persia (Iran) into spheres of influence; that Tibet be maintained as a buffer state under a degree of Chinese control; that Afghanistan be recognized as of special British interest; and that Russia could control the Bosphorus and the Dardanelles subject to other powers' agreement. *See also* TRIPLE ENTENTE.

Angola, republic of SW Africa, formerly the colony of Portuguese West Africa. Area: 1,247,000 sq km. Pop: 7,100,000 (est. 1983). Cap: Luanda. The country has rich mineral resources.

Civil uprisings in the 1960s were repressed, but the country achieved independence in 1975 following the change of government in Portugal. Civil war followed between the various liberation movements, principally the Marxist-Leninist MPLA and the South-African backed UNITA. With Soviet aid and the assistance of Cuban troops the MPLA achieved victory in 1976, though guerrilla warfare continues.

Anschluss, term referring to the political union of Austria and Germany, in effect 1938—45. Hitler's plans for union were checked in 1934 when Mussolini sent troops to the Brenner Pass to safeguard Austria's independence. By 1937 Mussolini was in the Axis camp and Hitler was able to put pressure on Chancellor SCHUSCHNIGG to legalize the Austrian Nazi Party. The Party stirred up unrest and in 1938 Hitler demanded that Schuschnigg postpone a planned plebiscite to determine Austria's future. Schuschnigg resigned and the Nazi SEYSS-INQUART became Chancellor. He invited the Germans to occupy the country and restore order. A plebiscite favoured formal union as the 'Greater Germany'.

Anti-Comintern Pact, an agreement between Germany and Japan (1936) declaring their hostility to international Communism. Italy joined the Pact in 1937; Hungary and Spain in 1939.

anti-Semitism, persecution of or descrimination against Jews. In Europe, insistence on religious conformity often concealed envy of Jewish commercial success. Racist prejudice was evident esp. in France, Germany and Tsarist Russia.

From the 1920s the Nazis represented the Jews as a scapegoat for every misfortune that had befallen Germany. A theory of an 'Aryan master race' was developed, though without any scientific basis. In the Nuremberg Laws (1935), Jews were forbidden to marry 'Aryan' Germans and denied German citizenship. Between 1939 and 1945 the Nazis killed more than one third of the total Jewish population of the world: over 6 million Jews died in CONCENTRATION CAMPS.

Since 1945, hostility towards the state of ISRAEL and ZIONISM, esp. in the USSR, has been seen as veiled anti-Semitism.

Antonescu, Ion (1882–1946), Romanian general and dictator, closely associated with the Iron Guard Fascist movement. In 1940, he became leader of a right-wing government and proclaimed himself 'Conducator', allying his country with the Axis powers in WWII. Heavy Romanian losses in the USSR undermined his position and he was executed in 1946.

ANZUS Pact, a tripartite security treaty concluded between Australia, New Zealand and the USA in 1951. It provided for collaboration should any of the countries be a victim of an armed attack in the Pacific area. For Australia and New Zealand the Pact meant a lessening of their dependence upon the UK and a closer collaboration with the USA. However, following New Zealand's adoption of a non-nuclear defence strategy in 1984, the USA has refused to cooperate with New Zealand on defence matters.

apartheid, the official South African government policy of racial segregation and 'separate development'.

In 1960 the introduction of identity cards for non-whites and the suspension of their parliamentary representation was followed by widespread demonstrations, often violently suppressed — as at SHARPEVILLE. Other aspects of the laws which have aroused hostility around the world and at the UN incl. segregated education, a prohibition of mixed marriages, and deportation of blacks from specified districts.

The policy of 'separate development' led to the Bantu Self-Government Act, which provided for the establishment of 7 native African areas with non-white chief ministers, e.g. the Transkei in 1963; these self-governing territories later became autonomous, though not widely recognized as such internationally. South Africa left the Commonwealth in 1961 rather than modify its apartheid policies. *See* SOUTH AFRICA.

appeasement, a form of foreign policy seeking to avert war by making concessions to a potential enemy. Such a policy was unsuccessfully adopted by British and French governments towards Germany between 1936 and 1939. *See also* RHINELAND, MUNICH AGREEMENT.

Arab-Israeli Wars, a series of conflicts, culminating 4 times (1948, 1956, 1967, 1973) in outright war between Israel and Arab countries over the existence in Palestine of the Independent Jewish state of Israel.

The 1948 War The proclamation of the state of Israel (1948) led to the immediate invasion by neighbouring Arab states, which was successfully resisted by Israel. The UN intervened and in 1949 established an armistice treaty: Jerusalem was partitioned, the WEST BANK became Jordanian, and the GAZA STRIP Egyptian.

The 1956 War As a result of Nasser's anti-Israeli Pan-Arab policy and Egyptian nationalization of the Suez Canal, the Israelis invaded Egypt in 1956, supported by British and French military action, and occupied the Gaza Strip and most of SINAI. The invasion was condemned by the UN, who secured a ceasefire and the withdrawal of the occupying forces. *See also* SUEZ CRISIS.

The 1967 War In 1967 the 'Six Day War' resulted from border incidents, increased action by Palestinian guerrillas, and the Egyptian blockade of the Gulf of Aqaba to Israeli shipping. Israel secured a rapid victory over Egypt, Syria and Jordan, and occupied Sinai, the Gaza Strip, the West Bank of the Jordan, and the Golan Heights.

The 1973 War In 1973 Egypt launched the 'Yom Kippur War', but after early Arab victories, Israeli forces crossed the Suez Canal. In 1974, after Arab states imposed an embargo on oil exports to the West, an agreement of disengagement with Egypt and Syria was reached.

After the CAMP DAVID AGREEMENT, in 1979 Egypt and Israel signed a peace treaty, following which Israel withdrew from Sinai; the other territories seized in 1967 remain occupied. Tensions in the area remain high despite international attempts to find a solution. *See also* LEBANON.

Arab League, an organization to promote inter-Arab cultural, technical and economic links and to minimize conflict between Arab states. A pact was signed in 1945 by 8 states. A council was established in Cairo, but the League remained an essentially loose association of states and never acquired a strong central authority. Until 1967 the League was concerned with organizing opposition to Israel, but since the PLO's increase in strength, the League has become a mouthpiece of moderate Arab opinion and a body favouring economic unity. It now has 19 member states.

Arab nationalism, a loosely defined sense of cultural and political solidarity expressed by members of Arab states in the face of outside influences and pressures.

The pan-Arab movement was led by Nasser from 1954—70. Plans for unification of the various Arab states did not conceal rivalries among the leadership nor tensions between various factions. Pan-Arab policy only tended to retain its appeal as long as it was directed against Israel (*see* ARAB-ISRAELI WARS). Attempts at unification by Egypt and Syria as a United Arab Republic (1958—61) were not very effective. Prime issues remain the existence of the Jewish state of Israel and the rights of Arab refugees driven from the West Bank, represented by the PALESTINE LIBERATION ORGANIZATION.

Arafat, Yasser (1929—), Palestinian guerrilla leader, and Central Committee Chairman of AL FATAH. Since 1969 he has been Chairman of the PLO, and accordingly in many international forums he has been received as a head of state (e.g. at the UN in 1974).

Ardennes Offensive (1944), the last major German attack of WWII when it was hoped to capture Antwerp and Liège by splitting the Allied armies. After initial success the German armies were driven back and their last reserves dissipated.

Argentina, republic of South America. Area: 2,776,000 sq km. Pop: 27,860,000. Language: Spanish. Religion: RC. Cap: Buenos Aires.

The country achieved independence from Spain in 1816. In the 20th cent. elected presidents have been overthrown by military coups on numerous occasions.

In 1946 Juan Perón was elected president. He propounded policies combining nationalism, populism and state socialism, known as Perónism. However his power was largely dependent on the popularity of his wife Eva (known as Evita). She died in 1952 and he was overthrown in 1955, returning from exile 18 years later to again become president with his second wife, Maria Estella, as vice-president. He died 9 months later and was succeeded by his wife, but economic crises and urban guerrilla activities led to her downfall in 1976.

The subsequent military regime carried out a 'dirty war' against its opponents, during which thousands of people disappeared. In 1982 the regime invaded the FALKLAND ISLANDS. Following the Argentinian defeat, the regime fell and was replaced by a democratically elected government, which has had to contend with high inflation.

armistice, an agreement between opposing armies to suspend hostilities in order to discuss peace terms.

The most important armistice negotiations at the end of WWI were between Germany on the one side and Britain, France and the USA on the other. The Allies had earlier signed armistices with Bulgaria, Turkey and Austro-Hungary.

In WWII, an armistice was concluded between Italy and the Allies in 1943, and the USSR signed with Romania, Finland and Hungary in 1944—45. No formal armistice was concluded with Germany or Japan in 1945: individual fighting fronts surrendered and there was no provision for a mere suspension of hostilities.

The Korean War was ended by the Panmunjom Armistice in 1953.

Arnhem, Battle of (1944), developed from the 1st Airborne Division's attempt to secure the bridge over the Rhine at Arnhem in Holland. The attempt failed owing to the slowness of the advance from the dropping zones, coupled with well-organized German resistance and countermeasures.

ASEAN, *see* ASSOCIATION OF SOUTHEAST ASIAN NATIONS.

Asquith, Herbert Henry, Earl of Oxford and Asquith (1852—1928), British Liberal statesman, PM (1908—16). He was Chancellor of the Exchequer (1905—08), and as PM his administrations were notable for the maintenance of free trade, the 'People's Budget' of 1909 (which precipitated the PARLIAMENT ACT of 1911), old age pensions, national insurance, payment of MPs, Irish Home Rule, the disestablishment of the Church of Wales, agitation for WOMEN'S SUFFRAGE, the EASTER RISING, and the first half of WWI.

Association of Southeast Asian Nations (ASEAN), an association established in 1967 in Bangkok by Indonesia, Malaysia, the Philippines, Singapore and Thailand to accelerate economic progress and increase stability in SE Asia.

Atatürk, Mustafa Kemal (1880—1938), the founder of modern Turkey, and president (1923—38). He participated in the Young Turks revolt (1908), and won fame as the defender of Gallipoli (1915). In the 1920s he led Turkish resistance to Allied plans for the division and subjugation of Turkey, and successfully repulsed the Greek invasion (1919—22).

After the Treaty of LAUSANNE (1923) was signed with the Allies, he ruled as a dictator and introduced radical reforms: the separation of state and religion, the introduction of Western law in place of Islamic, the abolition of the caliphate, the emancipation of women, and the abandonment of the Arabic for the Latin alphabet.

Atlantic, Battle of the, so called by Churchill to describe the struggle for control of the sea routes around the UK during WWII. It lasted for the whole period of the War but was particularly severe 1940—43 when Allied convoys were attacked by U-BOATS (frequently operating in packs), armed surface raiders, and long-range aircraft. Allied countermeasures included the escorting of convoys by warships, special escort aircraft carriers, armed merchant cruisers, submarines, land-based air cover, radar, and the underwater detection device, Asdic. Air attacks were also made on enemy naval bases and, in conjunction with the Royal Navy, on enemy warships at sea.

Atlantic Charter, a declaration of common objectives signed by Roosevelt and Churchill in 1941. It contained plans for the postwar world: the right of all peoples to choose their own governments and to live free from fear and want; no territorial changes without the consent of the peoples involved; the disarmament of aggressive nations; a wider and permanent system of international security; and access to essential raw materials through trade between all nations coupled with freedom of the seas.

atomic bomb, *see* NUCLEAR WARFARE.

Attlee, Clement (1883—1967), British statesman,

PM (1945—51). He became leader of the Labour Party in 1935. He entered the wartime coalition with Churchill, and was deputy PM (1942—45). As PM in the postwar Labour Government, he oversaw the creation of the WELFARE STATE. He ended his career as Leader of the Opposition (1951—55), receiving an earldom in 1955.

Australia, largest island and smallest continent, situated in the Southern Hemisphere between the Indian and Pacific Oceans. Area: 7,682,000 sq km. Pop: 15,452,000 (1983). Language: English. Religions: Protestant, RC. Cap: Canberra.

In 1900 the Australian Commonwealth Act united 6 former British colonies (now the 6 states) into an independent Commonwealth Dominion with a federated government, which came into being at the beginning of 1901. The Labour Party was the dominant political grouping in the new country, but was not strong enough to gain clear electoral victory until 1914. During WWI about 20% of the 300,000 volunteers were killed in Europe and the Middle East fighting for the Allies.

Between the Wars there was inter-state and federal friction over taxation in relation to defence expenditure, which nearly led to the break-up of the federation. That this did not happen was largely due to the rise in wool prices and the growing realization of Japan's aggressive intentions in the Far East and the Pacific.

Australia entered WWII in 1939, Australian forces being principally active in the Far East. As a result of WWII, strategic links were formed with New Zealand and the USA and resulted in troops being sent to serve in Vietnam in 1965.

Industrial growth was stimulated which incl. the huge Snowy River hydroelectric scheme in New South Wales. Trade with Japan and the USA has developed as it declines with Britain esp. after the latter joined the EEC in 1972. The Liberal Party (more or less equivalent to the British Conservative Party) has been dominant in government since WWII, Labour holding power only twice (1972–75 and 1983–).

Austria, federal republic of C Europe. Area: 84,000 sq km. Pop: 7,551,000 (est. 1983). Language: German. Religion: RC. Cap: Vienna.

With the defeat and dissolution of the AUSTRO-HUNGARIAN EMPIRE at the end of WWI, a republic was established in Austria in 1918, with Karl Renner (1870–1951) as Chancellor. The 1920s were marked by much social and political unrest, with frequent clashes between Fascist and socialist elements culminating in serious riots in Vienna in 1927. DOLLFUSS became Chancellor in 1932 but his home and foreign policies pleased neither left nor right and he was assassinated by a group of Nazis. He was succeeded by SCHUSCHNIGG, whose authority was undermined by increasing Nazi pressure leading to German annexation of the country (ANSCHLUSS) in 1938.

The country regained independence in 1945, again under Renner's leadership, but was occupied by the Allies until 1955, when it achieved full official sovereignty. The country has since maintained a neutral stance and has pursued generally moderate socialist policies under a succession of coalition governments. Bruno Kreisky (1911–)

coalition governments. Bruno Kreisky (1911–   ) was Chancellor 1970–83.

Austro-Hungarian Empire, a political unit which dominated C Europe from 1867 to 1918, incorporating what are now Czechoslovakia and parts of Italy, Poland, Romania, Yugoslavia and the Ukraine. There was a common monarch of the Hapsburg Dynasty (founded in 1153), and joint control of the armed forces and financial policies, but each state had its own parliament.

Independence and nationalistic issues, supported by the Allies at the end of WWI, caused the Empire's disintegration, formally recognized by the Treaties of SAINT GERMAIN (1919) and TRIANON (1920).

autarky or **autarchy,** a nationalist system or policy of economic self-sufficiency aimed at removing the need for imports by producing all requirements at home. Germany adopted such a policy in the 1930s to make herself blockade-proof.

authoritarian, (a) favouring or devoting strict obedience to authority, or to government by a small elite with wide powers; (b) despotic, dictatorial or domineering.

autocracy, (a) government by an individual with unrestricted authority (an autocrat); (b) the unrestricted authority of such an individual; (c) a country or society ruled by an autocrat.

autonomy, the right or state of self-government, esp. when limited.

Avon, Lord, *see* EDEN.

Awami League, *see* BANGLADESH.

axis, an alliance between a number of states to coordinate their foreign policy. In WWII, the Axis was the name given to the collaboration between Germany and Italy, which was based on the loose understanding achieved by the October Protocols in 1936. More broadly, the Axis powers in WWII were Germany, Italy and Japan, and their allies Hungary, Czechoslovakia, Romania and Bulgaria.

Ayub Khan, Mohammed (1908–74), Pakistani army officer, statesman. He became president in 1958 following a military coup and the declaration of martial law. He believed in the spread of democracy, ending martial law in 1962, and achieved limited land reforms, but he became unpopular owing to the repressive and militaristic form of his government. Imprisonment of the opposition led to serious student riots in 1968, followed by his resignation in 1969. He was replaced by YAHYA KHAN.

B

Ba'ath Socialist Party, a pan-Arab movement based upon the union of 1952 of 2 Syrian political parties, the Ba'ath ('resurrection') Party and the Socialist Party. The basic philosophy of the united Party is 'Freedom, unity and socialism in one Arab nation with an external mission'. The Party now rules Syria, and in Iraq the Ba'ath and Communist Parties rule as the Coalition National Progressive Front.

Bad Godesberg Meeting, *see* GODESBERG MEETING.

Badoglio, Pietro (1871–1956), Italian field marshal and politician. He was Governor of Libya (1929–33) and completed the conquest of Ethiopia (1936). He opposed Italian entry into WWII when Chief of the General Staff and resigned (1940) after the fiasco of the Greek campaign. Appointed PM (1943) by King Victor Emmanuel III after the fall of Mussolini, he concluded an armistice with the Allies and took Italy into WWII against Germany.

Baghdad Pact (1955), a defence and security agreement between Iraq and Turkey, subsequently joined by Pakistan, Iran and the UK. The SUEZ CRISIS (1956) and the Iraqi revolution (1958) practically ended the agreement, which survived only in truncated form as a basis for the CENTRAL TREATY ORGANIZATION.

balance of payments, the difference over a given time between total payments to and receipts from foreign nations, arising from exports and imports of goods and services, and transfers of capital, interest, grants, etc.

balance of power, the doctrine of maintaining a European system in which no single power is dominant. In the past many countries were concerned to support coalitions opposing one power gaining control over Europe, e.g. the German-Austro-Hungarian alliance balanced by the alliance between Britain, France and Russia prior to WWII.

balance of terror, *see* DETERRENCE.

Baldwin, Stanley, Earl Baldwin of Bewdley (1867–1947), British Conservative statesman. After serving as Chancellor of the Exchequer he became PM (1923–24, 1924–29 and 1935–37), and was Leader of the Conservative Party (1923–37). His main success was in uniting a divided party and in handling the ABDICATION CRISIS, but he had to deal with the problems of the General Strike, rearmament, and mass unemployment.

Balfour, Arthur James, 1st Earl of Balfour (1848–1930), British Conservative statesman, PM (1902–06). After holding several ministerial offices he became PM, but his government's split over PROTECTIONISM, FREE TRADE and tariff reform contributed to its defeat by the Liberals.

In the WWI coalition government he was First Lord of the Admiralty and Foreign Secretary and was responsible for the BALFOUR DECLARATION. As Lord President of the Council he played a prominent part in the postwar settlements, the establishment of the LEAGUE OF NATIONS and the drafting of the STATUTE OF WESTMINSTER.

Balfour Declaration (1917), statement by the

British Foreign Secretary A.J. BALFOUR declaring British support for a Jewish national home in PALESTINE provided that safeguards could be reached for the 'rights of non-Jewish communities in Palestine' and that Jewish political status in any other country should not be endangered.

The Declaration formed the basis of the League of Nations mandate for Palestine which was assigned to the UK in 1922 and lasted until 1948 when ISRAEL was established.

Balkan Pact (1934), defensive agreement between Greece, Romania, Turkey and Yugoslavia whereby they agreed to guarantee each other's frontiers. It was particularly aimed at Bulgaria which desired to recover territory previously lost to all 4 states. The signatories later formed an Entente, but this foundered (1940) when each state went its separate way in WWII.

Balkans, the, peninsula in SE Europe comprising Albania, Bulgaria, Greece, Romania, Yugoslavia (which has incorporated Serbia, Montenegro and Bosnia-Herzegovina) and European Turkey. Formerly it was an area of political and revolutionary upheaval characterized by the BALKAN WARS and involvement in WWI and WWII.

Balkan Wars (1912–1913), conflicts arising from territorial expansionist policies by various Balkan states against the OTTOMAN EMPIRE.

The First Balkan War arose when the Balkan League of Bulgaria, Greece, Montenegro and Serbia attacked Turkey and drove it out of what is now Albania, N Greece and S Yugoslavia.

The Second Balkan War arose when Bulgaria attacked its former allies, Greece and Serbia, which were joined by Romania and their previous enemy, Turkey. The Treaty of Bucharest (1913) produced a territorial settlement of both wars, resulting in territorial losses for Bulgaria and the Ottoman Empire. The resulting tensions contributed significantly to the outbreak of WWI.

Baltic States, collective name of Estonia, Latvia and Lithuania, territories of E Europe. Up to 1918 they were part of Russia, and were then independent republics (1919—40). In 1940 they were occupied by the Russians, since when they have been constituent republics of the USSR.

Banda, Hastings Kamuzu (1907—), Malawi statesman. He became leader of the Malawi National Congress (1958), PM of Nyasaland (1963) and led the country to independence as Malawi in 1964. He became President (1966) and subsequently has followed a cautious and moderate policy in relationships with South Africa. Internally he has created a 1-party state on dictatorial lines.

Bandaranaike, Sirimavo (1916—), Sri Lanka stateswoman who succeeded her husband, Solomon, as leader of the Freedom Party. She became the world's first female PM in 1960, but by following her husband's language and nationalization policies contributed to the Party's defeat in 1965. She regained power in 1970 on a platform of advancement to social democracy and held office until 1977.

Bandaranaike, Solomon (1899—1959), Sri Lankan statesman. He became involved with the Ceylon National Congress in the 1930s, a political alignment which led him to support the Sinhalese against the imigrant Tamils prior to independence

(1948). He founded the socialist Freedom Party
(1951), and on becoming PM (1956) closed all
British military and naval bases. His nationalization
programme and policy of making Sinhalese the sole
official language led to serious civil disturbances
and his assassination by a Buddhist monk.

Bandung Conference (1955), the first international political conference of African and Asian
states. The idea was to adopt a 'non-aligned and
neutral' attitude towards the Cold War confronta-
tions between East and West, and to create a
'united front' against colonial oppression.

   The increasing rivalry of India and China within
Asia, and the separate objectives of anti-
colonialism in Africa and Asia, weakened the
subsequent effectiveness of the Conference. The
Conference was a forerunner of the NON–ALIGNED
MOVEMENT.

Bangladesh, people's republic of S Asia. Area:
144,020 sq km. Pop: 89,940,000 (1981). Language: Bengali. Religion: Islam. Capital: Dacca.

   Until 1947 the country was part of India but then
became East Pakistan, separated from West
Pakistan by a large area of Indian territory. From
1954 the Awami League sought autonomy for East
Pakistan and the failure of talks to bring this about
precipitated a civil war, with INDIA actively inter-
vening to support the East in a 2-week war (1971).
The resulting peace enabled Bangladesh to be
established as an independent state (1972).

   In 1975 the PM and leader of the Awami League,
Mujibur RAHMAN, was assassinated in a military
coup led by Brigadier Khaled Mosharraf, who
himself was assassinated three months later. The

country has remained politically unstable, with alternating periods of military rule and parliamentary democracy.

'Barbarossa', German Supreme Command code name for the invasion of the USSR in 1941.

Basques, people of unknown origin living around the W Pyrenees in France and Spain. Since 1973 an extreme nationalist organisation (ETA) has sought Basque independence from Spain by a clandestine campaign of terrorism. A limited degree of autonomy was established in 1980.

Batista, Fulgencio (1901–73), Cuban dictator. After deposing President Machado (1933) he established a Fascist state, but in 1937 allowed opposition political parties to be formed. Free elections (1939) resulted in his appointment as President. He held office until 1944 when he went voluntarily into exile in the Dominican Republic.

As a result of another coup (1952) he returned to power, suspended the constitution and established a 1-party state. He was forced again to flee to the Dominican Republic (1958) following the army's refusal to support his corrupt and repressive regime against CASTRO'S successful guerrilla campaign.

Bay of Pigs (1961), site of an invasion of Cuba by 1,200 anti-CASTRO Cubans, trained by the CIA in the USA and using US military supplies. Most were killed or captured within a few days. In the same year Castro proclaimed Cuba a socialist nation.

Beaverbrook, Lord *see* AITKEN.

Begin, Menachem (1913–), Polish-born Israeli politician, PM (1977–83). He reached Palestine during WWII, and became leader of IRGUN ZVAI LEUMI, a member of the Knesset from 1948, and

leader of the Likud (Unity) Party (1973–83) which
won the 1977 general election.

His administration had to contend with high
inflation, Arab disturbances, and the maintenance
of Israeli authority on the occupied West Bank,
and PLO incursions from Lebanon. Begin was
jointly awarded with SADAT the 1978 Nobel Peace
Prize for efforts in achieving the CAMP DAVID
AGREEMENT.

Belgium, kingdom of NW Europe. Area: 30,513 sq
km. Pop: 9,863,000 (1981). Languages: Dutch,
French and German. Religion: RC. Cap: Brussels.

After being successively subject to many W
European states Belgium became an independent
kingdom (1830). At the outbreak of WWI, Germany invaded Belgium the same day as declaring
war on France. This disregard for Belgium's
guaranteed neutrality precipitated Britain's entry
into the War. In WWII Belgium was again overrun
by Germany.

The country occasionally suffers internal conflict
between the majority Dutch-speaking Flemish
population and the minority French-speaking
Walloons and the division is exacerbated by the
political separation of N and S, the former
supporting mainly the conservative Christian Social
Party and the nationalist Volksunie, while the latter
is more radically socialist in outlook. These
disagreements have led the country to be politically
unstable and governed by a succession of coalitions.
It is a member of the EEC and NATO.

Ben Bella, Mohammed Ahmed (1916–   ),
Algerian national revolutionary leader. After
WWII he became head of the extreme nationalist

'Special Organization'. Imprisoned by the French (1950) he escaped (1952) to Egypt where he founded the National Liberation Front (FLN) which played a leading role in the fight for Algerian independence. Again imprisoned by the French (1956) he was released (1962) to participate in the independence talks at Evian which also led to the end of hostilities. He became PM and, in 1963, President. He was overthrown (1965) in a military coup led by Colonel Boumedienne.

Benelux, customs union (1948) between Belgium, Luxembourg and the Netherlands which developed (1960) into an arrangement for the free movement of capital, goods and people between each state, and for joint commerical relations with other countries — principles merely restating factors imposed by EEC membership.

Beneš, Eduard (1884–1948), Czechoslovak statesman. During WWI he worked hard for his country's independence and became its first Foreign Minister (1918–35) and was PM (1921–22). His foreign policy was based on firm support for the League of Nations, the development of close associations with France and the USSR, and the strengthening of the LITTLE ENTENTE. He was President (1935–38, 1946–48), and headed a provisional government in France and England during WWII.

Ben Gurion, David (1886–1974), Israeli statesman. In 1930 he became leader of the Mapai Party, the strongest socialist grouping in Israel. He was PM (1948–53, 1955–63). Much of this time he led a country at war with the Arabs but was able to carry out agricultural and industrial reforms.

Beria, Lavrenti Pavlovich (1899—1953), Soviet politician and chief of the secret police. In 1938 Stalin appointed him Commissar of Internal Affairs, and he later became head of the Soviet Security Service (NKVD). During WWII he was Vice-President of the State Committee for Defence. It was widely assumed he had hastened Stalin's death in order to succeed him, and later the same year he was dismissed, tried and shot as a traitor. A ruthlessly ambitious plotter, he was a skilful organizer of espionage, forced labour and terror.

Berlin, city of N Germany, capital of united Germany 1871—1945. Since 1945 it has been divided into 2 sectors. The E sector is occupied by forces of the USSR, while the W sector is occupied by US, UK and French troops.

The E sector is capital of East Germany. Area: 403 sq km. Pop: 1,145,700. The W sector forms an enclave in East Germany closely associated economically and politically with West Germany. Area: 480 sq km. Pop: 1,898,900.

During 1948—49 the Russians imposed a rail and road blockade on the W sector, in response to the introduction of currency reform in West Germany, which the Soviet authorities refused to accept in Berlin. The UK and the USA organized an airlift of supplies, the success of which convinced the USSR of the futility of the blockade.

During this tense period 2 municipal authorities were established and the city administratively divided. In 1961, the East Germans built a wall dividing the sectors to halt the flow of refugees from E to W.

Berlin-Baghdad Railway, a misnomer since the proposed line was to run from the Bosphorus to the Persian Gulf, although it was to be engineered and financed by Germany. Turkey agreed to the project in 1899 but only a short section of the line had been constructed by the outbreak of WWI. There was considerable British and Russian opposition to the project which would have encroached into their spheres of influence.

Bevan, Aneurin (1897—1960), British Labour politician. He was Minister of Health (1945—51) and Deputy Leader of the Labour Party (1959—60). He pioneered the National Health Service and was on the left of the Party (unilateralist wing), opposing increased defence spending at the expense of investment on the Health Service.

Beveridge Report, the Report on Social Insurance and Allied Services prepared by the economist Sir William Henry (later Baron) Beveridge (1879—1963). Published in 1942 it became known popularly as a social insurance scheme 'from the cradle to the grave', which would overcome the prewar evils of poverty and unemployment. Beveridge was a Liberal but his proposals were espoused by the Labour Party, which implemented them when in power (1945—51). The report outlined the basis of the National Health Service and the WELFARE STATE as it is today.

Bevin, Ernest (1881—1951), British Labour politician. After a prominent career in the TUC (1921—1940), incl. the uniting of 50 unions into the Transport and General Workers Union, the largest in the world, he entered Parliament. He was Minister of Labour (1940—45), and then Foreign

Secretary (1945–51). He was noted for supporting
the creation of NATO, encouraging the adoption of
a nuclear defence policy, and for having a sense of
Commonwealth unity, which made him oppose
schemes for European union.

Bhutto, Zulfiquar Ali (1928–79), Pakistani
statesman. He joined President Ayub Khan's
government (1958), becoming Foreign Minister
(1963). He resigned (1966) and founded the
Socialist Anti-Indian People's Party (1967). It won
an Assembly majority in 1970, and in the following
year Bhutto became the first non-soldier to achieve
the Presidency. He led his country out of the
Commonwealth (1972) and initiated a new
constitution under which he took office as PM with
responsibility for foreign affairs, defence and
atomic energy (1973). He was overthrown by a
military coup (1977) and charged with conspiracy
to murder, for which he was executed.

Biafran War (1967–70), civil war in Nigeria
resulting from the secession of Biafra, the predominantly Ibo eastern region of the federated
republic. The secession was led by Colonel
Odamagwa Ojukwu, and had been preceded by
heightened inter-tribal conflict. Federal forces
intervened to quell the rebellion, and although the
main bases of Enugu and Port Harcourt were soon
occupied it was not until 1970 that Biafran
resistance was overcome and Ojukwu fled to the
Ivory Coast.

bipartisanship, the situation arising from the
mutual support of two or more countries,
organizations or political parties for each other's
general or specific policies.

Black and Tans, the armed force sent to Ireland in 1920 to strengthen the Royal Irish Constabulary in its effort to combat SINN FÉIN. The informal name derives from the uniform of dark green tunics (almost black) and khaki trousers.

Black Power, an economic, political and social movement of black people, esp. in the USA, to obtain equality with whites. The term was coined in 1965 by radical groups discontented with the failure of the CIVIL RIGHTS movement to obtain satisfactory legislation by means of non-violent action.

Black Shirts, members of a Fascist organization, esp. of the Italian Fascist party before and during WWII.

Blitz, the systematic nightime bombing of the UK (1940—41) by the Luftwaffe (the German air force). The intention was to terrorize the population, cause widespread destruction and disrupt industry. It failed due to the superiority of RAF Fighter Command and the strains imposed on Germany in waging war on Russia.

Blitzkrieg (Ger., 'lightning war'), term applied to a style of attack perfected by German generals in France in 1940. Essential elements were speed and surprise of attack (e.g. using tanks and dive bombing) resulting in shock and disorganization among enemy forces.

Blum, Léon (1872—1950), French socialist statesman. He became leader of the Socialist Party (1925) and the country's first socialist PM (1936), but held office for only a year, returning to power for a few weeks in 1938. He was put on trial during WWII by the VICHY GOVERNMENT as a scapegoat for the country's military inadequacies, and was imprisoned by the Germans in concentration camps. Freed in 1945, he headed an economic mission to the USA (1946) and was PM (1946—47).

Boer War (1899—1902), a conflict between the British and the Boers (descendants of Dutch settlers) in South Africa caused by Boer resentment of British colonial policy which it was feared would terminate the Transvaal's independence. After the British victory, the Treaty of Vereeniging (1902) transferred sovereignty over the Boer republics of the Orange Free State and the Transvaal to Britain.

Bolshevism, the policy pursued by the left wing of the Social Democratic Party which seized power in the RUSSIAN REVOLUTION (Oct. 1917). In 1918 the name of the policy was changed to 'Communism'.

The term derives from *Bolshevik* (Russ., 'majority') after the majority of the Social Democratic Party voted for LENIN'S revolutionary policy, as opposed to the more moderate policy of the Mensheviks (*Menshevik*, Russ., 'minority'). The term is also applied to any form of political radicalism, esp. if revolutionary.

boom, a period of high economic growth characterized by rising wages, profits and prices, full employment, and high levels of investment, trade and other economic activity. It is often followed by a DEPRESSION.

Bosnia-Herzegovina, region of C Yugoslavia. Capital: Sarajevo.

As separate provinces Bosnia and Herzegovina belonged to the Ottoman Empire (1463—1908), but by the Treaty of Berlin (1878) were then given to the Austro-Hungarian Empire with the agreement of the major European powers, although technically remaining part of the Ottoman Empire. In 1908 the Austro-Hungarian Empire annexed them, and in 1910 they became a joint province. Serbia was resentful of the annexation, and anti-Austro-Hungarian agitation culminated in the assassination of Franz Ferdinand at SARAJEVO and the start of WWI. After the War they became part of Yugoslavia (1918).

Botha, Louis (1862—1919), South African general and statesman. He fought for the Boers in the Boer War and then strove for reconciliation with his old enemies. He was PM of the Transvaal (1907—10) and first PM of the Union of South Africa (1910—19).

Botha, Pieter Willem (1916—   ), South African statesman. As PM (1978—84) and President (1984—   ) he has pursued a policy of moderate reform, while resisting internal and external pressure for the complete dismantling of APARTHEID.

bourgeoisie, (a) the middle classes, (b) in Marxist philosophy, the ruling class of the two basic classes of capitalist society, the other being the PROLETARIAT (working class). The bourgeoisie consists of bankers, capitalists, manufacturers and other employers, owning the most important of the means of production, with which it exploits the proletariat.

Bourguiba, Habib ben Ali (1903—   ), Tunisian statesman. He became PM (1956) when Tunisia gained independence, and President (1957—87). His moderate socialism found favour in France, and a close trading relationship has developed between both countries.

Boxer Rising (1900), an outbreak of anti-foreign violence in China organized by a secret society called 'The Society of Harmonious Fists' — hence the term 'boxer'. National resentment was aroused by European powers acquiring bases and developing commerical interests. The rising was suppressed with severity by the Europeans who, by the Peking Protocol (1901), imposed on the Chinese Government indemnity conditions which were not abrogated until 1943.

Brandt, Willy (1913—   ), West German Social Democratic Statesman. He started his political career (1930) as an anti-Nazi socialist worker, and from 1933 to 1945 he went into voluntary exile in Scandinavia. He entered the Bundestag (1949), was mayor of West Berlin (1951—66), and became chairman of the Social Democrats (1964).

    He was Foreign Minister in Kiesinger's coalition government (1966—69), and Chancellor (1969—74) in coalition with the Free Democrats. He worked hard for reconciliation with the Communist countries (*see* OSTPOLITIK) and treaties were concluded with Poland and the USSR, acknowledging East Germany and recognizing the ODER–NEISSE LINE (1972). He won the Nobel Peace Prize (1971).

Brandt Report (1979), paper prepared by the Independent Commission on International Development Issues, under the chairmanship of Willy BRANDT. The investigation leading to the Report was conducted by a group of international statesmen and leaders from many spheres from 19 countries, the UK's representative being Edward Heath.

The long and complex Report detailed long-term reforms required by 2000 and priority programmes for the 1980s to avert an imminent economic crisis. It proposed a new approach to international finance and development of the monetary system, and emphasized the anomalous situation created by the vast expenditure on armaments taking resources away from the urgent needs of Third World countries, which are desperately impoverished and have millions living below starvation level. Energy, food and trade were all discussed, emphasis being placed on the mutual interests of the industrialized and Third World nations, and the Report put forward proposals to reverse the decline in trade and the revival of the world economy.

Brazzaville Declaration (1944), resulted from a meeting in the French Congo between members of the Fighting French (*see* FREE FRENCH) and France's African colonies to discuss postwar relationships. The Declaration incl. proposals for the establishment of assemblies in each colony; the indivisibility of the empire; colonial participation in elections for the French parliament; equal rights of colonial subjects as citizens of the French Republic; economic reforms; and the progression of native populations in public services.

Brest-Litovsk, Treaty of (1918), peace agreement between the CENTRAL POWERS and Bolshevik Russia, under which the Russians lost Finland, Poland, the Baltic States, the Caucasus, the Ukraine and White Russia. The Treaty was invalidated later in the year by the ending of WWI.

Bretton Woods Conference (1944), agreement reached in New Hampshire, USA, by 28 nations to

establish a WORLD BANK and an INTERNATIONAL
MONETARY FUND (IMF), with the object of
preventing financial crisis developing like those
which had occurred in the interwar years. The Bank
was to advance loans for major projects designed to
aid a country's development. The Fund was to
operate a system of cash reserves on which members
states could rely to meet balance-of-payments
deficits.

Brezhnev, Leonid (1906–82). Soviet statesman.
He was President of the Supreme Soviet from 1960
to 1964 when he succeeded Khrushchev as First
Secretary of the Communist Party, emerging as
principal ruler of a collective leadership. He
resumed the Presidency (1977), retaining his party
offices and policy-making role.

He established the principle known as the
'Brezhnev Doctrine' in defence of the Soviet
invasion of CZECHOSLOVAKIA (1968), stating that a
socialist state should intervene in another socialist
state's affairs should its socialism be threatened by
internal or external attack or subversion. His period
of office was notable for the growth of DÉTENTE in
the 1970s, and its decline following the Soviet
invasion of AFGHANISTAN (1979).

Briand, Aristide (1862–1932), French statesman, originally a socialist but, on entering parliament (1902), inclined towards radicalism. He was
responsible for the separation of church and state
(1905) and was 11 times PM between 1909 and
1929, but such was the instability of government
during this period, his tenureship of the office only
totalled 58 months.

Briand was Foreign Minister (1925–32) and his

rapport with STRESEMANN, with whom he shared the 1926 Nobel Peace prize, helped Franco-German reconciliation, esp. by means of the Treaties of LOCARNO, Germany's admission to the League of Nations (1926), and the evacuation of the Rhineland (1930). He inspired the KELLOG-BRIAND PACT (1928), and advocated a federal 'United States of Europe'.

Britain, *see* UNITED KINGDOM.

Britain, Battle of (1940), fought over S England by the LUFTWAFFE and the RAF. In order to destroy British defences as a prelude to invasion, Germany launched a series of attacks against shipping, airfields and towns, using squadrons of bombers with massed fighter escorts. They were opposed by Hurricane and Spitfire fighters, and the Battle ended when Germany abandoned thoughts of invasion after losing 1,733 aircraft to the RAF loss of 915 fighters.

British Commonwealth of Nations, *see* COMMONWEALTH OF NATIONS, BRITISH.

British Empire, *see* COMMONWEALTH OF NATIONS, BRITISH, and IMPERIALISM.

British Union of Fascists (BUF), an amalgamation in 1932 of Sir Oswald Mosley's New Party and several small Fascist groups. The Fascist salute, black shirt and an extreme anti-Semitic line were adopted. Propaganda marches and meetings were deliberately used to provoke left-wing and Jewish elements but the Public Order Act (1936), prohibiting political uniforms and empowering the police to ban political processions, effectively put an end to the movement.

Brown Shirts, *see* SA.

Brüning, Heinrich (1885—1970), German statesman, Chancellor (1930—32). His expertise as an economist prompted President Hindenburg to appoint him Chancellor in an effort to stabilize the economy and halt the rise in popular eppeal of the Nazi Party. Without a Reichstag majority he governed by Presidential decree, thereby undermining the democratic process and favouring the progression to power of the Nazis who forced his resignation.

buffer state, small and usually neutral country between two rival powers, e.g. Poland prior to WWII acted as a buffer state between Germany and the USSR.

Bulganin, Nikolai (1895—1975), Soviet soldier and politician. He organized Moscow's defence against the German onslaught (1941) and was created a Marshal of the Soviet Union at the end of WWII. In 1946 he succeeded Stalin as Minister of Defence. He was Vice-Premier (1953—55) and PM (1955—58) when he was deposed by Khrushchev. Later that year Bulganin was dropped from the Party Presidium and became chairman of the State Bank.

Bulgaria, republic of SE Europe. Area: 110,911 sq km. Pop: 8,929,000 (1982). Language: Bulgarian. Religion: Eastern Orthodox. Cap: Sofia.

Under Turkish rule from 1395, it achieved autonomy in 1878 and became an independent kingdom in 1908 and a republic in 1946. Allied with Germany in both world wars, a Communist regime was established by occupying Russian forces after WWII. The country is a member of the COUNCIL FOR MUTUAL ECONOMIC ASSISTANCE and the

WARSAW PACT, and is a hard-line follower of Russian policy.

Burma, republic of SE Asia. Area: 678,030 sq km. Pop: 35,314,000 (1983). Language: Burmese. Religion: Buddhism. Cap: Rangoon.

Unified from small states (1752) it became part of British India (1885) and a British crown colony (1937). After Japanese occupation in WWII it achieved independence (1948) followed by a period of civil war. Parliamentary democracy was abolished in a military coup and a Revolutionary Council established (1962), and in 1974 the country became a single-party state. A non-aligned policy is followed in foreign affairs.

Butler, Richard Austen, Baron Butler of Saffron-Walden (1902—82), British Conservative statesman. As Minister of Education (1941—45) he was responsible for the EDUCATION ACT (1944). He was Chancellor of the Exchequer (1951—55), Home Secretary (1957—62), deputy PM (1962—63), and Foreign Secretary (1963—64). A supporter of the principles of the Welfare State, he was twice contender for the premiership (1957 and 1963).

C

cabinet (a) executive and policy-making body of a country, consisting of senior ministers, (b) advisory council to a head of state.

Caetano, Marcelo (1906—80), Portuguese politician. He was President of the National Union, the only permitted political party, Deputy PM (1955—58), and succeeded SALAZAR as PM (1968—74). He was removed from power by a military coup.

Cairo Conference (1943), meeting between Chiang Kai-shek, Churchill and Roosevelt during WWII when war Aims for the Far East were approved. These included Japanese unconditional surrender and the surrender by Japan of territories acquired since 1894, which would either be restored to China or become independent. At the Conference strategic discussions also took place between Churchill and Roosevelt and these were resumed after the TEHERAN CONFERENCE.

Callaghan, James (1912—), British Labour statesman, PM (1976—79). He was Chancellor of the Exchequer (1964—67), Home Secretary (1967—70), and Foreign Secretary (1974—76). He was elected Leader of the Labour Party (1976—81). As PM he tried to secure trade-union support for his counter-inflation policies. Lacking a Parliamentary majority, he had to enter into a pact with the Liberal Party (the 'Lib-Lab Pact'). He was created a life peer as Lord Callaghan of Cardiff in 1987.

Campaign for Nuclear Disarmament (CND),

organization founded (1958) to agitate for the UK's unilateral abandonment of nuclear weapons. In the early years it attracted considerable radical, and mostly youthful, support, largely devoted to public demonstrations which annually culminated in a march from the Atomic Weapons Research Establishment at Aldermaston, Berkshire, to a rally in Trafalgar Square, London. After the signing of the NUCLEAR TEST-BAN TREATY (1963) the CND's popularity waned, although a revival in strength began in 1980.

Campbell-Bannerman, Sir Henry (1836–1908), British statesman, Liberal PM (1905–8). His administration initiated trade-union legislation (*see* TAFF VALE CASE) and land reforms, and followed a policy of reconciliation following the Boer War, granting the Boers self-government in the Transvaal and Orange Free State.

Camp David Agreement (1978), accord reached at the US President's Maryland retreat between Egypt's President Sadat and the Israeli PM, Begin, promoting a Middle East settlement on which was based a peace treaty signed in Washington (1979). President Carter of the USA acted as mediator.

The agreement provided for the signing of a treaty within 3 months; the establishment of diplomatic and economic relations; for phased Israeli withdrawal from SINAI and demilitarized security zones along the frontier; and the development of a degree of Palestinian autonomy on the Jordan's WEST BANK within 5 years.

capitalism, an economic system based on private ownership of the means of production, distribution and exchange (capital), characterized by the freedom of the owners of capital (capitalists) to manage to operate their property for profit in competitive conditions.

Caporetto, Battle of (1917), scene of an Italian defeat by Austro-German forces on the River Isonzo. It was one of the greatest disasters suffered by the Allied armies during WWI, some 300,000 Italians being taken prisoner and even more deserting.

The village of Caporetto was Austrian until the end of WWI, when it became Italian. It was ceded to Yugoslavia (1947) and renamed Kobarid.

Carson, Sir Edward Henry, later **Baron** (1854–1935), Irish politician. Leader of the Ulster Unionists in the House of Commons (1910–21), he led the opposition in 1912 to the Irish HOME RULE Bill and raised the Ulster Volunteer Force, forcing Ireland to the verge of civil war before accepting the exclusion of Ulster from the Bill.

Carter, James ('Jimmy') (1924–   ), US Democratic President (1977–81). In the Presidential election he defeated Gerald Ford, but was himself defeated in 1980 by Ronald Reagan. He was successful in mediating between Egypt and Israel, resulting in the CAMP DAVID AGREEMENT. He was a champion of human rights abroad, and continued the policy of DÉTENTE until the Soviet invasion of AFGHANISTAN (1979).

Casablanca Conference (1943), meeting between Churchill and Roosevelt during which plans were discussed for the termination of the war in N Africa; the invasion of Sicily; and the increase in the bombing of Germany; the transfer of UK war resources to the Far East after the surrender of the

Axis powers, which was to be unconditional and not subject to negotiations; and preparation for a second front later in the year.

Casement, Sir Roger (1864–1916), Irish nationalist, and diplomat in the British consular service (1892–1911). He went to Berlin (1914) to solicit German support for Irish independence and endeavoured to enlist Irish prisoners of war into the German armed forces. Prior to the EASTER RISING (1916) he was landed by a U-boat in SW Ireland in order to participate in the SINN FEIN rebellion, but was arrested shortly after landing, and tried and executed in London for high treason.

Castro, Fidel (1927–), Cuban Communist politician. He came to prominence when he led an unsuccessful uprising against BATISTA'S oppressive regime (1953). He fled to the USA and Mexico where he organized a revolutionary movement, returning secretly to Cuba (1956) with a group which included GUEVARA. Waging guerrilla warfare he became something of a legendary figure, attracting more and more followers and achieving increasing successes over Batista's forces.

After capturing Havana he became PM and Minister of the Armed Forces (1959). He introduced far-reaching reforms in agriculture, education and industry and strengthened ties with China and the USSR, as well as endeavouring to promote revolutions in Latin America and encouraging African liberation movements, notably in Angola where thousands of Cuban troops are based.

CDU, see CHRISTIAN DEMOCRATS.

CENTO, see CENTRAL TREATY ORGANIZATION.

Central African Federation, *see* RHODESIA AND NYASALAND, FEDERATION OF.

Central Intelligence Agency (CIA), US security organization established (1947) to conduct and coordinate espionage and intelligence operations. Responsible to the National Security Council, it also plans secret operations for such purposes as the overthrow of governments or the downfall of persons hostile to the US and its allies. Successes as in Guatemala, Iran (both 1953—54), and Chile (1973) have been matched by disasters, such as the BAY OF PIGS, the failure to predict the 1973 ARAB-ISRAELI WAR and the 1974 CYPRUS crisis, and the Watergate Affair, which revealed that the CIA, among other government agencies, had infringed civil liberties.

Central Powers, collective term for Austria-Hungary, Germany and Italy, founder members of the Triple Alliance, established in 1882, joined in 1883 by Romania and during WWI by Bulgaria and Turkey, but left by Italy in 1914 and by Romania in 1916.

Although the number of Alliance members fluctuated during the War and finally resolved itself into a membership of 4, the term was retained to differentiate members of the Alliance from Britain, France and Russia, members of the TRIPLE ENTENTE. Italy and Romania eventually joined the Triple Entente members in fighting against their old allies of the Triple Alliance.

Before 1914 the Triple Alliance and Triple Entente had effectively divided Europe into 2 armed camps, thereby nurturing an atmosphere of secrecy and suspicion which developed into a contributory cause of WWI.

Central Treaty Organization (CENTO), economic and military alliance formed by Iran, Pakistan, Turkey and the UK in 1959, with the US as an associated member. It superceded the BAGHDAD PACT, which was dissolved following Iraq's withdrawal. Iran, Pakistan and Turkey withdrew in 1979, and the organization was effectively dissolved.

Chaco War (1928–35), a conflict between Bolivia and Paraguay over possession of the Chaco Boreal, a plain between the Andes and the Paraguay River. The eventual settlement divided the territory more than 2 to 1 in favour of Paraguay but guaranteed Bolivia access to the S Atlantic via the Paraguay River.

Chamberlain, Sir Austen (1863–1937), British Conservative statesman. As Foreign Secretary (1924–29) he participated in the discussions leading to the Treaties of LOCARNO and won the Nobel Peace Prize (1925). His leadership of the Conservative Party (1921–22) ended because of dissatisfaction with his support for Lloyd George, in whose War Cabinet he had served.

Chamberlain, Neville (1869–1940), Conservative statesman, PM (1937–40). He was Chancellor of the Exchequer from 1931 until he succeeded Baldwin as PM (1937). As PM he followed a policy of APPEASEMENT towards Nazi Germany, and signed the MUNICH AGREEMENT (1938). Although intended to avoid war, appeasement in fact encouraged Hitler's aggressive policies which led to WWII. Incompetence as a wartime leader led to his resignation in 1940.

Chanak Crisis (1922), situation in Anglo-Turkish relations resulting from the ceding of the port of Smyrna (now Izmir) and Turkey's European territories to Greece by the Treaty of SÈVRES (1920), which also established a neutral zone between Greece and Turkey on the E side of the DARDANELLES, the neutrality being subject to an Anglo-French guarantee.

A revolt led by Mustapha Kemal (ATATÜRK) against the Sultan resulted in Greece attempting to interfere on the Sultan's side, whereupon the rebels advanced on the Straits, after defeating the Greek army at Smyrna. This brought the guarantee into effect but France withdrew its troops and the outnumbered UK force had to negotiate an armistice, resulting in the Turks accepting the neutralization of the Bosphorus and Dardanelles in return for the restoration of Adrianpole and E Thrace and the ending of the Allied occupation of Constantinople (now Istanbul). The agreement formed the basis of the Treaty of LAUSANNE.

Within a fortnight of the armistice the UK coalition government was out of office because the Conservative Party withdrew support, due to what was considered Lloyd George's pro-Greek stance during the Crisis and his irresponsibility in taking the UK to the brink of war with Turkey.

Cheka, *see* SOVIET SECURITY SERVICE.

Chernenko, Konstantin Ustinovich (1911–85), Soviet statesman. General Secretary of the Communist Party and President of the USSR (1984–85).

Chiang Kai-shek (1887–1975), Chinese general, Nationalist statesman and KUOMINTANG leader. An

early associate of SUN YAT-SEN, he commanded the
army which accomplished China's unification
(1926–28), and was President (1928–31) and
Head of the Executive (1935–45). His efforts to
overcome army revolts, and the civil war with the
Communists, left little opportunity to resist the
Japanese occupation of Manchuria (1931). In 1936
he was kidnapped by dissident officers and released
when he agreed to call off the campaign against the
Communists and accept their support in resisting
Japanese advances.

The Japanese launched all-out war (1937) and
caused Chiang's withdrawal to Chongqing which
remained China's capital throughout WWII, during
which he became one of the 'big four' with
Churchill, Roosevelt and Stalin. He became
President again (1948–49) but, when the split with
the Communists intensified and they advanced
to occupy the whole country, Chiang and his
Nationalist followers fled to Taiwan. There, with
US military backing, they have remained,
maintaining they are China's legitimate government
and enjoying prosperity thanks to Japanese and US
economic support. Chiang resumed the Presidency
(1950) and held office until his death, but
effectively he was leader only of an island community.
China, People's Republic of, state of E Asia.
Area: 9,597,000 sq km. Pop: 1,008,175,000
(1982). Language: Chinese. Religion: largely
atheist, though Buddhism and Taoism are
prominent, with elements of Christianity and Islam.
Cap: Beijing (Peking).

The Manchu dynasty, which had ruled the
country since 1644, was overthrown (1911) by the

KUOMINTANG led by SUN YAT-SEN, who was succeeded by CHIANG KAI-SHEK. The Communist Party, founded in 1921, opposed the Kuomintang's military dictatorship, which had shown itself to be totally indifferent to the people's well-being. The factions were frequently in conflict, although during the SINO-JAPANESE WAR they cooperated in fighting the common enemy.

From 1945 onwards the internal struggle was resumed, the Communists under MAO ZEDONG making such rapid progress that by 1949 the Kuomintang had been driven off the mainland to seek refuge on the island of Taiwan. On the mainland, the Communists established the People's Republic, while on Taiwan a rival, US-backed government was set up by Chiang Kai-shek; each government has since claimed its right to the other's territory.

In the People's Republic, Mao Zedong's 2 great efforts at radical change, the GREAT LEAP FORWARD and the CULTURAL REVOLUTION, badly disrupted cultural, economic and social progress and were dramatic examples of Communist policy failures, as was the ideological friction resulting in the SINO-SOVIET SPLIT. In spite of all these difficulties, however, China had the technical competence to develop the atomic bomb (1964) and the hydrogen bomb (1967), thereby emphasizing its superpower status.

Although China's foreign policy has been opposed to the West in such matters as the KOREAN and VIETNAM WARS, in recent years there has been considerable DÉTENTE, commencing with President NIXON's visit to China, and the admittance of China to the UN with a seat on the Security Council (1971).

After Mao's death in 1976, DENG XIAOPING emerged as China's most prominent leader, and has reversed or moderated many of Mao's policies, implementing wide-ranging economic liberalization.

Chou En-lai, *see* ZHOU ENLAI.

Christian Democrats, members of the Christian Democratic Union (CDU) in West Germany, the Christian Democrat Party (DC) in Italy, and similar parties elsewhere.

The German **CDU** was founded in 1945. In some respects it is the successor of the Centre Party of the WEIMAR REPUBLIC and is politically akin to the British CONSERVATIVE PARTY. In association with its Bavarian wing it is called the Christian Social Union (CSU). It has held power on its own (1949—53) and in coalition (1953—57 and 1961—66) with the Free Democratic Party, successor of the Weimar Republic's liberal parties. The CDU's policies, based on united Catholic-Protestant principles, are moderately conservative, supporting maintenance of private enterprise and individual freedom, and commitment to the EEC and NATO.

The Italian **DC**, founded in 1943, is the successor of the Popular Party of the pre-Fascist period, which was inspired by Christian principles. Although not officially tied to the RC Church, the Vatican and clergy exert powerful influences on its anti-Communist and moderate social policies, and like the CDU it is committed to the EEC and NATO. It has had considerable electoral success, both on its own and in coalition, but is not as powerful on its own as the combined opposition, probably due to internal rivalries, the necessity of keeping happy its coalition partners, and outmoded administrative, educational and judicial systems.

Churchill, Sir Winston (1874—1965), British statesman, PM (1940—45 and 1951—55).

He entered Parliament as a Conservative (1900) but, a believer in FREE TRADE and laissez-faire, joined the Liberal Party (1904). He served as President of the Board of Trade (1908—10), Home Secretary (1910—11) and First Lord of the Admiralty (1911—15). The Conservative Party blamed him for the failure of the DARDANELLES campaign and he was driven from office. He returned to the Government as Minister of Munitions (1917), and was Secretary of State for War and Air (1919—21) and Colonial Secretary (1921—22).

He was out of Parliament (1922—24) and was then elected as a 'Constitutionalist' for Epping (1924), and served from then until 1929 as Chancellor of the Exchequer in the Conservative Government, rejoining the Party in 1925. From 1929 to 1939 he was out of office but consistently and vehemently warned Parliament and the country of the perils of German expansionism and the folly of pursuing an APPEASEMENT policy.

On the outbreak of WWII he returned to the Admiralty as First Lord and succeeded Chamberlain as PM (1940—45) of a coalition government. His inspired oratory and outstanding leadership qualities made him immensely popular and his 'bulldog' spirit encouraged and epitomized all that was best in the British people's determination to pursue the War to a successful conclusion through all vicissitudes.

The Conservative Party was defeated in the 1945 election, and Churchill did not achieve power again until 1951 when he once more became PM, finally resigning in 1955.

CIA, *see* CENTRAL INTELLIGENCE AGENCY.

Ciano, Count Galeazzo (1903–44), Italian diplomat, politician, and Mussolini's son-in-law. As Foreign Minister (1936–43) he developed Italo-German relations but, realizing German war aims, became anti-Nazi. Failing to change Mussolini's policies, he voted against him in the Fascist Grand Council (1943) for which he was tried for treason and executed.

civil defence, the organizing of civilians to deal with enemy attacks.

civil disobedience, (a) refusal to obey laws, pay taxes, etc., (b) non-violent method of protest or attempt to achieve political aims.

civil liberties, rights of individuals to certain freedoms of action and speech, the most important of which are the freedoms of assembly, association, conscience, publication, speech, worship, and peaceful demonstration, petition or protest.

civil rights, (a) personal rights of citizens upheld by law in most countries, but esp. as established by the 13th and 14th amendments to the US Constitution with particular application to the black American population; (b) equality of status between groups or races.

Civil Rights Acts, US legislative measures aimed at safeguarding civil rights from government and individual infringement. Several measures were enacted during the 19th cent., but they were largely ineffectual and it was not until 1957 that more positive measures began to be taken.

The Civil Rights Acts of 1957, 1960, 1964 and 1968, and the Voting Rights Act (1965), provided for the creation of a Civil Rights Commission and a Civil Rights Division of the Justice Department; penalties against the use of mob action to obstruct court orders; guaranteed access to public accommodation for black Americans; strengthened and expanded voting rights; the outlawing of job discrimination; the prevention of discrimination in programmes receiving federal government funds by the threat of such funds being withheld; the banning of discrimination in the sale and renting of houses; and anti-riot procedures with penalties for specified riot activities.

class, category or grouping of people according to economic, occupational or social status. In Marxist theory, the term refers exclusively to those persons with a common relationship to material production (*see* BOURGEOISIE and PROLETARIAT). Traditionally, society is divided into the upper, middle and working (lower) classes, according to socio-economic status.

Clemenceau, Georges (1841—1929), French Radical statesman, PM (1906—09 and 1917—1920). His first ministerial appointment was Minister of Home Affairs (1906) and by the year end he was PM. He was defeated (1909) because of his failure to expand the navy without having achieved many of the reforms he desired.

During WWI he was critical of the way it was

being conducted and in 1917 became PM and Minister of War. He inspired the armed forces and civilian population to resist the final German onslaught and assume the offensive, and played a major part in negotiating the Treaty of VERSAILLES. His intransigent hatred of Germany contributed to the harshness of the terms of the Treaty, which were possibly contributory factors in the outbreak of WWII.

CND, *see* CAMPAIGN FOR NUCLEAR DISARMAMENT.

coalition government, alliance or union between 2 or more political parties for some specific or temporary reason, usually in order to form a government where no party has an absolute majority. *See also* NATIONAL GOVERNMENTS.

Cold War, state of military tension and diplomatic and political hostility between 2 countries or power blocs, esp. that between the US and the USSR and their respective allies since WWII.

The Cold War has involved propaganda, subversion, threats, etc., and it has been characterized by assertive actions with limited objectives which have not been permitted to develop into direct military conflict, e.g. the invasions of HUNGARY, CZECHOSLOVAKIA and AFGHANISTAN; the SUEZ CRISIS; the CUBAN MISSILES CRISIS; the BERLIN blockade and wall; the ARAB-ISRAELI WARS; and LEBANON. The attempts by both sides to achieve DÉTENTE have met with only limited success.

collaboration, the act of cooperating with an enemy, esp. one occupying one's own country. Examples in WWII incl. the VICHY GOVERNMENT in France, and QUISLING in Norway.

collective security, a system of maintaining global peace and security by concerted action on the part of the nations of the world, or, in a limited area, by members of an association of states.

collectivization, (a) organization under collective control; (b) a social system based on the principle of the ownership of the means of production by a state, e.g. a collective farm (kolkhoz) in a Communist country. The system was opposed in the USSR in the 1930s by the kulaks, former peasants who had been allowed to become medium-sized farm owners before the Revolution. In order to achieve the first FIVE-YEAR PLAN, Stalin ordered the liquidation of the kulaks and about 10 million are thought to have died.

Collins, Michael (1890—1922), Irish politician and SINN FEIN leader who participated in the EASTER RISING. After WWI he organized the IRISH REPUBLICAN ARMY (IRA) and was a delegate to the London Conference (1921) which agreed to the establishment of Southern IRELAND as the Irish Free State, of which he became first PM. He was assassinated (1922) by a faction within the IRA which opposed the Conference agreements.

Colombo Plan, proposals initiated in 1950 at a Commonwealth ministers' meeting in Colombo, Ceylon (now Sri Lanka) for cooperative economic development of underdeveloped Commonwealth countries in S and SE Asia. Details were agreed at a Colombo meeting of the Commonwealth consutative Committee (1951) by which the principal recipients of economic advice, financial aid and technical training provided by Australia, Canada, New Zealand and the UK were to be

Burma, Ceylon (Sri Lanka), India, Malaya, Malaysia and Pakistan.

Eventually the Plan was expanded to include Japan and the USA as contributors, and Afghanistan, Bhutan, Cambodia (Kampuchea), Indonesia, Iran, Laos, the Maldives, Nepal, the Philippines, Singapore, South Korea, South Vietnam and Thailand as recipients.

colonialism, *see* IMPERIALISM.

COMECON, *see* COUNCIL FOR MUTUAL ECONOMIC ASSISTANCE.

Cominform (Communist Information Bureau), was established in 1947 for the exchange of information and coordination of activities by the Communist parties of Bulgaria, Czechoslovakia, France, Hungary, Italy, Poland, Romania, USSR and Yugoslavia, with HQ in Belgrade. It was dissolved in 1956 as a condition of reconciliation demanded by YUGOSLAVIA which had been expelled in 1948 for deviationist activities.

Comintern, the Communist or 3rd International, a movement established (1919) by Lenin to promote revolutionary Marxist international socialism as opposed to the reformist socialism of the 2nd International. In the early years the ideas of TROTSKY and Zinoviev prevailed but STALIN'S policies gradually took their place and served only Russian interests. The movement was dissolved (1943), probably to mollify disquiet amongst the Western allies of the USSR.

Common Agricultural Policy (CAP), EEC scheme for increasing agricultural productivity, stabilizing markets, and assuring the availability of supplies, reasonable consumer prices and fair living

Vatican City as an independent state and regulated
the position of the RC church in Italy. Indemnity
was also awarded to the Vatican for papal
possessions seized when Rome was occupied in
1870 during the progression to Italian unification.

Congress, the US legislature, established by Article
1 of the Constitution. It consists of the House of
Representatives and the Senate. The former, the
lower chamber, comprises members elected every 2
years from districts of roughly equal populations.
The Senate comprises 2 senators from each state,
elected for 6-year terms; every 2 years, a third of the
Senate comes up for election.

Congress Party, Indian political organization
known prior to independence as the Indian
National Congress. It was founded (1885) to draw
together regionally based, well-educated political
groups. Between the World Wars Mahatma
GANDHI'S doctrine of non-violent civil disobedience as a means towards Indian independence
dominated the Party, leading members of which
were interned (1942—45) because of opposition to
India's entry into WWII. Since independence the
Party has been in power continuously apart from
1977—80 under the successive leaderships of
NEHRU, SHASTRI, and Indira and Rajiv GANDHI.

conscription or **national service,** compulsory
military service, or the direction of conscientious
objectors into essential non-combatant duties, such
as agriculture, mining, etc. It was in effect in the UK
during the periods 1916—20 and 1939—60, and is
still used in a large number of countries.

Conservative Party, British political organization
which developed from the Tories of the 1830s.

It encourages property ownership, a mixed economy and strong defence, based (since 1945) on COLLECTIVE SECURITY against Communist expansion and subversion. Known from 1866 to 1922 as the Conservative and Unionist Party because of its opposition to Irish Home Rule, it has maintained adherence to established institutions coupled with moderate reforms, and its former imperialism has evolved into an affinity with the Commonwealth concept. Under THATCHER the Party has moved to the right, with a policy more radically in favour of free enterprise.

Constantinople Agreements (1915), secret assurances given to Russia by Britain and France that after WWI Constantinople (now Istanbul), the Bosphorus, the Dardanelles, and their hinterlands would be incorporated into Russia. The Agreements foreshadowed the partition of the OTTOMAN EMPIRE since they also provided for Britain and France acquiring unspecified areas of the Empire, the Russian acquisition being dependent on this happening. After the October Revolution (1917) the Bolsheviks repudiated the Agreements and published the secret texts, causing Turkey's resistance to stiffen and inciting liberal protests in Britain and the USA.

constitution, (a) fundamental political precepts on which a state is governed, esp. when it embodies the rights of subjects of that state, (b) a statute embracing such principals, e.g. the US Constitution.

constitutional monarchy, form of government in which supreme authority is vested in a single, usually hereditary, figure who rules according to a CONSTI-

TUTION that defines and limits the sovereign's powers.

containment, (a) act of restraining ideological or political power of a hostile country or operations of a hostile military force, (b) since 1947 a principle of US foreign policy that seeks to prevent Communist expansion. *See* TRUMAN DOCTRINE.

Contras, *see* NICARAGUA.

Coolidge, Calvin (1872–1933), US Republican statesman, Vice-President (1921–23), President (1923–29). On President Harding's mid-term death he succeeded to the Presidency, and set about restoring public confidence after the scandals of Harding's administration. He was a believer in unrestricted freedom in business which led to a rapid growth in commercial monopolies, and followed a policy of conservative ISOLATIONISM. After the left office the prosperity engendered by his policies was destroyed in the WALL STREET CRASH.

Council for Mutual Economic Assistance (COMECON), organization established (1949) for the improvement of trade between the member states — Albania, Bulgaria, Czechoslovakia, Hungary, Poland, Romania and the USSR. Albania was expelled (1961), but additional members are East Germany (1950), Mongolia (1962), Cuba (1972) and Vietnam (1978).

The USSR tried to enforce a common economic policy and trade pattern but strong opposition from Bulgaria and Romania forced a withdrawal of these proposals on the grounds that they interfered with the sovereignty of member states and would damage the less well-off members.

Council of Europe, established (1949) by a decision of the Consultative Council of the WESTERN EUROPEAN UNION. Its members are Belgium, Denmark, France, Eire, Italy, Luxembourg, the Netherlands, Norway, Sweden and the UK. Greece and Turkey joined (1949), Iceland (1950), West Germany (1951), Austria (1956), Cyprus (1961), Switzerland (1963), Malta (1965), Portugal (1976), Spain (1977) and Liechtenstein (1978). Greece withdrew (1969) because of opposition within the council to its violation of human rights.

The Council consists of a Committee of Ministers, and a Consultative Assembly of 170 members appointed or elected by the respective parliaments, usually from their own members but not necessarily so. The European Convention for the Protection of Human Rights (1950) is one of its major achievements. The Partial Agreement (1960) permits members to develop close cooperation, using Council facilities, without involving all members, and this has enabled group agreements to be reached on education, local government and social and public health matters.

The council's aims are the achievement of greater unity between members states and their economic and social progress, practically the only topic barred from discussion being that of a member state's national defence.

Council of Ministers, one of the 5 constituent bodies of the EEC, formed (1967) by a merger of the three existing Communities, ECSC, EEC and Euratom. It is composed of the foreign ministers of the member states who represent national as

opposed to EEC interests. Their decisions rest on
majority voting but unanimity is sought wherever
possible. The Presidency of the Council is held in
rotation for 6-month periods. Since 1974, heads of
state and government have met every 3 months to
discuss Community and foreign policy affairs.

Country Party, Australian political party founded
in 1920 with the objective of giving better representation to agricultural interests in a predominantly
urban-orientated parliament. By 1922 it held the
balance of power between Labour and Nationalists
and was a partner in coalition governments (1922—
29, 1934—41 and 1949—71).

coup d'état, a sudden, violent or illegal seizure of
government.

Cripps, Sir Stafford (1889—1952), British
Labour politician. As Chancellor of the Exchequer
(1947—50) he advocated austerity, but his policies
of strict taxation and a voluntary wage freeze failed
to solve the problem of inflation.

Cuba, see BATISTA, BAY OF PIGS, CASTRO, CUBAN
MISSILES CRISIS.

Cuban Missiles Crisis (1962), sequence of events
which brought about a grave risk of nuclear warfare.
US aerial reconnaissance showed that weapons
being supplied by the USSR to CASTRO'S Cuba were
ballistic missiles with atomic warheads capable of
reaching any part of the USA. President Kennedy
announced that the USA would blockade Cuba and
requested the USSR to remove all weapons that had
already reached the island and to order vessels
carrying more to return home. In exchange for the
removal of the weapons the USA pledged to lift the
blockade and refrain from invading Cuba. There is

no doubt that firm action by the USA prevented more serious circumstances developing, and Kennedy's prestige was enhanced at Khruschchev's expense.

Cultural Revolution (1965—68), major political movement in CHINA constituting an attack on bureaucracy and privilege, initiated by Mao Zedong. The country's educational, managerial and party elite and trends towards liberalism were criticized and purged, so that communications were dislocated and the economy threatened. The Red Guards, a mass youth movement, led the demonstrations by closing colleges and schools and participating in gigantic parades supported by widespread wall-poster campaigns. The Revolution ended when the army stepped in to restore order but its legacy still affects the country. The leaders of the Cultural Revolution (the GANG OF FOUR) were discredited after Mao Zedong's death in 1976.

Curragh Incident (1914), arose out of the possibility that the UK Government would have to use troops in Ulster owing to the threats of violent opposition by ULSTER LOYALISTS to Irish HOME RULE. Officers based at the Curragh, Dublin, were informed that they could resign their commissions and be dismissed from the Army if they did not wish to fire on Ulstermen. The Government withdrew the offer, when many of the officers said they were not prepared to fight in Ulster.

Curzon, George Nathaniel, Marquis Curzon of Kedleston (1859—1925), British Conservative statesman. As Viceroy of India (1898—1905) he introduced many administrative, financial, political and social reforms, incl. partition of Bengal and the establishment of the NW Frontier Province. He became Foreign Secretary (1919—24) when his main achievement was the conclusion of the Treaty of LAUSANNE (1923).

Curzon Line, proposed border along the 'ethnic line' separating Poles and Russians, suggested by the British Foreign Secretary, Lord Curzon, in 1919. As a result of the Polish-Soviet War the boundary was fixed by the Treaty of Riga (1921) well to the E of the Curzon Line. Following the Teheran Conference in 1944, the Curzon Line became the future E border of Poland.

Cyprus, Commonwealth island republic of the E Mediterranean. Area: 9,251 sq km. Pop: 618,000 (est. 1978). Languages: Greek and Turkish. Religion: Greek Orthodox and Islam. Cap: Nicosia.

The island, populated by both Greeks and Turks, was part of the OTTOMAN EMPIRE until 1914 when Britain annexed it because of the Turkish alliance with Germany during WWI, although Britain had held certain rights there since 1878. Cyprus became a colony in 1925, but from the 1930s the Greek population made increasingly vociferous demands for union with Greece (Enosis). The transfer of the UK's Middle East HQ from Egypt to Cyprus in 1954 precipitated a terrorist campaign organized against the British occupation forces (and civil war with Turkish Cypriots) by extremists of the pro-Enosis underground movement (EOKA) led by General George Grivas (1898—1974), a Greek Army officer.

In 1960 Cyprus became independent, and Archbishop MAKARIOS, having renounced Enosis, was elected President. However, civil war broke out again between the two communities (1963), only ending with the intervention of a UN peace-keeping force (1964). The conflict caused a widening rift between Greece and Turkey and in 1974 the Greek military junta backed a pro-Enosis coup which overthrew Makarios. This led to the invasion and occupation of the N part of the Island by Turkey, and open war between Greece and Turkey was narrowly avoided. These events contributed to the fall of the junta in Greece, and led to the movement of 200,000 Greek Cypriot refugees to the S of the island. The island is now effectively partitioned, despite the treaties between Cyprus, Greece, Turkey and the UK which forbid partition as well as Enosis. The UK still retains its sovereign military bases of some 158 sq km.

Czechoslovakia, federal republic of C Europe. Area: 127,871 sq km. Pop: 15,280,000. Languages: Czech and Slovak. Religion: RC. Cap: Prague.

The state consists of the former Austro-Hungarian provinces of Bohemia, Moravia, Silesia and Slovakia and was established (1918) as part of the WWI peace settlements. Tómaš Masaryk (1850—1937), who had organized the Czechoslovak independence movement during the War, became President (1918—35) and did much to weld the disparate provinces into a united nation which was to become the most progressive and prosperous of the new European states.

After the Nazis achieved power in Germany the population of the SUDETENLAND in N Bohemia, mostly German in origin, campaigned for the area to be ceded to Germany, and this was accomplished under the terms of the MUNICH AGREEMENT (1938). In 1939 Germany occupied the rest of Czechoslovakia, and the country remained under occupation until 1945.

Immediately after the War the coalition government was in power with Tómaš Masaryk's son Jan (1886–1948) as Foreign Minister. In 1948 the Communists under GOTTWALD seized control, and shortly afterwards Jan Masaryk died in suspicious circumstances. Gottwald established a hard-line and repressive Communist system which was perpetuated after his death (1953) by NOVOTNÝ.

In 1968 pressures for change brought about the so-called 'Prague Spring', when DUBČEK attempted to introduce liberalizing policies, only to see the popular support he received ruthlessly suppressed when the country was occupied by the armed forces of the WARSAW PACT states (except those of Romania). Dubček was replaced by HUSÁK under whom the country returned to its previous position as a hard-line member of the Warsaw Pact and Comecon.

D

Daladier, Édouard (1884–1970), French statesman, Radical Party PM (1933–34 and 1938–40). The governments he led favoured APPEASEMENT and he was a signatory of the MUNICH AGREEMENT. He served in Reynaud's government (1940) and, after the collapse of France, he tried to form a government in N Africa opposed to the VICHY GOVERNMENT, but was arrested and tried for taking France unprepared into war, imprisoned until 1945 he never held ministerial office again.

Danzig (German; Polish, *Gdánsk*), Polish port at the mouth of the Vistula. Formerly belonging to Prussia, the Treaty of VERSAILLES constituted it a Free City to allow Poland an outlet to the Baltic. The Treaty also granted territory to Poland to give it access to Danzig. This territory was known as the Polish Corridor, and it divided East Prussia from the main part of Germany.

In 1938 Germany demanded that Poland should return the city and allow extra-territorial routes across the Polish Corridor to East Prussia. Poland's ultimate rejection of these demands led to the country's invasion by Germany and the outbreak of WWII.

Dardanelles (ancient name, 'the Hellespont'), strait linking the Sea of Marmara and the Aegean Sea, part of the strategic waterway connecting the Black Sea and the Mediterranean.

In 1915 an Anglo-French fleet tried to force a way through to Constantinople (Istanbul) but suffered heavy losses. The purposes of the attempt were to drive Turkey out of WWI, establish Allied predominance in the Balkans and open the Black Sea route to Russia. The failure of this imaginative strategic plan was due to bad coordination, inadequate planning, lack of persistence, and loss of surprise because of preliminary bombardments.

This disaster was followed immediately by another, when Australian, New Zealand and British forces landed on the Gallipoli peninsula at the S end of the strait. After 8 months of fighting the troops were withdrawn, leaving Turkey the victor yet again. Inadequate planning, bad coordination, confused leadership and high-ranking British and French opposition to the attack were causes of the failure.

Darlan, François (1881—1942), French admiral and politician. Early in WWII he became Secretary of State for Foreign Affairs and the Navy. After the collapse of France (1940) he became Minister of National Defence in the VICHY GOVERNMENT and its representative in N Africa, where he had to deal with the victorious Anglo-American forces. He was assassinated in Algiers.

Dawes Plan (1924), scheme initiated by a US banker, Charles Gates Dawes (1865—1961), while chairman of the Allied Reparations Committee. The plan assisted Germany to fulfil its treaty commitments in the period 1924—29 by permitting annual REPARATIONS payments on a fixed scale, and the reorganization of the German State Bank to assist currency stabilization. Dawes was awarded the Nobel Peace Prize (1925) for his work towards German reconciliation.

Dayan, Moshe (1915–81), Israeli general and politician. He was Chief of Staff (1953–58), directing the Sinai campaign against Egypt (1956). As a Labour member of the Knesset (Parliament) he served as Minister of Agriculture (1959–64). He was Minister of Defence (1967–74), responsible for the successful outcome of the 1967 and 1973 ARAB-ISRAELI WARS. After becoming critical of the government he joined the opposition and became Foreign Minister (1977–79) in Begin's coalition government.

D-Day *see* NORMANDY LANDINGS.

decolonization, (a) granting of independence to a colony, (b) freeing from colonial status.

Britain divested itself of its larger colonies in a gradual process starting in the 19th cent. Canada gained independence in 1867, Australia in 1901, New Zealand in 1907 (more fully in 1931), South Africa in 1910, India and Pakistan in 1947, Sri Lanka in 1948, Ghana in 1957, Nigeria in 1960, Tanzania in 1961, Uganda in 1962, Kenya and Malaysia in 1963. Most of Britain's smaller colonies have subsequently been granted independence, notable exceptions being Gibraltar and the Falkland Islands.

France lost Indo-China (1954) and Algeria (1962) after violent wars of independence, but most of her other colonies (principally in Africa) had a peaceful transition to independence in the 1950s and 1960s. Pressure for independence mostly came from the growth of nationalism led by a Western-educated elite.

De Gaulle, Charles (1890–1970), French general and statesman, President (1945 and 1959–69). After a distinguished military career he escaped to England after the fall of France (1940) in WWII and became leader of the FREE FRENCH and head of the French Committee of National Liberation (1943). He never courted popular favour and his sense of aloofness and arrogance made him a difficult person to work with as Churchill and Roosevelt soon discovered.

He returned to France (1944) and the same year became head of the Provisional Government when France was liberated. He was elected President (1945) but resigned after 10 weeks in office because his proposals for the Fourth Republic were not accepted by the constituent assembly.

De Gaulle remained in retirement until the fall of the Fourth Republic when he formed a 'government of national safety' and a constitution for the Fifth Republic (1958). President again (1959), he resolved the Algerian War by means of the Evian Agreements (1962), determined on France having an independent nuclear deterrent, and insisted on the UK's exclusion from the EEC, with whose members he declined to cooperate because of antagonism to the EEC's agricultural policy. He then withdrew France from NATO and insisted on the removal of its installations from the country because of disagreements with the USA. He was forced to make economic concessions (1968) due to serious student unrest over high taxation for military purposes at the expense of education, health and social services requirements (*see* PARIS STUDENT DEMONSTRATIONS). He resigned (1969) after proposals for senate and regional reforms were rejected in a referendum.

democracy, government by the people or their elected representatives; a political or social unit governed by all its members. The term implies that free elections are held at regular intervals, with the participation of an unlimited number of political parties. The absence of democracy is variously termed AUTOCRACY, DICTATORSHIP and TOTALITARIANISM.

Democratic Party, one of the two main political parties in the USA. Founded (1828), its first 20th-cent. Presidential success was that of Woodrow Wilson (1913–21). The Party urged government action to stimulate industry and reduce unemployment after the interwar depression, and the proposals were incorporated in F.D. Roosevelt's NEW DEAL. Under Wilson, Roosevelt, Truman and Kennedy the Party displayed a sense of worldwide responsibility, in contrast to Republican isolationism. From the early 1960s civil rights, social welfare and aid to underdeveloped countries have been priorities.

Deng Xiaoping or **Teng Hsiao-ping** (1904–   ), Chinese Communist statesman. He achieved enormous power on becoming Party Secretary (1954). His organizational skills, moderation, pragmatism and dislike of uncontrolled radicalism caused his disaffection from Mao Zedong and his affinity with Liu Shaoqi. During the CULTURAL REVOLUTION he disappeared from the Chinese hierarchy, was rehabilitated (1973), dismissed again (1976), and rehabilitated again and made deputy PM and Party Vice-Chairman (1977).

Although he has retired from many of his official posts he remains perhaps the most powerful figure in the Chinese leadership.

depression or **slump,** in economic terms a decline in trade and general prosperity. The Great Depression of 1929–34 was worldwide, starting with an agricultural recession followed by financial panic and collapse, known as the WALL STREET CRASH, in the USA. This in turn affected financial institutions and money markets in other parts of the world and caused a run on the pound in the UK. The result was a decline in internal consumption and exports in industrialized countries, factory closures and massive unemployment.

desegregation or **integration,** the policy of ending the forced separation of racial, political or religious groups within a society.

In the 1950s the US federal government ordered the end of separate schooling for blacks and whites in the southern states. This policy met with widespread white opposition, culminating in race riots in Little Rock, Arkansas (1957), where federal troops were used to enfource school integration.

In South Africa, the policy of APARTHEID opposes racial desegration.

Desert Campaign, *see* NORTH AFRICA CAMPAIGN.

détente, the easing or relaxing of tension, esp. between nations. More specifically the term is used for the improvement of relations between East and West from around 1969. In 1972 the USA and the USSR embarked on the STRATEGIC ARMS LIMITATION TALKS. East-West relations deteriorated after the Soviet invasion of AFGHANISTAN

(1979), although they have improved to an extent since GORBACHEV came to power. *See also* COLD WAR.

deterrence, prevention of hostilities by the possession of a weapon or combination of weapons, esp. nuclear, held by a state or allied states, in order to deter attack by another state or states. There is a 'balance of terror' where opposing groupings each possess such weapons, thereby deterring each other between NATO and Warsaw Pact powers.

De Valéra, Eamon (1882–1975), Irish statesman. After joining SINN FEIN, he participated in the EASTER RISING (1916). He was captured by the British but released in the 1917 amnesty. From then until 1926 he was President of Sinn Fein, but then formed a new political party, FIANNA FÁIL, which, with Labour, formed a coalition government (1932). He remained PM for 16 years, an office he again held (1951–54 and 1957–59). He was instrumental in forming a new constitution (1937) which severed the final links with the UK by creating the Republic of Eire, of which he was President (1959–73).

deviationism, ideological deviation, esp. from orthodox Moscow-line Communism, such as practised by YUGOSLAVIA since the 1950s and advocated by W European Communist parties (*see* EUROCOMMUNISM).

devolution, transfer or allocation of authority, esp. from a central government to regional governments or particular interests; such as certain functions and powers passed to Northern Irish, Scottish and Welsh authorities by the UK government.

dictator, a ruler who is not effectively restricted

by a constitution, laws, recognized opposition, etc. Examples incl. Hitler, Mussolini and Stalin.

dictatorship, (a) office, government or period of rule by a DICTATOR, (b) country ruled by a dictator, (c) absolute or supreme power of authority.

Dien Bien Phu, village in North Vietnam, the scene of a decisive victory (1954) by the VIET MINH over the French in the war of independence in INDO-CHINA. The French defeat led to the end of French colonial rule in Indo-China and the partition of VIETNAM following the 1954 Geneva Agreement.

disarmament, the reduction of defensive or offensive fighting capability by an armed force or nation. Before and after WWI and WWII many attempts have been made to achieve meaningful disarmament, firstly between the Fascist states and the democracies of Europe and America and, during the last 30 years, between NATO and Warsaw Pact countries. There was no success before WWII and only limited progress has been made since, notably in the NUCLEAR TEST BAN TREATY (1963), a Non-Proliferation Treaty (1968), a germ warfare agreement (1972), the STRATEGIC ARMS LIMITATION TALKS (1969–72 and 1979), and the INTERMEDIATE NUCLEAR FORCES TREATY (1987).

Governments on both sides have generally pursued a policy of mutilateralism, i.e. that no country should abandon nuclear weapons until all agree to do so. Vocal pressure groups in the West such as the CAMPAIGN FOR NUCLEAR DISARMAMENT have called for a policy of unilateralism, i.e. that their own country should abandon nuclear weapons as an example to others.

Dogger Bank Incident (1904), event arising during the RUSSO-JAPANESE WAR when the Russian Baltic Fleet was despatched to the Far East. Steaming through the North Sea it encountered what were thought to be Japanese torpedo boats but actually were Hull fishing vessels. The warships sank one vessel, killing 2 of its crew, thereby rousing such anger in Britain that an armed conflict was barely avoided. International arbitration and Russian acceptance of compensation claims eased tension, and long-term relations between the 2 countries were unimpared.

Dollfuss, Engelbert (1892–1934), Austrian statesman. After WWI he joined the Christian Social Party, becoming Chancellor (1932–34). Fearing a socialist revolt he suspended parliamentary government (1933), and ordered the army to suppress a demonstration by attacking housing estates in the Viennese suburbs (1934). His introduction of a new and Fascist constitution (1934) brought about his downfall. Hated by the Nazis, who wanted ANSCHLUSS, and by the Marxists, he was assassinated in the Chancellery by Nazis attempting to stage a coup d'état.

dominion, (a) formerly applied to self-governing divisions of the British Empire, i.e. Australia, Canada, India, New Zealand and South Africa; (b) an area of control or sphere of influence; (c) the land governed by a government or ruler.

domino theory, the idea that a Communist takeover of a country will lead to Communist takeovers in neighbouring states; an allusion to a line of dominoes, each standing on end, all of which fall when one is pushed. The theory was invoked by those in the USA who opposed withdrawal of US forces from the Vietnam War.

Dönitz, Karl (1891–1980), German admiral and leading member of the High Command during WWII and, for 3 weeks in 1945, Hitler's successor. In violation of the Treaty of VERSAILLES he was principally involved in the reorganization of the U-boat fleet in the 1930s and became C-in-C of the Navy in 1943. The Allied Military Tribunal at Nuremburg sentenced him in 1946 to 10 years imprisonment for war crimes.

Douglas-Home, Sir Alec, Baron Home of the Hirsel (1903–   ), British Conservative statesman, PM (1963–64). He was twice Foreign Secretary (1960–63 and 1970–74). After Macmillan's resignation (1963), Douglas-Home was elected leader of the Conservative Party, and became PM. An experienced politician and diplomat, the success of his 'caretaker' premiership drastically reduced the size of Labour's majority in the 1964 election.

dreadnought, a class of big-gun battleship named after HMS *Dreadnought,* launched in 1906. The class carried 10 × 12-in guns, had a speed of 21 knots, and was able to outrange and outpace any other warship. The introduction of this class of ship started a full-scale naval armaments race which reached a climax in WWI.

Dresden, an industrial city of East Germany. Pop: 1,809,000. A beautiful Baroque city, it was almost totally destroyed by Allied bombing in 1945 with a loss of c. 135,000 lives, an action which caused considerable criticism as being unnecessary at such a late stage in WWII.

Dreyfus, Alfred (1859—1935), French army officer, of Jewish origin, falsely convicted for treason (1893—94). Charged with passing military intelligence to Germany, he was court-martialled and imprisoned on Devil's Island. The case split France in two: liberals, radicals and socialists maintained his innocence, being opposed by the military, monarchists and RCs, who stirred up considerable anti-Semitic and anti-German feelings. Dreyfus was eventually released in 1906. Final proof of innocence was established when documents of the German military attaché were published in 1930.

Dubček, Alexander (1921—   ), Czechoslovak politician. His reforms as First Secretary of the Communist Party (1968—69) prompted the Warsaw Pact occupation of CZECHOSLOVAKIA (1968) and his enforced resignation. He was expelled from the Party in 1970. His fall from power was due to his desire to liberalize the economy, to widen the area of discussion within the Party without deviation from the Warsaw Pact's external policies, and to reduce the party's totalitarian character.

Dulles, John Foster (1888—1959), US diplomat and statesman. As Secretary of State (1953—59) he caused tension with America's allies, esp. during the SUEZ CRISIS. A firm supporter of European unity, he did much to strengthen international alliances against Communism, and his shrewd exposition of US strength was instrumental in safeguarding West Berlin's status, and the retention of the Pescadores, Quemoy and Matsu (islands off the Chinese mainland) by the Chinese Nationalists against Communist harassment.

Duma, Russian elective legislative assembly established by TSAR NICHOLAS II (1905) and overthrown by the Bolsheviks (1917). The upper chamber was the Council of State and the lower chamber, the State Duma, elected on a limited FRANCHISE. There were 4 Dumas during the period 1905—17. The Tsar retained the power of dissolution and veto, and ministers were responsible to him and not to the Duma, which was allowed only limited control of the budget.

Dumbarton Oaks Conference (1944), a series of meetings held near Washington by delegates from Britain, China, the USSR and the USA to discuss structural proposals for the UNITED NATIONS ORGANIZATION, with special reference to the Security Council and the individual members' use of veto powers.

Dunkirk, port of NW France, scene in WWII of the evacuation of the British Expeditionary Force and the French 1st Army (1940). About 336,000 men were rescued by an improvised flotilla of vessels of all descriptions, strongly supported by the RAF. Shortly afterwards France capitulated, but the success of the evacuation did much to strengthen British morale.

E

Easter Rising (1916), rebellion seeking
independence for IRELAND, centred on the Dublin
GPO from where a provisional government of the
Irish Republic was proclaimed. Hopes of German
assistance did not materialize and twelve rebel
leaders, incl. James Connolly of SINN FEIN and
Patrick Pearse of the Irish Republican Brotherhood,
were executed. Others, incl. Eamon DE VALÉRA,
were imprisoned but subsequently released by an
amnesty (1917).

East Germany, *see* GERMANY.

EC, *see* EUROPEAN COMMUNITY.

ECSC, *see* EUROPEAN COAL AND STEEL COM-
MUNITY.

Eden, Sir Anthony, 1st Earl of Avon
(1897–1977), British Conservative statesman,
PM (1955–57). He was also Foreign Secretary
(1935–38, 1940–45 and 1951–55). His administration's handling of the SUEZ CRISIS (1956)
aroused widespread opposition and this, coupled
with poor health, caused his resignation.

Education Act (1944), legislation sponsored
by R.A. BUTLER, then Minister of Education. The
Act transformed the Board of Education into a
Ministry; reorganized state-assisted education into
primary, secondary and further education spheres;
raised the school-leaving age to 15; abolished fees
for grammar schools; and stipulated daily collective
undenominational worship. Secondary education

was split into grammar, technical and modern categories, those attending grammar schools having been successful in the '11-plus' examination, which resulted in these schools receiving the more academically gifted children. Since the 1960s, state secondary schools have gradually been transformed into comprehensive schools, which take pupils of all abilities.

Edward VII (1841–1910), King of Great Britain and Ireland (1901–10). The eldest son of Queen Victoria, his playboy image weakened Victorian conventions and so earned the Queen's disapproval, with the result that she denied him official responsibilities. However, throughout his 9-year reign he was a popular and well-loved monarch.

Edward VIII, *see* ABDICATION CRISIS.

EEC, *see* EUROPEAN ECONOMIC COMMUNITY.

EFTA, *see* EUROPEAN FREE TRADE ASSOCIATION.

Egypt, republic of NE Africa. Area: 1,002,000 sq km. Pop: 47,000,000 (est. 1983). Language: Arabic. Religion: Sunni Islam. Cap: Cairo.

In 1914 Egypt was declared a British protectorate, prior to the formal recognition of independence (1922). In 1936 an Anglo-Egyptian Treaty provided for the gradual withdrawal of British forces (except from the Suez Canal Zone), but this was hindered by WWII.

The creation of the state of Israel led to Egyptian involvement in the ARAB-ISRAELI WARS (1948, 1956, 1967, 1973), and to the intensification of nationalist feeling. In 1952 the monarchy was overthrown by General Neguib, who proclaimed a republic in 1953. Neguib was in turn ousted by the radical Colonel NASSER (1954). After the SUEZ CRISIS (1956), Egypt increasingly depended on aid from the USSR, and formed the United Arab Republic (UAR) with Syria (1958–61). The 1967 war with Israel led to the loss of Sinai, which Egypt unsuccessfully attempted to recover in the 1973 war.

Nasser died in 1970 and was succeeded by SADAT, who reorientated the country towards the West. The CAMP DAVID AGREEMENT (1978) led to a peace treaty with Israel (1979) by which Egypt recovered Sinai, but which left the country temporarily isolated in the Arab world. In 1981 Sadat was succeeded by MUBARAK.

Eire, *see* IRELAND.

Eisenhower, Dwight D. (1890–1969), US general, Republican President (1953–61). As Allied C-in-C, N Africa, he directed the NORTH AFRICA CAMPAIGN and the invasion of Italy during WWII (1942–43). As supreme commander of the Allied Expeditionary Force in W Europe he was responsible for the NORMANDY LANDINGS (1944), the expulsion from occupied territory of the German forces, and their ultimate unconditional surrender. He was widely criticized for not allowing the Allied armies to take Berlin, Prague and Vienna before the Russians, so weakening the West's bargaining powers in the postwar settlements.

As President, his integrity and conciliatory flair balanced his political inexperience. His Presidency was marked by 2 CIVIL RIGHTS ACTS, the passing of social-security laws, and efforts to achieve better understanding with the USSR while supporting mutual security programmes to combat Communism (*see* EISENHOWER DOCTRINE).

Eisenhower Doctrine, principle recommended by President Eisenhower to Congress (1957) that US forces should be used to protect any state in the Middle East subject to aggression by any nation 'controlled by international Communism'. Military advice and economic aid to any state in the area which considered its independence threatened was also proposed. The Doctrine was withdrawn (1959) owing to the fact that those countries it was designed to assist believed it was against the principles of Arab nationalism.

Elizabeth II (1926–), Queen of Great Britain and Northern Ireland (1952–). She married Philip Mountbatten in 1947 and succeeded her father George VI in 1952. Her reign has been characterized by closer relationships with her subjects both at home and overseas than that of any previous monarch, and she has maintaned and developed Commonwealth ties and relationships between the UK and foreign countries.

Energy Crisis, *see* OIL CRISIS.

Entente Cordiale, a term first used in the 1840s to denote the friendly relationship between France and Britain; nevertheless severe strains have been imposed upon the friendship from time to time.

Many differences between the countries were resolved in 1904 when a convention was concluded (the Anglo-French Entente) which settled outstanding colonial disputes, policy disagreements over Egypt and Morocco, and Newfoundland fishing rights. *See also* TRIPLE ENTENTE.

In 1923 there was trouble over the RUHR, and again in 1940 when the Royal Naval attacked the

French fleet in the Mediterranean to prevent it falling into enemy hands in WWII. The Treaty of Dunkirk (1947) sought to reactivate the Entente's ideals but in recent years fresh strains have arisen, especially over EEC matters.

Erhard, Ludwig (1897–1977), West German statesman. After becoming a Christian Democrat member of the Bundestag (1949) he was appointed Minister of Economic Affairs, a position he held until 1963, when he became Chancellor. As Economics Minister he presided over West Germany's transition from wartime devastation to prosperity. He was not so successful as Chancellor, and proposed taxation increases resulted in his resignation (1966).

Eritrea, province of ETHIOPIA on the Red Sea. It became an Italian colony (1890) and was a base for attacks on Ethiopia (1895–96 and 1935–36). During WWII it was occupied by the British from 1941, who remained until 1952 when it was united federally with Ethiopia, which absorbed it in 1962. A guerrilla separatist movement has been active since 1963.

Estonia, *see* BALTIC STATES.

Ethiopia, republic of NE Africa; formerly known as Abyssinia. Area: 1,221,900 sq km. Pop: 31,000,000 (est. 1981). Language: Amharic. Religion: Coptic Christian and Islam. Cap: Addis Ababa.

Menelik II (1844–1913) defeated Italy's attempt to colonize the country at the Battle of Adowa (1896), but Italy reoccupied the country (1936) until driven out by Allied forces (1941). Emperor HAILE SELASSIE ruled the country from

1930, but was an autocratic monarch, permitting parliament little real authority. He was deposed in 1974 by an army coup.

The country is now governed by a Provisional Military Administrative Council which has had to contend with famine, social distress, a guerrilla separatist movement in ERITREA, and a war over disputed territory with Somalia.

Euratom, *see* EUROPEAN ATOMIC ENERGY COMMUNITY.

Eurocommunism, a term denoting the liberalized form of Communism as practised by Western European Communist parties since 1975 when the French and Italian parties issued a joint policy declaration. This recognized the right of other parties to exist, advocated democratic elections, guaranteed civil liberties and the right of opposition, and abandoned the principle of the dictatorship of the proletariat (*see* MARXISM).

European Atomic Energy Community (Euratom), was established in 1957 by a treaty between the 6 members of the EEC. In 1967 it was absorbed into the general European Community. Its objectives are the rapid large-scale production of nuclear energy for peaceful purposes, and technical development of nuclear research.

European Coal and Steel Community (ECSC), came into existence in 1952 as a result of the SCHUMAN PLAN of 1950 proposing a union of the Franco-German coal, iron and steel industries. Belgium, Italy, Luxembourg and the Netherlands joined France and West Germany in the union, and in 1967 the ECSC was merged with the EEC and Euratom. The objectives of the organization were to eliminate tariffs and other restrictions and promote a free labour market.

European Commission, one of the constituent bodies of the EEC whose members are appointed by agreement among the member governments for a 4-year renewable term. France, Italy, the UK and West Germany each have 2 Commissioners and the other states have 1 each.

The Commissioners are pledged to be independent of government, national or special interests. The Commission acts as a mediator between member governments in Community matters, and is the custodian of Community Treaties and the initiator of Community action.

European Community (EC), the joint executive of the ECSC, EEC and Euratom, formed in 1967.

European Economic Community (EEC), also known as the Common Market, international organization established in 1958, a year after the Treaty of ROME was signed by Belgium, France, Italy, Luxembourg, the Netherlands and West Germany. These states were already members of the EUROPEAN COAL AND STEEL COMMUNITY, and the EEC was an expansion of the earlier organization based on discussions by its members at the Messina Conference (1955).

The EEC provides for free movement of capital and labour, joint financial and social policies, FREE TRADE, and the abolition of restrictive trading practices. Veto powers were available to enable a member to block proposed new entries, and France used these powers (1963 and 1967), in defiance of the wishes of the other members, to prevent the UK joining. Denmark, Eire and the UK became members in 1973. Greece in 1981, and Spain and Portugal in 1986. The EEC has special links with the EUROPEAN FREE TRADE ASSOCIATION and with Third World states by means of the LOMÉ CONVENTIONS.

European Free Trade Association (EFTA), became effective (1960) when Austria, Denmark, Norway, Portugal, Sweden, Switzerland and the UK joined in promoting economic expansion and trade between themselves. Finland became an associate member (1961) and Iceland joined in 1970.

Denmark and the UK left to join the EEC (1972), and the remaining members negotiated an agreement with the EEC making provision for free trade in industrial products between the two organizations.

European Parliament, originated (1952) as part of the EUROPEAN COAL AND STEEL COMMUNITY and was expanded by the Treaties of ROME (1957) to cover EEC and Euratom affairs. It became (1967) one of the constituents of the European Community. Until 1979 the Parliament comprised members nominated by the national parliaments of the member states. It was then decided that every 5 years the electorate of each state should elect its own representatives. The membership is split on party lines similar to those prevailing in the national parliaments.

executive, (a) branch of government responsible for carrying out laws, decrees, etc., (b) an administration, (c) function of carrying into effect plans, orders, laws, etc. *See also* SEPARATION OF POWERS.

F

Fabian Society, an association of British socialists (founded 1884) advocating the establishment of democratic socialism by gradual reforms within the law. Notable early members were George Bernard Shaw and Sidney and Beatrice Webb.

Falange, Fascist movement founded in Spain in 1933 by José Antonio Primo de Rivera (1903–36). It was the only legal party under the FRANCO regime.

Falkland Islands, (Span. *Islas Malvinas*), crown colony of the UK, in S Atlantic Ocean. Area: 12,100 sq km. Pop: 2,400. Cap: Port Stanley.

Settled by British colonists in the 19th cent., the islands have long been claimed by Argentina. In April 1982 Argentinian forces occupied the islands. Attempts by the USA and UN to bring about a diplomatic solution were unsuccessful, and the UK despatched a task force to retake the islands. After heavy fighting, the UK force eventually recaptured the Islands in June 1982. Argentina has continued to claim sovereignty, which the UK continues to refuse to negotiate.

Fascism, the ideology and political system of Benito MUSSOLINI, which encouraged militarism and extreme NATIONALISM, organizing Italy along right-wing hierarchial authoritarian lines fundamentally opposed to democracy and liberalism. The term is also applied to any ideology or movement inspired by such principles, e.g. German NATIONAL SOCIAL-

ISM and the Spanish FALANGE.

federation, the union of several provinces, states, etc., to form a federal union; a political unit formed in such a way. The members of such a union usually reserve a degree of autonomy, maintaining their own executive and legislature to govern internal affairs, although the federal government normally deals with defence, foreign affairs, etc. Examples of federations incl. the USA, the USSR, Australia and West Germany.

FGR, *see* GERMANY.

Fianna Fáil, Irish political party founded (1926) by DE VALÉRA, originating from the faction of SINN FEIN opposed to the Anglo-Irish Treaty (1921), and sympathetic towards republican ideals (*see also* FINE GAEL).

It achieved power in 1932 and has been the governing party for much of the time since. In the 1930s it took steps to distance Eire from the UK, incl. the abolition of the Governor-Generalship, the introduction of high protective tariffs, the differentiation of Irish nationality from that of the UK, and the inclusion of claims to a united Ireland in the 1937 Constitution.

fifth column, a group of Falangist sympathisers within Madrid during the SPANISH CIVIL WAR who aided the 4 columns of rebel troops marching on the city. The term is now applied to any group of hostile or subversive infiltrators.

Fine Gael, Irish political party originating from the faction of SINN FEIN sympathetic to the Anglo-Irish Treaty (1921).

It formed the first government of the Irish Free State but, after FIANNA FÁIL achieved power

(1932), it has been unable to re-establish itself in government since 1945 except for short periods when it was supported by some of the minor parties, during the first of which the last connections with the UK were severed.

Finland, republic of N Europe. Area: 304,643 sq km. Pop: 4,844,000 (1982). Languages: Finnish, Swedish. Religion: Lutheran. Cap: Helsinki.

The country was ceded to Russia by Sweden (1809) but gained independence (1917). Invasion by the USSR in 1939 was repulsed, but important land areas were ceded to the USSR in the peace treaty (1940). Being Germany's ally in WWII resulted in further territorial losses in the peace treaty (1947). Since the war a series of coalition governments has pursued a non-aligned policy in international affairs.

First World War, *see* WORLD WAR ONE.

Fisher, John, Baron Fisher of Kilverstone (1841–1920), British Admiral of the Fleet. He rose to be First Sea Lord (1904–10 and 1914–15). He did much to prepare the Navy for WWI, scrapping outdated ships and introducing the DREADNOUGHT.

Fiume (Italian; Serbo-Croat, *Rijeka*), a Hungarian port on the Adriatic claimed by Italy and Yugoslavia at the PARIS PEACE CONFERENCE (1919). Whilst deliberations were going on an Italian nationalist, Gabriele D'Annunzio, seized the port and held it until 1921. In 1924 Yugoslavia recognized the incorporation of the port into Italy but it was ceded to Yugoslavia in 1947 as part of WWII peace settlements.

Five-Year Plan, in socialist economies a government plan for economic development over a period of 5 years. In the USSR Stalin introduced a series of 3 such plans, starting in 1928, which involved rapid industrialization and the COLLECTIVIZATION of agriculture.

Foot, Michael (1913–), British politician. Leader of the Labour Party (1980–83).

Ford, Gerald (1913–), US statesman, Republican President (1974–77). He was chosen by Nixon to be Vice-President on the resignation of Spiro Agnew, and when Nixon himself resigned, Ford succeeded him as President, becoming the only person in US history to hold such offices in a non-elected capacity. He continued Nixon's policies of withdrawal from Vietnam and DÉTENTE.

Fourteen Points, a peace programme to follow the end of WWI, outlined by President Woodrow Wilson to the US Congress in 1918.

The points were: (1) renunciation of secret diplomacy; (2) freedom of the seas; (3) removal, where possible, of economic barriers; (4) reduction in armaments; (5) impartial adjustment of colonial claims; (6) Germany and its allies to leave USSR territory; (7) restoration of Belgium; (8) liberation of occupied France, and the return to France of Alsace-Lorraine; (9) Italian frontiers to be adjusted along clearly recognizable lines of nationality; (10) autonomous development for the peoples of the Austro-Hungarian Empire; (11) occupation forces to withdraw from Romania, Montenegro and Serbia, with Serbia receiving access to the sea; (12) self-development for non-Turkish peoples within the Ottoman Empire, and free passage of the Dardanelles; (13) formation of an independent Poland with access to the sea; (14) the creation of a general association of nations to guarantee the political independence of all states.

The majority of these points were implemented at the PARIS PEACE CONFERENCE, and point (14) led to the foundation of the LEAGUE OF NATIONS.

France, republic of W Europe. Area: 543,965 sq km. Pop: 54,335,000 (1982). Language: French. Religion: predominantly RC. Capital: Paris.

The Third Republic (1871—1946) was established after the overthrow of the Emperor Napoleon III in the Franco-Prussian War. Because of a fear of authoritarian, anti-republican rule, its constitution favoured weak and unstable governments — for example, between WWI and WWII there were 44 governments, led by 20 different PMs. The Franco-Russian Alliance (*see* TRIPLE ENTENTE) led to France's involvement in WWI, and the instability of its governments led to near-defeat. However, with the Allied victory, France regained ALSACE-LORRAINE from Germany.

In the 1930s, France, like Britain, pursued a policy of APPEASEMENT towards Hitler, and the instability of its governments was again a factor in its defeat (1940) and occupation by Germany in WWII, when the collaborationist VICHY GOVERNMENT came to power (1940—44). DE GAULLE and the FREE FRENCH, together with resistance groups in France, continued to oppose German occupation until the liberation (1944).

The Fourth Republic (1946—58) was just as unstable as the Third Republic, 23 governments holding power in 12 years. Under the Republic, the economy was revitalized after the ravages of war, and France became a founder member of the EEC.

The unsuccessful attempt to hold onto the French colonies in INDO-CHINA discredited the Republic, and its plans for the independence of ALGERIA led to a threatened rebellion by French settlers in the colony and by elements in the army. The crisis led to the return to power of De Gaulle, and his establishment of the Fifth Republic (1958).

The Fifth Republic (1958–   ) gave extensive powers to the President, and put an end to government instability. As President, De Gaulle, having survived an army rebellion in 1961, eventually settled the Algerian problem when independence was granted in 1962. In the late 1950s and early 1960s France also granted independence to most of its other colonies, principally in Africa, but it has maintained close economic, political and cultural links with them.

De Gaulle's ambition was to establish France as leader of a united Europe independent of US and Soviet influence. He withdrew French forces from NATO (1966), and twice blocked the UK's application to join the EEC (1963 and 1967), fearing that France's dominant position might be usurped. He insisted that France develop its own nuclear deterrent, and in foreign affairs followed an independent line, e.g. by visiting Warsaw Pact countries, and by opposing Western policies in conflicts such as the Middle East and Vietnam. At home, crises developed over the value of the franc and over a lack of educational and social investment. These, combined with substantial wage demands, culminated in a general strike and the PARIS STUDENT DEMONSTRATIONS (1968).

De Gaulle resigned following a referendum

defeat in 1969, and was succeeded as president by POMPIDOU (1969—74), GISCARD D'ESTANG (1974—81), and MITTERAND (1981—   ). French opposition to expansion of EEC membership was dropped, and France has been more amenable to cooperating with the West's political and economic policies, although still opting for an independent military approach.

franchise or **suffrage**, the right to vote, esp. for representatives in a legislative body. In the UK, following agitation for WOMEN'S SUFFRAGE, the Representation of the People Act (1918) gave the vote to all women over 30 and all men over 21. A further Act in 1928 enabled all women over 21 to vote. In 1969, the voting age was lowered to 18.

Franco, Francisco (1892—1975), called el Caudillo, Spanish general and statesman. He was Commander-in-Chief of the nationalist rebels in the SPANISH CIVIL WAR (1936—39), defeating the republican socialist government with German and Italian military aid and establishing a dictatorship. He kept Spain neutral during WWII, and afterwards made a pact with the USA for military bases in Spain in return for economic aid. He prepared the country for a return of the monarchy and the restoration of democracy after his death. *See also* SPAIN.

Franco-Russian Alliance, *see* TRIPLE ENTENTE.

Franz Ferdinand, *see* SARAJEVO.

Franz Josef I (1830—1916), Emperor of Austria (1848—1916) and King of Hungary (1867—1916). His autocratic reaction to the 1848 revolutions led him to distrust all forms of party government and adhere to bureaucratic administration, under a benevolent dynasty, at the expense of constitutional rule. The last years of his reign were marked by WWI.

Free French, the name given in 1940 to supporters of General DE GAULLE during WWII. The movement represented a political alternative to the VICHY GOVERNMENT as well as a rallying-point for French patriots. It was renamed the Fighting French in 1942.

free trade, international trade that is free of such government influence as import quotas, export subsidies, protection tariffs, etc. The opposite to free trade is PROTECTIONISM. Free trade was the policy of 19th-cent. Liberalism in the UK, and was in force until IMPERIAL PREFERENCE was introduced in 1931. Such international organizations as the EEC and EFTA promote free trade between member states.

G

Gaddafi, Mu'ammar Muhammad al-
(1942–), Libyan army officer and statesman. He
has held power since the overthrow of the monarchy
(1969). He proclaimed a programme intended to
involve the people more closely in the running of the
state (1973), and in 1977 renamed the country the
Socialist People's Libyan Arab Jamahiriyah ('state
of the masses').

Gaddafi is a fanatical Moslem and revolutionary,
who uses intimidatory tactics to achieve his ends
and supports terrorist movements elsewhere with
Libyan oil wealth. His attempts to foster Arab unity
(e.g. the planned unification of Libya and Egypt in
1973) have largely failed because of his extremism,
which has antagonized a large number of other
countries.

Gaitskell, Hugh (1906–63), British Labour politician. As Chancellor of the Exchequer (1950–51),
he became unpopular with the left wing of the Party
by introducing prescription charges under the
National Health Service. He became Leader of the
Labour Party (1955–63), and remained in conflict
with the Left over unilateral nuclear disarmament
and nationalization. He defeated moves to oust
him from the leadership in 1961.

Gallipoli, see DARDANELLES.

Gandhi, Indira (1917–84), Indian stateswoman.
Congress Party PM (1966–77 and 1980–84). The
daughter of NEHRU, she succeeded SHASTRI as PM.

Her methods alienated older Hindu Congressional members, who eventually formed a dissident movement which charged her with corruption during the 1971 electoral campaign. She was barred for 6 years (1975) from public office, but retaliated by having 676 of her opponents arrested under the Maintenance of Internal Security Act, and by being granted dictatorial powers by Parliament, so bringing India to the verge of civil war (1976). She resigned after the dissidents gained overwhelming victory in the 1977 election, but was re-elected in 1980. She was assassinated by Sikh extremists.

Gandhi, Mohandas Karamchand (1869–1948), Indian nationalist leader and social reformer, known as 'Mahatma' (Great Soul). He spent several years in South Africa opposing discriminatory legislation against Indians, and on his return to India during WWI started a campaign for raising the economic and social standards of its peoples.

As leader of the Indian National Congress (*see* CONGRESS PARTY) he adopted a non-cooperation policy of civil disobedience, supported by hunger strikes, directed against British rule in India. He spent several years in prison, but lived to see independence achieved (1947). Having opposed violence all his life, he was assassinated by a Hindu fanatic opposed to his efforts to achieve communal harmony between Hindus and Moslems.

Gandhi, Rajiv (1942–   ), Indian statesman. He became PM (1984–   ) following the assassination of his mother Indira. He has had to deal with the problems of Sikh separatists in the Punjab and the civil war in SRI LANKA. He also initiated a major crackdown on corruption.

Gang of Four, radical faction within the Chinese Communist Party, consisting of Jiang Qing (Mao Zedong's widow), Zhang Chunqiao, Wang Hongwen and Yao Wenyuan. It emerged as a political force (1976) but was denounced 6 months later by Party Chairman Hua Guofeng for leading the excesses of the CULTURAL REVOLUTION, and was again denounced at the Party's 11th congress (1977). The members of the gang were brought to trial and sentenced to life imprisonment. The term has also been applied to the founders of the UK SOCIAL DEMOCRATIC PARTY.

GATT, *see* GENERAL AGREEMENT ON TARIFFS AND TRADE.

Gaza Strip, area of about 160 sq km on the E Mediterranean coast around Gaza. Formerly part of the British Mandate for Palestine it was administered by Egypt (1949—56), and frequently used as a base for terrorist missions against Israel. Israel occupied it during the 1956 ARAB-ISRAELI WAR, and it was placed under UN control (1957—67). It was occupied during the 1967 War by Israel which subsequently administered it as 'occupied territory'.

GDR, *see* GERMANY.

General Agreement on Tariffs and Trade (GATT), multilateral international treaty signed by 86 states in 1948. It was designed to expand international trade and promote economic development, esp. by the elimination or reduction of import quotas and tariffs. Special attention is given to the trading problems of developing countries.

Since its inception, 7 rounds of negotiations have been concluded, and participating countries now account for some 80% of world trade. In addition to its members the Agreement has 31 de facto adherents who participate under special arrangements.

General Strike (1926), the climax to several years of industrial unrest and of attempts by the miners' unions to secure sympathetic support for their grievances from workers in other major industries.

The miners, threatened by further wage cuts, succeeded in persuading the TRADES UNION CONGRESS to bring out all major industries — transport workers, printers, builders, workers in heavy industries, and engineers. The Government used troops to maintain food supplies. The TUC ended the strike as it felt the Government had been better prepared for the strike than had the unions. A legacy of bitterness was left on all sides.

Geneva Convention, series of 4 international agreements, signed as a group (1949) by 59 governments, for the protection of war victims. The oldest (1864) set out regulations for the care of sick and wounded. Naval combatants were covered in 1907, treatment of prisoners of war in 1929, and treatment of non-combatants in 1949.

George V (1865–1936), King of Great Britain and Ireland (1910–36). His reign was marked by the PARLIAMENT ACT, WWI, the Irish troubles, the GENERAL STRIKE, the Great DEPRESSION, the choice of Baldwin as PM, and the formation of a NATIONAL GOVERNMENT (1931).

George VI (1894–1952), King of Great Britain and Northern Ireland (1936–52). His reign was marked by the aftermath of his brother Edward VIII's abdication, WWII, the formation of the first

Labour government with an overall majority, and the start of the dissolution of the Empire.

George, David Lloyd, *see* LLOYD GEORGE.

Germany, former state of NC Europe (Cap: Berlin), partitioned since 1949 between the German Democratic Republic (GDR) and the Federal German Republic (FGR), also known respectively as East Germany and West Germany.

The Empire (1871−1918) was established following the Franco-Prussian War. For centuries Germany had been divided among a large number of independent states, but in 1871 they were united into a federal system, with the King of Prussia becoming Emperor (*Kaiser*) of Germany. Imperial and military rivalry with Britain and France, encouraged by Kaiser WILHELM II, combined with the Austro-German Dual Alliance, precipitated Germany's involvement in WWI. After its defeat (1918), the Allies forced punitive terms on Germany at the Treaty of VERSAILLES, incl. the loss of territory and the obligation to pay substantial REPARATIONS. Attempted Communist revolts, such as the SPARTACIST RISING (1919), were successfully suppressed.

The Weimar Republic (1919−33) was established following Wilhelm II's abdication, and was named after the town where it was established. Its constitution was democratic, but it suffered from severe economic problems caused by the aftermath of WWI and REPARATIONS, made worse by the Depression and mass unemployment. The economic situation paved the way for HITLER's rise to power, and the Nazi Party (*see* NATIONAL SOCIALISM) was elected to power in 1933 and introduced a new constitution.

The Third Reich (1933—45) became a 1-party Nazi state (1934), with Hitler as its dictator. Against the terms of the Treaty of Versailles, Hitler initiated a massive programme of rearmament, and ordered the occupation of the SAARLAND and the RHINELAND. Encouraged by Britain and France's policy of APPEASEMENT, Germany then annexed Austria (*see* ANSCHLUSS), the SUDETENLAND (following the MUNICH AGREEMENT), and then the rest of Czechoslovakia. However, Germany's invasion of Poland in 1939 in pursuit of further territorial demands prompted the UK and France to declare war (*see* WORLD WAR TWO). After Germany's eventual defeat by the Allies, it was divided (1945—49) into UK, French, US and Soviet occupation zones, until the establishment of East and West Germany in 1949. *See also* BERLIN.

East Germany Area: 108,177 sq km. Pop: 16,740,000. Language: German. Religion: Protestant and RC. Cap: East Berlin.

Formed from the Soviet occupation zone, the state has continued to be Soviet-dominated, and is ruled by a hard-line Communist regime. It is a member of the COUNCIL FOR MUTUAL ECONOMIC ASSISTANCE and the WARSAW PACT. Under ULBRICHT it adopted the Soviet system of agricultural collectivization with a similarly poor result, and this coupled with bad social and industrial conditions led to an uprising which was put down with the aid of Soviet troops (1953). Conditions failed to improve and nearly 4 million people emigrated to the West. To halt this drain on manpower the Berlin Wall was erected in 1961.

Since the friendship treaty with the FGR in 1972 (*see* OSTPOLITIK), relations with the West have been less frigid.

West Germany Area: 248,667 sq km. Pop: 61,333,000 (1983). Language: German. Religion: Protestant and RC. Cap: Bonn.

The state was formed from the British, French and US occupation zones, and parliamentary democracy established. Its membership of the EEC and NATO has contributed towards its remarkable economic and political recovery from the ravages of WWII and its acceptance as one of the Western democracies. Like many other states in W Europe, governments frequently have to rely on coalition partners to stay in office. Chancellors since 1949 have incl. ADENAUER, ERHARD, KIESINGER, BRANDT, SCHMIDT and KOHL.

Gestapo, Nazi Germany's secret state police, headed by HIMMLER, and notorious for its ruthless interrogation methods.

Ghana, republic of W Africa; formerly the Gold Coast. Area: 238,305 sq km. Pop: 14,000,000 (est. 1984). Official language: English. Cap: Accra.

The original Gold Coast was established as a British colony in 1874 after being purchased from the Dutch in 1871. Ashanti and the Northern Territories were incorporated in 1901 and the former German colony of Togoland was incorporated as a mandated territory after the WWI peace settlements.

The country became independent as Ghana in 1957, with NKRUMAH as PM. In 1960 Ghana became a republic within the Commonwealth, and in 1964 Nkrumah established a 1-party state. He was overthrown by a military coup in 1966, since when the country has been ruled by a succession of civilian and military governments, which have, however, failed to deal with the problems of widespread corruption.

Gibraltar, self-governing British crown colony at the W end of the Mediterranean Sea, at the S end of the Iberian Peninsula. Area: 5.5 sq km. Pop: 30,000 (est.). Language: English. Religion: RC.

The Rock was captured from Spain by the British (1704), possession being confirmed by the Treaties of Utrecht (1713), Paris (1763) and Versailles (1783), but Spain has constantly pressed for its return. The inhabitants voted overwhelmingly in a referendum to stay British (1967) and Spain closed its frontier and severed communications with the colony in 1969 until 1985 when Anglo-Spanish relationships improved. Gibraltar was of great strategic importance during WWII.

Gierek, Edward (1913–   ), Polish Communist politician. He replaced GOMULKA as First Secretary (1970–80). From 1976 onwards he faced considerable industrial and social unrest, manifested in riots and strikes, caused by the raising of prices without comparable wage increases. In 1980 his government signed the 'Gdansk Agreements' with SOLIDARITY.

Giscard D'Estaing, Valéry (1926–   ), French statesman, President (1974–81). As leader of the Independent Republicans (allied to the Gaullists), he became the youngest President of France since 1848, and was faced with difficult economic circumstances with mounting inflation and uncertain political support, esp. from his Gaullist PM,

Jacques Chirac. Giscard maintained a strong French position within the EEC and on defence matters.

glasnost, (Russ.) openness. The term is applied to the Soviet policy of political and social liberalization embarked upon under GORBACHEV since 1985. *See also* PERESTROIKA.

Godesberg Meeting (1938), discussion between the British PM Neville Chamberlain and Hitler, at which Chamberlain refused to agree to the German occupation of the SUDETENLAND, the German-speaking area of Czechoslovakia. A week later, Chamberlain, with Daladier and Mussolini, signed the MUNICH AGREEMENT, agreeing to the German occupation.

Goebbels, Joseph (1897–1945), German Nazi politician. He was an early follower of Hitler, and controlled the party propaganda machine from 1929. From 1933 to 1945 he was Minister of Enlightenment and Propaganda, and his control of press, radio and cinema contributed enormously to the establishment of a totalitarian Nazi state. He committed suicide with his family in 1945 in Hitler's bunker.

Goering, Herman (1893–1946), German Nazi politician, Luftwaffe officer. An early Nazi, he joined with Hitler in the Munich PUTSCH. In 1932 he became President of the Reichstag, and from 1933 he was Minister of Aviation, building up the Luftwaffe (German air force) into a formidable fighting machine, used with great success in the BLITZKRIEG tactics of WWII. Following the victories of 1940, he was created Reichsmarshal, but thereafter his influence declined. He committed suicide after the Nuremberg Trials (1946) in which he had been sentenced to death for WAR CRIMES.

Golan Heights, range of hills astride the NE Israeli and SW Syrian frontier N of the Sea of Galilee. This strategic area was the scene of heavy fighting between the two countries during the 1967 ARAB-ISRAELI WAR, and was finally occupied by Israel. After the 1973 War it was occupied by UN forces.

Gold Coast, *see* GHANA.

Gomulka, Wladyslaw (1905–82), Polish Communist politician. He became General Secretary of the Communist Polish Workers' Party (1943). He was Vice-President in the first postwar government, but his nationalist deviation from orthodox Stalinist Communism led him to be dismissed from office and imprisoned (1951–55).

He was rehabilitated in 1956 and, amidst growing political unrest, later in the same year became the country's leader as First Secretary of the Party, a position he held until replaced by GIEREK (1970). Economic stagnation, and serious rioting which arose from substantial food price increases, contributed to his downfall.

Gorbachev, Mikhail Sergeevich, (1931–), Soviet statesman. As General Secretary of the Communist Party (1985–) he has embarked on policies of social and political liberalization (GLASNOST) and economic reform (PERESTROIKA). In 1987 he signed the INTERMEDIATE NUCLEAR FORCES TREATY with President Reagan of the USA.

Gottwald, Klement (1896–1953), Czechoslovak Communist politician. He was General Secretary of the Party (1929–53). He became PM of a coalition government (1946) and established a 1-party state

by using the police and workers' militia to effect a
coup d'état (1948), since when the country has been
Communist controlled. Gottwald succeeded BENEŠ
as President (1948—53).

Gowon, Yakubu (1934—), Nigerian politician
and general. He emerged as head of state
(1966—75) after a military coup. He introduced a
new federal system of 12 states, later increased to
19. In the BIAFRAN WAR (1967—70) Gowon
successfully crushed the rebel forces. In 1975 he was
removed by another army group.

Great Britain, *see* UNITED KINGDOM.

Great Leap Forward (1958—61), slogan used to
describe the massive upheaval in China aimed at
transforming the country, economically and
politically, to the level of advanced nations.

Inspired by MAO ZEDONG it had radical aims:
to sweep away backwardness by the condemnation
of old customs and usages; to establish a com-
mune system encompassing agriculture, education,
industry, local defence, trade and welfare; to di-
versify industry and the economy; to reduce consumption; to establish a truly communistic society;
and to mobilize the population's latent talents.

It failed due to a variety of causes: a series of
national disasters; managerial difficulties; withdrawal of Soviet technological advice; bureaucratic
opposition; Party pragmatism; and substandard
harvests.

Great War, *see* WORLD WAR ONE.

Greece, republic of SE Europe. Area: 131,986
sq km. Pop: 9,740,000 (1981). Language: Greek.
Religion: Christian (Greek Orthodox). Cap:
Athens.

The country was a monarchy until 1973 apart from republican periods (1926–35, 1941–46). Greece fought on the Allied side in both World Wars. It defeated the Italian invaders in WWII, but was then occupied by German forces. Two guerrilla groups were in action during the War, one Communist-inspired and the other pro-monarchist organization. Both conspired to overcome the Germans but then resorted to conflict between themselves (1945–49), so that British troops had to intervene to try to prevent civil war; they stayed in the country until 1950 but were unable to stop the warfare. The Communists controlled the N of the country, receiving aid from Albania, Bulgaria and Yugoslavia, which only ceased after Yugoslavia's expulsion from the COMINFORM.

During the 1950s and 1960s there were frequent changes of government and a state of political chaos reigned. Fears of civil war and a left-wing takeover resulted in a right-wing army coup (1967) after which left-wing organizations were banned, civil liberties suspended, opponents of the regime arrested, and the press censored. A dictatorial military JUNTA lasted until 1974 when democracy was restored, partially as a result of the crisis in CYPRUS.

Greece is a member of NATO, became an associate member of the EEC, achieving full membership in 1981. The long-standing dispute between Greece and Turkey over Cyprus and exploration rights in the Aegean Sea has caused misgivings in NATO because of the danger that a vital part of the defence system against Communist expansion would be endangered if war broke out between them, resulting in either or both not being able to honour their NATO obligations.

Grey, Edward, Viscount Grey of Fallodon (1862–1933), British Liberal Statesman. He was Foreign Secretary (1905–16), and Ambassador to the USA (1919–20). A great believer in international dialogue, he concluded the ANGLO-RUSSIAN ENTENTE (1907), played a leading part in the peace negotiations following the BALKAN WARS, and was a firm supporter of the LEAGUE OF NATIONS. He convinced a deeply-divided cabinet of the necessity of entering WWI, and was largely instrumental in persuading Italy and the USA to join in hostilities.

Gromyko, Andrei (1909–   ), Soviet diplomat and statesman. He became Deputy Foreign Minister and permanent UN delegate (1946), Foreign Minister (1957–85), and President (1985–   ). He accompanied Bulganin and Khrushchev to the UK (1956), and Khrushchev to Vienna for the meeting with President Kennedy (1961). Although involved in DÉTENTE, he was nevertheless a relentless protagonist of the COLD WAR philosophy.

Guernica, see SPANISH CIVIL WAR.

Guevara, Ernesto ('Che') (1928–67), Argentinian revolutionary. He joined the exiled CASTRO in Mexico where he was planning the Cuban revolution. They fought together in Cuba to oust BATISTA, and Guevara became Minister of Industries in the new regime. His revolutionary ideals did not contain him for long and he left Cuba to rouse Bolivian tin-miners to insurrection, but was captured by the army and executed. His guerrilla techniques have influenced revolutionary movements elsewhere.

Gulf States, collective name for the oil-producing states of the Persian Gulf: Bahrain, Iran, Iraq, Kuwait, Oman, Qatar, Saudi Arabia, and the United Arab Emirates.

Gulf War, a conflict between Iran and Iraq. The war started in 1980 with an Iraqi attack in pursuit of disputed territory. Enormous offensives by both sides have resulted in huge numbers of casualties, but no resolution to the conflict has been achieved, despite diplomatic efforts by other states. The hostilities have also involved attacks on neutral shipping in the Persian Gulf.

H

Hague Peace Conference (1907), assembly attended by delegates from 44 countries to discuss international ARBITRATION and DISARMAMENT. Its declaration against the arms race was ineffectual and it achieved very little, except that a proposition to establish an international court came to fruition in 1920 (*see* INTERNATIONAL COURT OF JUSTICE) having been postponed by the outbreak of WWI.

Haile Selassie (1892–1975), Emperor of Ethiopia (1930–74). One of the founders of modern ETHIOPIA, he westernized the country's institutions, and improved education and health. He resisted the Italian invasion (1935), but was forced into exile in England (1936). He returned to Ethiopia (1941) after the Italians had been driven out during WWII, and set about restabilizing the country. However, from 1955 onwards he lost touch with the enormous social problems facing the country, and in 1974 was deposed by a group of left-wing army officers. From 1963 he took a leading part in the ORGANIZATION OF AFRICAN UNITY.

Halifax, Earl of, *see* WOOD.

Hammarskjöld, Dag (1905–61), Swedish politician. He was Secretary-General of the UN (1953–61), and was internationally respected for the impartial and skilful manner in which he carried out his duties, particularly during the SUEZ CRISIS and the turmoil arising from the granting of independence to the Belgian Congo (Zaïre). He was killed in an air crash in Zambia while dealing with the Congo Crisis, and was posthumously awarded the Nobel Peace Prize (1961).

Hapsburg Dynasty, *see* AUSTRO-HUNGARIAN EMPIRE.

Hardie, Keir (1856–1915), Scottish Labour politician. He was MP for Merthyr Tydfil (1900–15), and helped to found the INDEPENDENT LABOUR PARTY (1893), of which he was Chairman (1893–1900 and 1913–15). A man of honour and integrity and an excellent speaker, he was influential in the formation of the LABOUR PARTY (1906), leading it in the House of Commons after the 1906 general election. He campaigned for international socialism and against unemployment, opposed Liberal influence in the trade unions and, as an implacable pacifist, opposed the Boer War and WWI.

Harriman, Averell (1891–1986), US financier and diplomat. As a close friend of President F.D. Roosevelt, he was prominent in the establishment of the NEW DEAL, in which he displayed his wide business abilities. In 1941 Roosevelt sent him to London to supervise the LEND-LEASE programme, and he played an important role as US ambassador to the USSR (1943–46). He was Secretary of Commerce (1946–48), and special assistant to President Truman (1950–51), helping to organize NATO. He negotiated the NUCLEAR TEST BAN TREATY (1963), and led the US delegation to the Vietnam peace talks in Paris (1968–69).

Heath, Edward (1916–   ), British Conservative statesman, PM (1970–74). As Lord Privy Seal (1961–63) he conducted unsuccessful negotiations towards the UK's entry into the EEC (1963). He was elected Leader of the Party (1965), and became PM (1970).

Under his leadership the UK joined the EEC (1973), but his Industrial Relations Act and incomes policy antagonized the trade unions, and strike action by the miners caused the country to be placed on a 3-day working week (1974). To gain public support Heath called an election (1974) but was defeated, and in 1975 Margaret THATCHER displaced him as Party leader.

hegemony, ascendancy or domination of a power or state within a group of neighbouring states, a confederation, league, etc., or of one social class over others.

Helsinki Conference, assembly attended by delegates from 35 countries to discuss security issues, with the aim of reducing international tension. The initial stage of the negotiations took place in Helsinki (1973) and the process was continued intermittently at Geneva (1973—75). Agreements were reached on: economic and technological cooperation; the upholding of human rights, coupled with closer links between peoples of different states; and measures aimed at preventing accidental confrontation between opposing power blocs. A separate agreement was reached on Mediterranean problems.

Henderson, Arthur (1863—1935), British Labour politician. He joined the Coalition Cabinet (1915) and the 5-man War Cabinet as minister responsible for labour affairs (1916—17). He was Home Secretary (1924) and Foreign Secretary (1929—31), but refused to join Macdonald's NATIONAL

GOVERNMENT, preferring to fight for the Labour Party's recovery from the 1931 election defeat. A crusader for disarmament, he was President of the World Disarmament Conference (1932) and was awarded the Nobel Peace Prize (1934).

Herriot, Édouard (1872–1957), French Radical-Socialist statesman. He was PM (1924–25). His government recognized the USSR, championed the cause of disarmament, COLLECTIVE SECURITY and the League of Nations, and withdrew troops from the RUHR. Internal economic problems brought down the government, but Herriot again became PM in 1926 (for 2 days) and in 1932. He was imprisoned by the VICHY GOVERNMENT and the Nazis during WWII, and elected President of the National Assembly (1947–53) and afterwards for life.

Hertzog, James Barry Munnick (1866–1942), South African soldier and statesman. Having served as a general in the Boer army in the BOER WAR, he founded the anti-British National Party (1913), which advocated independence for the country and opposed cooperation with Britain during WWI. He was PM (1924–39), partly in coalition with the Labour and United Parties. His advocacy of neutrality at the start of WWII led to his electoral defeat.

Herzegovina, *see* BOSNIA-HERZEGOVINA.

Hess, Rudolf (1894–1987), German Nazi politician. He joined the Nazi Party and became Hitler's political secretary in 1920 and in 1923 participated in the Munich PUTSCH. He became deputy Party leader (1934) and successor-designate to Hitler after Goering (1939). He flew alone to Scotland (1941) to try to arrange a negotiated peace settlement of WWII, but was interned for the rest of the War. He was sentenced to life imprisonment at the Nuremburg Trials and from 1966 was the sole remaining prisoner in Spandau Gaol, Berlin, the Russians having consistently rejected pleas by the Americans, British and French for his release.

Himmler, Heinrich (1900–45), German Nazi politician. He became deputy leader of the SS in 1927 and leader in 1929. He was made commander of the unified German police forces in 1936, head of Reich Administration in 1939, and Minister of the Interior in 1943. His ruthless direction of the secret police (Gestapo) made him a sinister figure among the Nazi leaders, and he was responsible for many atrocities, incl. the enforcement of Nazi extermination policies (*see* CONCENTRATON CAMPS). He committed suicide in 1945 shortly after being arrested by British forces.

Hindenburg, Paul von (1847–1934), German soldier and statesman. In WWI he commanded the 8th Army, defeating the Russians at TANNENBERG and the Masurian Lakes (1914). He became a field marshal and Chief of the General Staff (1916), and with LUDENDORFF controlled civil and military policy for the last months of the war. He advised Kaiser Wilhelm II to abdicate, and retired from the army himself in 1919. He was President (1925–34), defeating Hitler in the 1932 election but appointing him Chancellor (1933) on Von PAPEN'S advice.

As President, Hindenburg supported STRESE-MANN'S conciliatory foreign policy at the expense of alienating extreme right-wing elements. In the early 1930s no party could achieve a Reichstag majority, with the result that during BRÜNING's chancellorship Hindenburg had to rule by decree, and during that of von Papen he had to rule through a non-party government. This political chaos was a factor in the Nazi rise to power.

Hirohito (1901–   ), Emperor of Japan (1926–   ). His reign was marked in its early stages by rapid militarization, later manifesting itself by aggression against Manchuria and China, and then by Japan's involvement in WWII.

Hirohito never held any real power in the government of the country, but from the 1930s to the end of WWII the cult of the Emperor was a crucial factor in the growth of nationalism and Japan's aggressive territorial expansion, the Emperor traditionally being worshipped as a god. After WWII the Allies allowed Hirohito to remain as a constitutional monarch, and in 1946 he renounced all claims to imperial divinity.

Hiroshima, Japanese port on the island of Honshu. It was destroyed (1945) by the USA by means of an atomic bomb, the first wartime use of a nuclear weapon. A second bomb was dropped in NAGASAKI 3 days later, which led to Japan's unconditional surrender to the Allies.

Hitler, Adolf (1889–1945), Austrian-born German dictator. He became leader of the National Socialist German Workers' Party — the Nazi Party — in 1920 (*see* NATIONAL SOCIALISM). Like many of his compatriots he was bitterly opposed to the Treaty of VERSAILLES. He soon commanded attention and a growing following with his flamboyant oratory, which he used to expound anti-democratic, anti-Semitic and racialist policies, and to demand the return of Germany's lost territories. He also built up a myth of the superiority of Aryan peoples, of whom the Germans were the 'master race'.

Parliamentary strong-arm squads, the SA, were formed by Party members and Hitler soon felt able to challenge the Bavarian Government, attempting its overthrow in the so-called 'beer cellar' PUTSCH in Munich (1923). The Putsch failed and Hilter spent several months in jail when he dictated to HESS the first part of *Mein Kampf* ('My Struggle'), his autobiography and political philosophy.

The Nazi Party won 12 seats in the Reichstag election (1928) and by 1932 had become the largest in the country, helped to that position by the bitterness, desolation, fear and resentment caused by the mass unemployment accompanying the world DEPRESSION. Hitler became Chancellor (1933), declaring a 1-party state following the REICHSTAG FIRE (1934), and started on a massive programme of military and territorial expansion which led to the outbreak of WWII. This policy was coupled with a ruthless elimination of all opposition and systematic persecution of Jews. His mega-lomania reached such a state that by 1941 he was personally directing the military campaigns of WWII to the disquiet of his field commanders, and refused to consider the possibility of defeat even after Allied forces had crossed the German frontiers. Beseiged in the Berlin Chancellory, he committed suicide surrounded by the burning ruins of the city. *See also* NATIONAL SOCIALISM, GERMANY, WORLD WAR TWO.

Hoare-Laval Pact (1935), proposals for terminating Italo-Abyssinian hostilities (*see* ETHIOPIA) prepared by the UK Foreign Secretary, Sir Samuel Hoare, Viscount Templewood (1880—1959), and the French PM, Pierre LAVAL, at the request of the League of Nations. The agreement outraged UK public opinion and such was the uproar that the Government rejected the plan and Hoare resigned. The proposal, if accepted, would have made substantial economic and territorial concessions to Italy based on the assumption that no state would be likely to go to war over Abyssinia.

Ho Chi Minh (Vietnamese, 'seeker of englightenment'), orig. Nguyen Van Thann (1892—1969), Vietnamese Communist politician. He founded the Communisty Party in INDO-CHINA (1930). After an abortive uprising against the French (1940) he fled to S China and founded a resistance movement of Communists and Nationalists (VIET MINH) to fight the Japanese, then occupying Vietnam during WWII.

After the Japanese surrender the French returned and Ho Chi Minh then led the Viet Minh in successful operations against tham (1946—54) having managed to establish a provisional government (1945). He continued to fight for independence in the jungle and, after finally succeeding, became PM (1954—55) and President of North Vietnam (1955—69).

After his victory in the North, Ho Chi Minh set about gaining control of South Vietnam by sending supplies along a secret route through the jungle (the Ho Chi Minh Trail) to the VIET CONG nationalists still fighting for independence. After the US military intervention in support of the South (1965), he despatched regular army units to support the rebels. *See* VIETNAM WAR.

In spite of the devastation and turmoil of War, Ho Chi Minh introduced drastic land reforms, increased heavy industrial output in the North and was a highly popular leader among his own people.

Hohenzollern Dynasty, *see* WILHELM II.

Holocaust, term used to describe the genocide of European Jewry by the Nazis during WWII. *See* CONCENTRATION CAMPS.

Home, *see* DOUGLAS–HOME.

Home Rule, self-government for IRELAND, the goal of the Irish Nationalists from 1870 to 1920 at a time when the whole of Ireland was part of the UK. It was achieved for the 26 southern counties when the Irish Free State (Eire) was created by the Anglo-Irish Treaty (1921). The 6 northern counties (NORTHERN IRELAND) opted to stay within the framework of the UK but were granted Home Rule within that framework with a parliament at Stormont Castle (suspended from 1972).

Hoover, Herbert (1874–1964), US Republican President (1929–33). His administration was uneventful apart from the WALL STREET CRASH (1929). He was rejected in favour of F.D. ROOSEVELT at the 1932 election because of the effect the DEPRESSION was having on the country and because of his refusal, despite increasing hardship, to allow the government to assume responsibility for the unemployed.

Horthy [de Nagybanya], Miklós (1868–1957),

Hungarian admiral and regent. He organized a counter-revolution against the Communist regime of Béla KUN (1919—20), and in 1920 he became Regent of Hungary, a post he held for 24 years. He followed conservative policies at home, and worked for the revision of the Treaty of TRIANON.

Although he took Hungary into WWII in 1941 (Hungarian forces assisted in the occupation of Yugoslavia), his support for Hitler was half-hearted and his attempt to negotiate a separate peace led to his overthrow and imprisonment by the Nazis (1944). The Americans captured him at the end of WWII but refused to hand him over to the Yugoslavs to stand trial for war crimes, and he went into exile in Portugal.

'Hot Line', direct telephone, teletype, or other communications link between heads of government for emergency use. The 'Hot Line' between the President of the USA and the leadership of the USSR was established in 1963 following the CUBAN MISSILES CRISIS.

House of Commons, see PARLIAMENT.

House of Lords, see PARLIAMENT, PARLIAMENT ACTS.

House of Representatives, see CONGRESS.

Hoxha, Enver (1908—85), Albanian Communist politican. In 1943 he became Secretary-General of the Albanian Communist Party and leader of the resistance forces during WWII. After the War he headed a provisional government and, with Soviet backing, established a Stalinist-style dictatorship. Disillusioned by Soviet attempts to make him a subservient puppet he turned to China for aid and understanding (1968) but that association was terminated by China in 1978.

Hua Guofeng or **Hua Kuo-feng** (1920–   ),
Chinese Communist statesman. He was severely
criticized during the Cultural Revolution but
survived to be nominated by Mao Zedong as his
successor. He became PM (1976–80) and
Chairman of the Central Committee (1976–81).
His denunciation of the GANG OF FOUR led to the
arrest of its members and their subsequent
imprisonment.

**Huggins, Sir Godfrey, Viscount Malvern of
Rhodesia and Bexley** (1883–1971), Southern
Rhodesian statesman. He was PM of Southern
Rhodesia (1933–53) and of the Federation of
RHODESIA AND NYASALAND (1953–56), of which
he was a staunch advocate. He held a firm belief in
white rule, with the result that black Africans had
little opportunity for political activity.

Hull, Cordell (1871–1955), US Democratic
statesman, Secretary of State (1933–44). He
initiated the 'good neighbour' policy towards Latin
America; this consisted of the concept of 'equal
partnership' between the US and Latin American
states, and a commitment to mutual assistance and
joint defence, coupled with renunciation of armed
intervention by the USA in Latin America. At the
start of WWII, Hull was a proponent in favour of US
aid to the Allies (*see* LAND-LEASE). Known as the
'father of the UN', he was awarded the Nobel Peace
Prize (1945) for his part in its establishment.

Hungary, republic of E Europe. Area: 93,032
sq km. Pop: 10,710,000. Language: Hungarian
(Magyar). Religions: of the 20 authorized de-
nominations the principal are RC, Calvinist and
Lutheran. Cap: Budapest.

The country achieved independence under the
leadership of Count Mikály Károlyi (1875—1955)
after the collapse of the AUSTRO-HUNGARIAN
EMPIRE (1918). Károlyi was overthrown by Béla
KUN who established a Communist system of
government (1919), which was itself replaced with a
monarchial constitution (1920) by HORTHY, who
left the throne vacant while himself acting as
Regent.

Between the World Wars Hungary endeavoured
to redress the impositions of the Treaty of TRIANON,
resulting in close association and eventual alliance
with Germany during WWII.

After the War the Smallholders' Party was in
power until replaced by the United Workers' Party
under Mátvás Rákosi (1892—1971). Hostility to
the Party's ultra-Communist policies resulted in
the replacement of Rákosi in 1953 by Imre Nagy
(1895—1958), whose liberalizing reforms included
the freeing of political prisoners, relaxation of
economic and political controls, and the termination of compulsory agricultural collectivization.
Less than 2 years later Rákosi returned to power
only to be removed again from office as a result
of the anti-Stalinist demonstrations preceding the
national uprising.

In 1956 Nagy returned to power, and at the same
time fighting broke out between Hungarians and
Soviet forces. Nagy secured a Soviet withdrawal,
and his coalition government withdrew the country
from the WARSAW PACT, tried to establish a neutral
position in foreign affairs, permitted the re-forming
of political parties, and released the Primate of
Hungary, Cardinal Jósef Mindszenty (1892—

1975), who had been imprisoned in 1949 for his hostility to Communism. The government fell when Soviet forces, despite fierce resistance, re-occupied the country. KÁDÁR formed an administration sympathetic to the USSR, and Nagy was executed.

In recent years cautious liberalizing policies, educational reforms and decentralized economic planning under Kádár's leadership have made the country the most prosperous and least repressive of all the Soviet bloc states.

Hunger Marches, demonstrations by unemployed workers in the 1920s and 1930s to draw attention to the plight of the depressed areas of the UK. The first march, organized by Communists and socialists, was from Glasgow to London (1922). The National Unemployed Workers' Movement was founded (1929) by a Communist, Wal Hannington, and became the organizing body for such displays of working-class solidarity. The best remembered march was from Jarrow to London (1936), organized by the town's MP, Ellen Cicely Wilkinson (1891–1947). WWII brought an end to the demonstrations, which had become a commonplace method of protest.

Husák, Gustáv (1913–), Czechoslovak Communist politician. He was one of the organizers and leaders of the Slovak uprising in WWII (1944). He was imprisoned for 'bourgeois-nationalist' deviation because of his championship of Slovak rights (1951–1960), and his climb to political power was slow. He was a strong advocate of DUBČEK's proposed reforms, and was appointed Deputy PM (1968). Having deserted Dubček's policies in favour of coming to terms with the facts of the Warsaw Pact occupation of the country (1968), he became First Secretary of the Party (1969–87) and President of the Republic (1975–87).

Hussein [ibn Talal] (1935–   ), King of Jordan (1952–   ). He has maintained a robust and highly personal rule necessitated by the political upheavals inside the country and in the surrounding states. He has sought to keep on good terms with other Arab states, while at the same time maintaining friendly ties with the West, particularly the UK.

His antipathy to Israel resulted in Jordan signing a defence agreement with Egypt (1967). Israel, surrounded by hostile states, included Jordan in its offensive action during the 1967 ARAB-ISRAELI WAR and occupied E Jerusalem and the WEST BANK.

In addition Hussein had to contend with his country being used as a base by the PALESTINE LIBERATION ORGANIZATION for terrorist attacks on Israel and elsewhere. Finally, after bitter fighting, Hussein put a stop to these activities by expelling the PLO (1970).

Hu Yaobang, (1915–   ), Chinese Communist statesman. He was General Secretary of the Party (1981–87).

hydrogen bomb, *see* NUCLEAR WARFARE.

I

ILO, *see* INTERNATIONAL LABOUR ORGANIZATION.
ILP, *see* INDEPENDENT LABOUR PARTY.
IMF, *see* INTERNATIONAL MONETARY FUND.
Imperial Conferences (1911–37), meetings in London of the PMs of the UK and the Dominions. Under the title of Colonial Conferences, 4 similar meetings had taken place earlier, and since WWII such gatherings have been called Commonwealth Conferences.

The first 3 Imperial Conferences (1911, 1917–18 and 1921) were characterized by the growing desire of the Dominions to control their own foreign policies free from British interference, and for the status of the Dominions to be more precisely defined. The next 2 Conferences (1923 and 1926) detailed proposals on these matters and the agreed formula was embodied in the STATUTE OF WESTMINSTER (1931). Little of consequence arose at the 1930 and 1932 Conferences. The last Conference (1937) was devoted to the worsening international situation.

imperialism or **colonialism,** the policy or practice of extending a state's rule over other territories, and of incorporating such colonized territories into an empire.

The European powers began building empires in the Americas and Asia in the 15th cent., but from c. 1880 to 1914 there was a rush to gain previously uncolonized territory, esp. in Africa, in order to satisfy the need for raw materials and for new markets for manufactured goods. Apart from such economic motives, the prestige of the imperial powers was also involved, as was the desire to offset strategic dangers (real or imagined). Imperial competition between the European powers in this period contributed to the tensions that eventually broke out in WWI.

Since WWII, the European powers have gradually granted independence to most of their colonies (*see* DECOLONIZATION), though the economic domination of the Third World by the developed countries has been called 'neo-imperialism'.

Imperial Preference, economic arrangement between members of the British Empire, and later the COMMONWEALTH, by which preferential TARIFFS were operated between them. In the early years of the 20th cent. the princple was bitterly opposed by those in favour of FREE TRADE. These incl. the Liberal Party and a section of the Conservative Party, which was split on the issue, and it was not until 1932 that preferences were established on a significant scale. The GENERAL AGREEMENT ON TARIFFS AND TRADE (1948) prevented any further extension of preferences and the scheme was phased out after the UK joined the EEC (1973).

Independent Labour Party (ILP), socialist organization founded (1893) in Bradford by Keir HARDIE. It was one of the constituent members of the Labour Representation Committee (1900), the forerunner of the LABOUR PARTY (founded 1906). After WWI its influence waned, and following policy disagreements it disaffiliated from the Labour Party (1932). Although still in existence its influence is of little consequence.

India, federal republic of S Asia. Area: 3,159,530 sq km. Pop: 683,880,000 (1981). Official languages: Hindi and English. Religion: predominantly Hindu. Cap: New Delhi.

India was part of the British Empire from the 18th cent. The slow progress made by Britain in the early years of the 20th cent. in granting India a degree of self-determination stimulated the organization of a strong nationalist movement after WWI. The nationalists were strengthened by the outrage felt at the AMRITSAR massacre and disappointment engendered by the Government of India Act (1919), which transferred only some powers to elected Indian officials.

Under Mahatma GANDHI, the Indian National Congress (*see* CONGRESS PARTY) was reorganized into an effective protest body and instigator of CIVIL DISOBEDIENCE campaigns, and from 1930 Congress demanded complete independence. The 1935 Government of India Act established elected governments in the provinces, but the failure to grant immediate independence led to India's less than enthusiastic support for the Allied cause during WWII. Indeed an Indian National Army was formed in Singapore (1943) by Subhas Chandra Bose to fight on the Japanese side.

Meanwhile, suspicions that Congress was becoming Hindu-dominated prompted the MOSLEM LEAGUE under JINNAH to agitate for an independent Moslem state. The postwar British Labour Government offered Indian independence in 1946, but tensions and violence between Moslem and Hindu communities led to the decision to partition the country on independence between India and Pakistan (1947). Partition was accompanied by massacres of Hindus by Moslems and vice versa, and by vast movements of refugees.

On independence, NEHRU became PM (1947—64), and in 1950 India became a republic within the Commonwealth. Nehru was succeeded by SHASTRI (1964—66), Indira GANDHI (1966—77 and 1980—84), and Rajiv GANDHI (1984—   ).

The traumas of Partition have continued to arouse animosity and suspicion between India and Pakistan, which have fought wars over the disputed territory of KASHMIR (1947—49 and 1965) and over the secession of BANGLADESH from Pakistan (1971). India has also had frontier problems with China, leading to open conflict in 1962. India has, however, steered a middle course in foreign affairs and has become a leader of the NON-ALIGNED MOVEMENT, although signing aid agreements and a treaty of friendship and cooperation with the USSR. As a result, Pakistan has drawn closer to China.

Internally the problems are enormous, with slow industrialization, backward agriculture, rising birth-rate, food shortages, illiteracy, poverty and religious and social intolerance all inhibiting government attempts at modernization and economic and social reforms. There has also been violent agitation by various minorities (such as the Sikhs) for independence.

Indo-China, former French dependency in SE Asia comprising the colonial territory of Cochin

...hina and the protectorates of Annam, Cambodia (KAMPUCHEA), Laos and Tonkin. The Indo-China union lasted from 1887 until 1949 when VIETNAM was established by the merger of Annam, Cochin China and Tonkin. The French connection was broken when Cambodia, Laos and Vietnam became independent states in 1954.

Indonesia, *see* SUKARNO, SUHARTO.

inflation progressive increase in the general level of prices caused by (a) an expansion in demand for goods and services and an increase in the amount of money in circulation, or (b) an increase in costs. The increase in prices means that the value of money decreases.

Intermediate Nuclear Forces Treaty (INF) Treaty, treaty signed in 1987 by the USA and the USSR banning all short and medium-range land-based nuclear missiles.

International Bank for Reconstruction and Development (World Bank), UN financial organizaton established (1945) to assist economic development in member states by the provision of loan capital. It supports programmes which it considers to be sound investments, based on normal economic criteria.

International Brigades, volunteer units organized to fight in the SPANISH CIVIL WAR (1936—39) against FRANCO's forces. All were imbued with anti-Fascist ideals and many were Communists. The volunteers totalled some 40,000 men drawn from most European countries and the Americas.

International Court of Justice, principal judicial body of the UN established in 1945 to adjudicate on international disputes. The Court meets in The Hague and comprises 15 judges, no 2 of whom may be nationals of the same state. They are elected by the General Assembly and the Security Council for a 9-year term. Any party failing to adhere to the Court's judgement may cause action to be taken by the Security Council to enforce it at the instigation of the offended party.

International Labour Organization (ILO), agency with HQ in Geneva, established (1919) by the Treaty of VERSAILLES as an affiliated body of the LEAGUE OF NATIONS. Since 1946 it has been a specialized agency of the UN and now has a membership of 144 states. Its aims are: the promotion of peace through social justice; the establishment of international labour standards for the improvement of working conditions and the protection of human rights; the maintenance of a technical assistance programme to developing countries; research and dissemination of information on aspects of economic activity in order to improve economic and social welfare; and the provision of productive work to mitigate the evils of unemployment. The ILO was awarded the 1969 Nobel Peace Prize.

international law, body of rules that affect or control nations' relations with each other. In 1921 the League of Nations established the Permanent Court of International Justice, based at the Hague, and after WWII it was succeeded by the INTERNATIONAL COURT OF JUSTICE of the UN.

International Monetary Fund (IMF), UN agency with HQ in Washington, DC, established in 1945. Its aims are: to support currency stability by defending currencies that are under pressure and by keeping exchange rates stable; to promote international monetary cooperation and expansion of trade; and to make the Fund's resources available to alleviate imbalance in the BALANCE OF PAYMENTS of member states, usually subject to conditions and controls imposed by the IMF. The Fund's assets are raised from member states by means of a quota system.

International Socialism, concept of worldwide fraternity and solidarity between working-class peoples, first propounded by Engels and Marx (1848). The Second International (founded 1889) still survives as a loose association of social democratic parties. The Third International was the COMINTERN.

IRA, see IRISH REPUBLICAN ARMY.

Iran, republic of SW Asia; formerly known as Persia. Area: 1,648,000 sq km. Pop: 39,190,000 (est. 1982). Language: Iranian (Persian). Religion: Islam. Cap: Teheran.

Despotic Shahs of the Qajar dynasty ruled the country until 1925 when the National Assembly (Majlis) deposed the dynastic ruler, Ahmed Shah, and elected Colonel Reza Khan (1878—1944) as Shah. Reza Khan had led a military coup (1921) and assumed dictatorial powers before his formal election. He adopted the dynastic name 'Pahlavi' and commenced the nation's modernization, imposing European dress, breaking the power of the mullahs (Islamic clerics), abolishing the veil for women, and developing the armed forces, hospitals, railways, roads and schools. Because of his pro-German sympathies during WWII, UK and Soviet forces occupied the country (1941—46), and he was forced to abdicate in favour of his son, Mohammed Reza PAHLAVI.

Nationalistic, anti-American and anti-British attitudes developed (1947—51), culminating in clamour for the nationalization of the oil industry, which had been controlled by the Anglo-Iranian Oil Company since 1909. An attempt was made on the Shah's life and the PM and Education Minister were assassinated in the disturbances, which were condoned, even incited, by the fanatical Mohammed Mussadiq (1881—1967) who was PM (1951—53). Although the oil industry was nationalized, the expected economic benefits did not materialize, since the expert personnel left the country following the UK's severance of diplomatic relations, with the result that the installations became practically unworkable. The promised break-up and distribution of large estates also failed and civil turmoil returned to the streets, resulting in the Shah's dismissal of Mussadiq.

There followed a period of economic consolidation and expansion, the emancipation of women and a series of welfare measures, but they did not satisfy the traditionalists. Islamic fundamentalist demonstrations commenced (1977) in support of the return of the Ayatollah KHOMEINI who had been exiled for opposing the Shah's reforms. Serious rioting occurred and the Shah was forced to flee the country. In retaliation for the USA giving him sanctuary, student extremists occupied the US embassy and held 63 members of staff hostage (1979—81). Meanwhile Khomeini had returned to Iran (1979) and established an Islamic republic, under which thousands of the Shah's supporters and other opponents of the regime were exterminated. To add to these internal stresses, Iran became involved in the GULF WAR with Iraq from 1980.

Ireland, island of the British Isles, partitioned since 1921 into NORTHERN IRELAND (still part of the UK) and Southern Ireland, successively known as the Irish Free State, Eire, and the Republic of Ireland.

The English colonization of Ireland began in the 12th cent. and was complete by the end of the 16th. Agitation for independence, exacerbated by the fact that the majority of the inhabitants remained RC at the Reformation, broke out in several unsuccessful rebellions over the centuries.

In an attempt to solve the 'Irish Question', UK governments in the late 19th cent. twice attempted to grant HOME RULE to Ireland, but the legislation was defeated in Parliament. A new Home Rule Bill in 1912 led to a threat of armed rebellion by the Protestants of Northern Ireland, who feared subjection to what would have been a Catholic-dominated Irish parliament. The nationalists also began to arm, and civil war was only averted by the outbreak of WWI, which resulted in the postponement of plans for Home Rule.

The SINN FEIN nationalists rebelled unsuccessfully in the EASTER RISING of 1916, but more protracted guerrilla war broke out in 1919–21, with the IRISH REPUBLICAN ARMY fighting British government forces. The Government of Ireland Act (1920) established separate parliaments for Northern and Southern Ireland, and the 1921 Anglo-Irish Treaty gave Southern Ireland dominion status within the Commonwealth, followed in 1922 by the establishment of the Irish Free State.

Southern Ireland, state formed from the southern 26 counties of Ireland. Area: 69,893 sq km. Pop: 3,443,000 (1981). Languages: English and Irish (Gaelic). Religion: RC. Cap: Dublin.

The establishment of the Irish Free State split Sinn Fein into those who supported dominion status and those who wanted a fully independent republic. These two factions became respectively FINE GAEL and FIANNA FÁIL, the latter led by DE VALÉRA. De Valéra came to power in 1932 and in 1937 introduced a new constitution abolishing the Irish Free State, declaring Eire a sovereign independent state under a president, and refusing to recognize the partition of Ireland. Eire remained neutral in WWII and in 1949 left the Commonwealth and declared itself fully independent as the Republic of Ireland.

The Republic's foreign policy has remained one of neutrality, and although it joined the EEC in 1973, it has refused to join NATO. Due to the number of political parties and splinter groups, formation of majority governments has proved difficult, the largest party having to rely on coalition support to remain in office.

Irgun Zvai Leumi, revisionist Zionist underground organization founded (1937) for the defence of Jewish settlers against Arab attacks in PALESTINE. It was subsequently in opposition to the British mandated forces, though it declared a truce in 1939 leading to the breakaway of the STERN GANG. It resumed hostilities in 1944 and blew up, with the loss of 91 lives, Jerusalem's King David Hotel (1946) while it was being used as the British administrative HQ. BEGIN was its leader before it was absorbed into the Israeli Army.

Irish Free State, *see* IRELAND.

Irish Republican Army (IRA), Irish irregular military organizaton founded (1919) as the armed wing of SINN FEIN. Its purpose was to carry out guerrilla operations against British institutions and troops. Its successes contributed to the formation of the Irish Free State (1921) but it then split into factions that either accepted or refuted the Anglo-Irish Treaty (1921).

The hardline republicans continued to agitate and fight for the unification of the whole of IRELAND. Bombing campaigns were mounted in England on a spasmodic basis from 1939 onwards and intensified after 1970, accompanied by similar attacks and assassinations in NORTHERN IRELAND which are now so prevalent that a large British army presence has been mounted in the province. The attacks, in addition to being on members of the police force and the armed services, are sectarian in character with elements of the minority republican Roman Catholic population waging a mini civil war against the majority loyalist Protestants, who have developed their own retaliatory paramilitary organizations. The IRA is an illegal organization in both Northern Ireland and the Republic.

Iron Curtain, term used by Churchill (1946) to describe the ideological division and physical barriers preventing interchange of people and ideas between the West and the Soviet-dominated countries in Eastern Europe, which later became members of the WARSAW PACT.

isolationism, a policy of nonparticipation in, or withdrawal from, international affairs, esp. as practised in the USA. The concept has been adhered to during much of the 20th cent. The sinking of the LUSITANIA strained this attitude and contributed to eventual US entry into WWI, but the policy returned in the interwar years, gradually being relaxed at the start of WWII and shattered by the Japanese attack of PEARL HARBOUR. A vociferous minority has advocated the return of the policy of 'fortress America' in recent years.

Israel, republic of the Middle East, bordering on the Mediterranean. Area: 20,770 sq km. Pop: 3,922,000. Language: Hebrew. Religion: Judaism. Cap: Jerusalem.

From the end of the 19th cent. it had been the aim of ZIONISM to create a homeland for the Jews in PALESTINE, from where many had been dispersed all over Europe, N Africa and the Middle East at the time of the Roman Empire. After the defeat of the Ottoman Empire in WWI, Palestine became a British MANDATE (1922—48) and the BALFOUR DECLARATION pledged the UK government to the eventual creation of a Jewish national home. Jewish immigration increased enormously as a result of Nazi persecution in Europe, and this led to violent opposition from the native Arab population. The UK referred the problem to the UN, which partitioned Palestine between Jews and Arabs.

The state of Israel was founded (1948) when the British mandate ended. Immediately the neighbouring Arab states attacked the new nation, refusing to recognize its existence. By the time of the

1949 armistice, Israel had increased its land area by c. 25%. The creation of the state of Israel led to the exodus of large numbers of Palestinian Arabs, and it is their desire for a homeland that has been at the root of much of the subsequent conflict in the Middle East (*see* ARAB-ISRAELI WARS and PALESTINE LIBERATION ORGANIZATION.

In the 1967 War, Israel further increased its territory to incl. the GAZA STRIP, the WEST BANK of the River Jordan, the GOLAN HEIGHTS, and SINAI. Israel has had to rely heavily on US economic and military aid, and it was through US pressure that the CAMP DAVID AGREEMENT (1978) was signed with Egypt, following which Sinai was returned to Egypt. However, the provision for a degree of Palestinian autonomy on the West Bank has failed to materialize. Between 1982 and 1985 Israel was involved in the war in LEBANON, and there remains a state of hostility between Arabs and Israelis.

Internally, Israel has established many modern industries and with the use of irrigation has transformed what was once desert into productive agricultural land. Due to the enormous cost of defence, Israel suffers from high inflation and BALANCE OF PAYMENTS problems. The country is governed by a single-chamber legislative assembly (the Knesset), elected by proportional representation, which has meant that most governments have had to rely on coalition support to remain in power.

Italy, republic of SC Europe. Area: 301,245 sq km. Pop: 56,830,000 (1983). Language: Italian. Religion: RC. Cap: Rome.

Since the collapse of the Roman Empire, Italy

had been divided into numerous independent states and areas ruled by foreign powers. The nationalist movement of the 19th cent. eventually unified the country as a monarchy in 1870, although Italy continued to claim sovereignty over certain other territories. By the Treaty of LONDON (1915). Italy joined the Allied side in WWI on the understanding that it would gain these territories following an Allied victory. At the peace settlement, only some of the promised territories were granted to Italy, and the resulting disillusionment, combined with social unrest, parliamentary instability and fear of Communism, assisted the rise of FASCISM and the appointment of MUSSOLINI as PM (1922).

By manipulating electoral laws and the role played by King VICTOR EMMANUEL III, Mussolini crushed parliamentary opposition and established a Fascist dictatorship, which lasted from 1925 to 1943. Mussolini's ideas of aggrandisement and colonial expansion led Italy into the conquest of Abyssinia (see ETHIOPIA) and support for the nationalist rebels in the Spanish Civil War. Italy formed the AXIS alliance with Germany in 1936, joined the ANTI-COMINTERN PACT in 1937, and in 1940 entered WWII on the German side in the hope of territorial gains. In 1943 the Allies invaded Italy, resulting in Mussolini's resignation, Italy's surrender, and its declaration of war on Germany. German forces immediately occupied much of the country and put up a stubborn resistance until 1945.

In 1946 a referendum decided in favour of the establishment of a republic, and parliament now consists of a Chamber of Deputies and a Senate. Since the War Italy has been ruled by a succession of unstable coalition governments. Economic difficulties, financial crises, unemployment and the poverty of S Italy have contributed to the growth of the Communist Party, which is now the largest W of the Iron Curtain, but which has failed to overcome the dominance of the Christian Democrats in national government. Extreme left-wing and neofascist groups have taken advantage of the unstable conditions to carry out terrorist campaigns. Italy is a founder member of the EEC and NATO.

J

Japan, island monarchy of E Asia. Area: 369,660 sq km. Pop: 118,390,000 (1982). Language: Japanese. Religion: Buddhism and Shintoism. Cap: Tokyo.

Japan underwent a process of rapid industrialization in the last quarter of the 19th cent., and by the early 20th cent. was able to defeat Russia in the RUSSO-JAPANESE WAR (1904—5). In WWI Japan fought on the Allied side.

Between the Wars, extreme nationalists in the army increasingly controlled political life, reviving traditional beliefs — such as the divinity of the Emperor HIROHITO — to create an autocratic state. The military, backed by nationalist sentiment at home, embarked on a policy of colonial expansion to relieve pressure on the overpopulated country. This led to the conquest of MANCHURIA (1931), the invasion of China (1937), and the SINO-JAPANESE WAR. Japan withdrew from the League of Nations (1933), and, wary of the USSR, joined Germany in the ANTI-COMINTERN PACT, which was consolidated by the Tripartite Pact (1940).

Japan entered WWII as one of the AXIS powers in 1941 with its attack on the US navy at PEARL HARBOUR. This was followed by the rapid conquest of large parts of SE Asia and the Pacific. Japan was eventually forced to surrender following the dropping of atomic bombs on Hiroshima and Nagasaki, and was occupied until 1952 by Allied Forces.

Japan has made a remarkable recovery from the effects of WWII, and has become one of the world's principal industrialized nations, developing close ties with the West, esp. the USA. The country is now a parliamentary democracy, having in the 1946 constitution abandoned the doctrine of the Emperor's divinity with its consequent authoritarian overtones. The constitution also renounces war, and the country's defence is guaranteed by the US-Japan Security Treaty (1960).

Jarrow Marchers, *see* HUNGER MARCHES.

Jaruzelski, Wojceich (1923–), Polish general, statesman. He became First Secretary (1981–), PM (1981–85) and head of State (1985–). He imposed martial law (1981–83), banning SOLIDARITY and imprisoning many of its leaders.

Jinnah, Mohammed Ali (1876–1948), Pakistani statesman. He joined the Indian National Congress, the Indian Moslem League and the Viceroy's Legislative Council before WWI. He resigned from Congress because of dislike of Gandhi's disobedience campaign and Hindu dominance of the independence movement. He was President of the MOSLEM LEAGUE from 1984. He gave support to the UK during WWII when Congress refused to do so and from 1940 was a leading advocate to the partition of the subcontinent into separate Hindu and Moslem states. When this happened (1947) he became his country's first Governor General, having to contend with problems of fighting, rioting and refugees, and the delicate relationship with India.

Johnson, Lyndon Baines (1908–73), US

Democratic President (1963–69). He became Vice President (1961) and after Kennedy's assassination succeeded him as President (1963), retaining the position after the 1964 election. During his administration Congress approved legislation affording limited improvements to the position of black Americans (*see* CIVIL RIGHTS ACTS), together with other social reforms. However, Johnson's escalation of US involvement in the VIETNAM WAR led to growing opposition which caused him to decide not to stand for re-election (1968).

judiciary, (a) branch of a state's authority concerned with the administration of justice, (b) a country's court system, (c) the bench, i.e. judges collectively. *See also* SEPARATION OF POWERS.

junta, a ruling group of officers in a military government, esp. after a coup d'état or revolutionary seizure of power. The term is also applied to an executive or legislative council in several Latin American states.

Jutland, Battle of (1916), an important naval engagement between the Royal Navy and the German High Seas Fleet. The British lost 14 vessels to Germany's 11. As the Germans were able to return to port, despite British dominance in ships and firepower, the battle was tactically indecisive. However, Jutland was regarded as a strategic victory for Britain since the German High Seas Fleet never again ventured to seek out the British fleet.

K

Kádár, János (1912–   ), Hungarian Communist politician. He became Minister of the Interior (1948) but was imprisoned (1951–53) for displaying 'Titoist' sympathies, i.e. independence from hard-line Stalinist principles. He had been First Secretary of the Party since 1956.

When the anti-Soviet revolution commenced (1956) he was a member of NAGY'S 'national' anti-Stalinist government but a few days later formed a counter-government with Soviet support. He took control of the post-revolutionary regime as PM (1956–58) and instituted a period of severe repression. He was again PM (1961–65), and has pursued a policy of gradual liberalization and national reconciliation.

Kampuchea, republic of SE Asia; formerly known as Cambodia and the Khmer Republic. Area: 181,000 sq km. Pop: 6,000,000 (est. 1981). Language: Khmer. Religion: Theravada Buddhism until the Constitution of 1976 ended it as the state religion. Cap: Phnom Penh.

The country was part of INDO-CHINA from 1887 until it achieved independence from France in 1954. Prince Norodom Silhanouk (1922–   ) dominated political life until 1970 when he was deposed as a result of the country's increasing economic difficulties and intensifying indirect involvement in the VIETNAM WAR.

After the establishment of the Khmer Republic

(1970), Marshal Lon Nol became PM and, in 1972, President. A civil war developed between the US-backed Republic and the Communist KHMER ROUGE backed by China and North Vietnam. After their victory in 1975 the Khmer Rouge, led by Pol Pot, imposed a severely regimented regime, expelled all foreigners, cut off contacts with the rest of the world and compelled the urban population to undertake agricultural work.

War with Vietnam broke out in 1977, and Vietnamese troops occupied the capital in 1979. A puppet regime was established, but Khmer Rouge forces continue fighting in remote parts of the country.

Kashmir Dispute, territorial disagreement between India and Pakistan concerning ownership of the northernmost region of the Indian sub-continent.

At the time of the partition of India and Pakistan (1947), Kashmir had a largely Moslem population but was ruled by a Hindu Maharajah who decided to permit the state to be integrated with India. Fighting broke out between Hindus and Moslems, with the result that Pakistani troops moved into the state to support the Moslem population and came into conflict with elements of the Indian army.

India branded Pakistan as an aggressor and appealed to the UN, which appointed a peace commission to establish a provisional boundary line. This left most of the state under Indian control, but when arbitration was suggested as a means of achieving a final settlement it was opposed by India on the assumption that, as the majority of the population was Moslem, most of the region would be absorbed by Pakistan if the issue depended on the principle of self-determination.

Kashmir has continued to be a subject of hostilities between India and Pakistan, notably in 1965 (*see* TASHKENT CONFERENCE), and in 1971 during the conflict over the secession of Bangladesh from Pakistan. The dispute remains unresolved, although bilateral negotiations resulted in the Simla Agreement (1972), which delineated a new demarcation line.

Kaiser, *see* WILHELM II.

Kaunda, Kenneth (1924–), Zambian politician. To further African emancipation, he joined the Northern Rhodesia National Congress (1949) and then founded the Zambia National Congress (1958) which was later banned because of its opposition to colonial rule and the Federation of Rhodesia and Nyasaland. He became leader of the United Nationalist Independence Party (1960) and PM of Northern Rhodesia (1964) and, after independence, President of Zambia (1964–), establishing a 1-party state and assuming autocratic powers (1972).

Kellogg-Briand Pact (1928), in 1927 the French Foreign Minister, BRIAND, proposed that France and the USA should sign a pact renouncing war. Frank Kellogg (1856–1937), the American Secretary of State, proposed that the whole world should be involved. Eventually 65 states signed, agreeing to renounce war as an instrument of national policy. The signatories incl. Germany, the USA and the USSR, even though the latter were not members of the League of Nations. The Pact made no provision for punishing aggressors, and therefore had a very limited power, and by the end of the 1930s the Pact had become more or less meaningless.

Kennedy, John Fitzgerald (1917–63), US statesman, Democratic President (1961–63). His charisma, youthful appearance, effective organization and political style made him the most popular President this century.

Foreign affairs dominated his administration. They included the BAY OF PIGS fiasco; discussions with KHRUSHCHEV in Vienna; the building of the BERLIN Wall; the launching of the Peace Corps, the purpose of which was to develop assistance to underdeveloped countries, and the Alliance for Progress, an aid programme for Latin America (1961); the CUBAN MISSILES CRISIS; and the conclusion of the NUCLEAR TEST BAN TREATY (1963).

Domestically his civil-rights (*see* CIVIL RIGHTS ACTS) and social-reform programmes (the New Frontier) met opposition in Congress but eventually became law some 3 years after he had proposed them. He was assassinated by Lee Harvey Oswald in Dallas, Texas.

Kenyatta, Jomo (?1891–1978), Kenyan politician. He was a pioneer of African nationalism and a campaigner for African rights and land reform. He became President of the Kenya African Union (1947) which advocated extreme nationalism and was a screen for MAU MAU terrorist activities. Although Kenyatta eventually denounced these excesses he was distrusted by the UK government and sentenced to imprisonment (1953–61). While still in jail he was elected

President of the Kenya Africa National Union (KANU) (1960) and when it came to power (1963) he became PM, playing a prominent part in negotiations towards independence (1963). He was President of the Republic (1964—78).

Kerensky, Alexander (1881—1970), Russian soldier and politician. A democratic socialist, he became War Minister and weeks later PM in the Provisional Government following the February Revolution of 1917, urging the vigorous prosecution of WWI. His attempts to mount a formidable offensive in the summer ran counter to the feelings of the Russian people who were anxious for peace. He was pushed out of office by the Bolsheviks in the October Revolution of 1917. *See also* RUSSIAN REVOLUTIONS.

KGB, *see* SOVIET SECURITY SERVICE.

Khan, *see* AYUB KHAN and YAHYA KHAN.

Khmer Rouge, the Cambodian (now Kampuchean) Communist Party. It seized power following its victory in the civil war (1970—75), and under Pol Pot instituted a harsh, regimented regime, expelled all foreigners, and cut off the country from contact with the rest of the world. Cities and towns were forcibly evacuated and their populations made to take up agricultural work. After the country's invasion by Vietnam in support of an uprising by the Kampuchean National United Front (1978) and the fall of the capital Phnom Penh (1979), the Khmer Rouge went underground and is now waging a guerrilla war.

Khomeini, Ruholla (1900—   ), Iranian Islamic fundamentalist leader. As Ayatollah of the Shi'ite sect, he came into prominence when he condemned

the Shah's Western-type reforms, especially
women's emancipation (1963). He was sent into
exile, from where he called on the Iranians to
overthrow the Shah and establish an Islamic
republic. This was accomplished after the Shah fled
the country (1979), Khomeini returning in triumph
to Teheran shortly afterwards. There followed
a period of drastic repression and terror when
thousands of the Shah's followers and others
opposed to Khomeini's radical fundamentalist
reforms were summarily executed or imprisoned.
Khomeini effectively became head of state with
an administration organized by a Revolutionary
Committee of Shi'ite clergymen.

Khrushchev, Nikita (1894–1971), Soviet
statesman. He became First Secretary of the Party
(1953–64) following Stalin's death. At the 20th
Party Congress (1955) he made a remarkable attack
on Stalin's 'personality cult' and other misdeeds.
He was PM (1958–64) while remaining First
Secretary, and undertook a series of overseas visits,
talking much about peaceful intentions yet
accompanying them with threats, although in 1963
he signed the NUCLEAR TEST BAN TREATY.

He was responsible for instigating the CUBAN
MISSILES CRISIS, allowed relations with China to
deteriorate (*see* SINO-SOVIET SPLIT), and disrupted
the economy by encouraging agricultural decentralization and the production of consumer
goods at the expense of heavy industrial output. His
responsibility for these crises, together with
accusations of nepotism, the revival of a personality
cult, and authoritarian and unruly handling of state
and Party affairs, resulted in his deposition and

enforced retirement (1964). He was succeeded as First Secretary by BREZHNEV and as PM by KOSYGIN.

kibbutz, Israeli collective agricultural settlement, administered and owned by its members and on which children are collectively raised. The first was established by Jewish settlers in Palestine in 1910.

Kiesinger, Kurt Georg (1904–), West German Christian Democrat Chancellor (1966–69). His government was a coalition of the Christian and Social Democrats. It succeeded in arresting the recession which had led to the downfall of ERHARD's government and re-established diplomatic relations with Romania (1967) and Yugoslavia (1968) which had been broken off during WWII. Kiesinger was a believer in reconciliation with the Warsaw Pact countries (*see* OSTPOLITIK) and an advocate of European unity.

Kim Il Sung, orig. Kim Songju (1912–), North Korean Communist marshal and politician. He joined the Party (1931) and organized and led the Korean People's Revolutionary Army against the Japanese (1932–45). He was put in charge of administration by the Soviet army of occupation (1945), quickly established himself, and became PM on the formation of the Democratic People's Republic (1948–72).

He was Supreme Commander of the Army in the KOREAN WAR, and during and after the War his position was precarious. However, he managed to eliminate his rivals in a 'cultural revolution' and became the focus of a personality cult, aiming to centre the country on himself and to make it completely self-reliant. He has been the Republic's

President since 1972.

King, Martin Luther (1929—68), US Baptist minister and civil-rights leader. He advocated non-violent confrontation as a weapon of social protest. In Montgomery, Alabama, he organized a boycott of buses by the black American community in protest at racial segregation, which eventually produced a federal court desegregation order (1955). This success encouraged him to extend the campaign, and in many parts of the country peaceful demonstrations were held opposing racial discrimination in matters such as employment, housing and schooling. This agitation contributed towards the passing of several CIVIL RIGHTS ACTS, and in 1964 King was awarded the Nobel Peace Prize. He was assassinated in Memphis, Tennessee, by James Earl Ray.

Kinnock, Neil (1942—), British politician. Leader of the Labour Party (1983—).

Kissinger, Henry (1923—), US diplomat, b. Germany. He was President Nixon's Special Adviser on National Security (1969—73), visiting China and the USSR in efforts to obtain some form of DÉTENTE and the easing of tension between East and West. For his efforts to secure peace in the VIETNAM WAR he was awarded the Nobel Peace Prize (1973). He was Secretary of State (1973—77), practising a conservative and pragmatic style of diplomacy. He became particularly well known for his 'shuttle diplomacy' in the Middle East where on several visits he flew from country to country in efforts to secure peace between Israel and its Arab neighbours, notably helping to negotiate a ceasefire in the 1973 ARAB-ISRAELI WAR.

Kitchener, Horatio Herbert, Earl Kitchener of Khartoum (1850—1916), British field marshal. He was C-in-C (1900—2) in the BOER WAR, and became Secretary for War (1914—16) in WWI. He raised an army of 70 divisions with the aid of the famous recruiting poster carrying the slogan, 'Your country needs you', accompanied by his portrait. He was drowned on his way to Russia when HMS *Hampshire* was mined and sank off the Orkneys.

Kohl, Helmut (1930—), West German statesman. As leader of the Christian Democratic Party (1976—) he was elected Chancellor (1982—).

Korea, peninsula of NE Asia, now divided into North Korea and South Korea.

Korea was annexed by Japan (1910), and after Japan's defeat at the end of WWII, forces of the USSR and the USA occupied the country. For mutual military convenience the occupiers divided the territory into 2 regions along the 38th parallel of latitude, in accordance with terms agreed at the YALTA CONFERENCE. The ultimate objective was a unified democratic country, but it soon became evident that North and South were polarized in their allegiances, the former towards the USSR and the latter towards the USA, and so it has remained since negotiations between the Americans and Russians broke down (1946). In 1950 North Korea invaded the South, marking the start of the KOREAN WAR (1950—53).

North Korea Area: 122,370 sq km. Pop: 18,000,000 (est. 1982). Language: Korean. Religions: all repressed since 1945; formerly Buddhism, Confucianism, Chondokyo and Shamanism. Cap: Pyong-yang.

The People's Democratic Republic of North Korea was proclaimed (1948) under the leadership of KIM IL SUNG, who has remained in power ever since.

South Korea Area: 98,447 sq km. Pop: 39,000,000 (est. 1982). Language: Korean. Religions: Animism, Buddhism, Christianity and Confucianism. Cap: Seoul.

The Republic of South Korea was proclaimed (1948) with Syngman Rhee (1875–1965) as President. This right-wing nationalist presided over a corrupt regime and it was overthrown in 1960, being replaced (1962), after a period of instability, by an administration headed by Major General Park Chung Hee (1917–79), who was assassinated by the head of the Korean Central Intelligence Agency. South Korea's first fully democratic presidential elections were held in 1987, although there were widespread accusations of corruption.

Korean War (1950–53), conflict resulting from the partition of KOREA into the Soviet-occupied North and the US-occupied South along the 38th parallel of latitude (1945). After both occupying forces were withdrawn (1948) border clashes developed and eventually escalated into a full-scale invasion of the South by 8 North Korean divisions. Within 3 days the South Korean capital, Seoul, fell and the UN Security Council, which at the time was boycotted by the USSR, approved the despatch of armed forces to drive out the North Koreans. Contingents were sent from 15 nations, and they were placed under the command of the US C-in-C, Far East, General MacArthur.

Within a fortnight the North Koreans were back

on their own side of the partition line, but then
China warned that it would enter the War should
the UN forces approach the Yalu River (the North
Korean-Chinese border). This warning was
ignored, and this and a desire to prevent the
decimation of the North Korean forces prompted
China to intervene with such force that the UN
forces were compelled to retreat for a time. Finally
counter-offensives forced back the Chinese and the
partition line was restored. Peace talks commenced
(1951) but an armistice agreement was not reached
for 2 years (*see* PANMUNJOM ARMISTICE).
All attempts at peaceful reunification of Korea
have failed and the country remains divided as
before.

Kosygin, Alexei (1904—80), Soviet statesman. He
held a multiplicity of state and party appointments
before becoming Chairman of the Council of
Ministers (1964—80), effectively sharing power
with BREZHNEV. He concentrated on internal
matters at the expense of foreign matters, being
concerned with economic development and reform,
particularly the decentralization of agriculture and
industry, although in the foreign sphere he was
notably successful in mediating between India and
Pakistan at the TASHKENT CONFERENCE.

Kremlin (Rusian, 'citadel'), former imperial palace
in Moscow, now the administrative HQ of the
USSR government. Hence the term is also used for
the central government of the USSR.

Kronstadt Mutiny (1921), revolt by the Soviet
garrison (consisting largely of peasant recruits) of
the Kronstadt naval base on Kotlin Island in the
Gulf of Finland.

The mutineers were concerned by rural disturbances taking place all over the USSR and they issued a variety of demands: fresh elections to the Soviets by secret ballot; freedom of assembly for peasant and trade-union movements; freedom of speech and the press for all left-wing parties; re-establishment of a free market for the peasants; and disbandment of grain-requisitioning squads.

Although the mutiny was eventually put down by loyal troops it was not unsuccessful since some policy changes (e.g. the NEW ECONOMIC POLICY) were made in line with the mutineers' demands.

Krupps, German industrial combine founded (1811) for steel manufacture but later expanding into armaments, mining, shipbuilding and agricultural and railway machinery. It remained a family concern for 5 generations. It was vitally important to Germany's ability to wage both World Wars, and was notorious for its exploitation of occupied countries and the use of slave labour.

Ku Klux Klan, US secret society of white Southerners formed after the Civil War to fight Northern domination and black emancipation. Largely a Protestant organization it has directed its hostility towards blacks, Catholics, Communists, Jews and alien minorities. Its symbol is a fiery cross and its members disguise themselves in white masks and robes, their leaders being given fanciful names such as Grand Wizard, Grand Dragon, etc. Murder, lynch law and intimidation were practised but its effectiveness has waned in recent years.

kulaks, *see* COLLECTIVIZATION.

Kun, Béla (1886–1937), Hungarian Communist dictator. He was captured in WWI by the Russians, who after indoctrination returned him to Hungary as an agitator. He succeeded in overthrowing the liberal government and establishing a regime noted for its cruelty and ruthlessness (1919) although it only survived a few months. The country was invaded by Czechoslovakia and Romania and a counter-revolutionary government established by HORTHY, causing Kun to flee to the USSR where he perished in the purges.

Kuomintang, Chinese nationalist political movement. Under SUN YAT-SEN it helped in the overthrow of the Manchu dynasty (1911). CHIANG KAI-SHEK took over as leader (1925—75) and set out to reunify China by extending the movement's political influence and military domination. Superficially this objective was achieved (1928) and the Kuomintang was China's ruling party until 1949.

However, the movement became increasingly army-dominated, right-wing and authoritarian, and the economic, political and social reforms advocated by Sun Yat-sen were not carried out. This was in some degree owing to the need to fight the Japanese invasion (1937—45).

Chiang had purged the Communists from the movement in 1927, and engaged in an intermittent civil war with them until 1949, when the Communists under MAO ZEDONG drove the Kuomintang from the mainland. Chief causes of the Kuomintang's downfall were its manifest corruption and inefficiency, the devastation caused by years of war, and the resulting inflation. Since 1949 it has been the ruling party of Taiwan.

L

Labour Party, British and Australian socialist movements.

The **British Labour Party** was founded in 1900 as the Labour Representation Committee, an amalgam of various socialist bodies. The Committee became the Labour Party (1906) and its adherents grew rapidly as a result of unemployment and the TAFF VALE CASE judgement. The Party's policies of industrial reform, WOMEN'S SUFFRAGE, slum clearance and old-age pensions steadily won it by-elections and local-government elections, so building on the successes of the 1906 general election.

The first experience of office held by Labour members was the WWI coalition government. In 1922 the Party became the offical Opposition, and in 1924 formed a minority government, with Ramsay MACDONALD as PM, which survived less than a year. The Party regained power in 1929 but was unable to deal with the financial crisis and unemployment caused by the Depression. When a NATIONAL GOVERNMENT was formed (1931) the Party split over MacDonald's decision to serve as PM.

The party was represented in the WWII coalition government but its first real taste of power was after the 1945 general election when it obtained an overwhelming majority. With ATTLEE as PM, it brought in extensive NATIONALIZATION measures, established the National Health Service and many other features of the modern WELFARE STATE, and granted independence to India, Pakistan and Burma. The Party was in opposition (1951—64), a period marked again by internal stresses, and when it returned to office with WILSON as PM (1964—70), it faced rising inflation, BALANCE OF PAYMENTS problems and industrial unrest, problems that also confronted the Labour government of 1974—79, in which Wilson, then CALLAGHAN, served as PM. This period was also marked by a widening gulf between the left and right within the Party. Since then, the Party has been led in opposition by FOOT and KINNOCK.

The **Australian Labour Party** formed coalition governments with the Liberal Party (1904 and 1908) before being able to form majority governments (1910 and 1914). These began the construction of the transcontinental railway and the development of land, established the Commonwealth Bank, and begun the taxation of income. During WWI the Party was split over the issue of conscription and thereafter was out of office from 1916—41 except for 1929—31 when its policies were disrupted by the Depression.

It was again in power (1941—49) and in the post-WWII period launched economic, immigration and reconstruction programmes designed to achieve full employment and social security. Industrial unrest, the retention of wartime controls, and attempted bank nationalization brought about its defeat, and it did not regain power until 1972. This period of office (1972—75) was characterized by internal dissention and parliamentary upheavals. Finally the

Governor General intervened and unprecedentally dismissed the PM's government. The Party came to power again in 1983.

Lateran Treaties, *see* CONCORDAT.

Latvia *see* BALTIC STATES.

Lausanne, Treaty of (1923), the final peace settlement between Turkey and the Allies after WWI, following the refusal of the Turkish Republic to consider the Treaty of SÈVRES binding.

Turkey surrendered all claim to former territories of the OTTOMAN EMPIRE occupied by non-Turks. Greeks were confirmed in possession of all Aegean Islands, but they surrendered the Turkish port of Izmir (Smyrna). Italy annexed the islands of the Dodecanese, and the UK annexed Cyprus. The Bosphorus and DARDANELLES were demilitarized, and Turkey recovered E Thrace. Following the territorial changes dictated by the Treaty, considerable exchanges of population occurred.

Laval, Pierre (1883–1945), French statesman. A socialist until 1920, he moved further and further to the right. He was PM (1931–32 and 1935–36) and Foreign Minister (1934–36), but public indignation over the HOARE-LAVAL PACT forced him to resign. He subsequently supported the ideas of PÉTAIN, and joined his VICHY GOVERNMENT (1940), later becoming PM (1942–44). He avoided any military commitment to the Nazis, and in trying to convene a National Assembly in 1944 he was arrested by the Germans. Laval fled to Spain but returned to France in 1945 to be tried for treason, and was shot.

Law, Andrew Bonar (1858–1923), British Conservative statesman, PM (1922–23). He became leader of the Conservative Party in 1911. In the WWI coalition government, Law was Chancellor of the Exchequer (1916—18). Law's brief premiership set the fashion for tranquillity and 'safety first' which was to mark British Conservatism throughout the interwar period.

Lawrence, Thomas Edward (1888—1935), British soldier. He became known as 'Lawrence of Arabia' because of his leadership of the Arabs in the revolt (1917—18) against the OTTOMAN EMPIRE in WWI. During the revolt Lawrence led raids on the Hejaz railway, took part in the capture of Aqaba and Damascus and maintained close Arab liaison with General Allenby's Palestinian army. He was trusted implicitly by the Arabs, opposed the BALFOUR DECLARATION, and supported the Arab cause at the PARIS PEACE CONFERENCE.

League of Nations, international organization created (1920) to preserve the peace and settle disputes by arbitration or conciliation. Its Covenant was incorporated into the Treaty of VERSAILLES and other post-WWI treaties, the MANDATES created by these treaties becoming the League's responsibility.

Though the creation of the League had been advocated by the US President Wilson (among others), the USA was never a member. The League's only weapon against wayward members was SANCTIONS, and it failed to prevent aggression among member states: Japan in Manchuria and China, Italy in Abyssinia (Ethiopia), the USSR in Finland. Brazil left the League in 1926, Germany and Japan in 1933, Italy in 1937, and the USSR in 1940. The League did however succeed in resolving international disputes in the Balkans and South America. It was dissolved in 1946, transferring its services and property to the UNITED NATIONS ORGANIZATION.

Lebanon, republic of the Middle East, on the E coast of the Mediterranean. Area: 10,400 sq km. Pop: 2,780,000 (est. 1984). Language: Arabic. Religion: Christian and Islam. Cap: Beirut.

Until 1918 the country was part of the OTTOMAN EMPIRE. It was captured by Britain and France in WWI and then mandated to France (1920) by the League of Nations.

Lebanon became a fully independent state in 1946, having achieved degrees of independence in 1926 and 1941. Postwar economic and political instability was caused by the high cost of living, rising unemployment, loss of wartime trade, and increasing antagonism between the Christian and Moslem communities. These problems resulted in rioting and near civil war, so that the Government requested US assistance to restore order (1958).

The country has tried to avoid taking sides in inter-Arab disputes and avoided involvement in wars against Israel. This has succeeded only partially since large numbers of Palestinians sought refuge there after being driven out of Jordan (1970) and immediately the PLO started the organization of terrorist activity across the frontier into Israel, using Lebanon as a base from which to shell Israeli troops and settlements. The arrival of the Palestinians aggravated the situation between the Christians and Moslems and the fighting that ensued provoked Syria into sending in troops to oppose the Christians. The Israelis reacted by giving support to the Christians and occupied Lebanon S of the Litani River (1978). In 1982–85 Israel extended its military involvement as far north as Beirut, forcing the PLO leadership to leave the country.

Lebanon was once the Middle East's banking and commercial centre but now large parts of it are in ruins and occupied by foreign troops, while numerous mutually hostile factions continue the civil war. A UN force has vainly tried to keep the peace since 1978.

Lebensraum (Ger., 'living space'), term coined by the Nazis for the non-German-speaking territories to the E of Germany which they thought the German people should settle. Hitler attempted to implement this policy in his invasions of Poland (1939) and the USSR (1941). These territorial objectives were in addition to Hitler's claims to countries already settled by Germans.

Lee Kuan Yew (1923–   ), Singaporean statesman. He founded the People's Action Party (1954) and was elected to the Legislative Assembly (1955) after campaigning for 'an independent, democratic, and non-Communist Malaya' that would include Singapore. He became first PM of SINGAPORE (1959) after separation from Malaya and then led it into the Federation of Malaysia (1963) and out again (1965). Since then he has encouraged foreign industrial development, and in foreign affairs has pursued a policy of non-alignment and regional cooperation.

legislation, (a) act or process of passing laws, (b) laws so made.

legislature, group (not necessarily elected) vested

with power to enact, repeal or amend laws for a
political unit. In the UK, PARLIAMENT is the
legislature, and in the USA, CONGRESS. *See also*
SEPARATION OF POWERS.

Lend-Lease Act (1941), US legislation author-
izing the lease, loan, transfer or exchange of equipment required by any state recognized as being
of vital importance to the defence and security of
the USA. Practically, this meant the immediate
release of vast quantities of war materials to the UK,
and later to China and the USSR, and placed US
industry on a war footing even before the country
entered WWII. Lend-Lease ended (1945) after
some $50 billion worth of aid had been granted.

Lenin, Vladimir Ilyich (1870–1924), Russian
statesman. He studied Marx as a student, and
during a spell in Western Europe he became
recognized as the leader of the Bolsheviks, the
militant wing of the Russian Social Democrats (*see*
BOLSHEVISM).

Returning to Russia in 1917 he led the October
Revolution (*see* RUSSIAN REVOLUTIONS), becoming
head of the new government, the Council of
People's Commissars. He ordered an armistice with
Germany in 1918 following the Treaty of BREST-
LITOVSK. His attempt to achieve a Communist
economic revolution while waging civil war led to
the virtual collapse of the economy, but by 1920 he
had successfully established the Soviet Union. In
1921 he introduced the NEW ECONOMIC POLICY in
reaction to economic difficulties and internal
unrest.

Leningrad, Siege of (1941–44), heroic defence of
the USSR's second city during WWII when Finnish

and German armies encircled and practically cut it off from the rest of the country. About 1½ million civilians and troops perished from cold and hunger even though a counter-offensive partially relieved the city (1943). The complete lifting of the siege occurred after the Germans had been forced to retreat by massive Soviet counter-attacks.

Leopold III (1901–83), King of Belgium (1934–51). As C-in-C of the Army in WWII, he ordered it to capitulate to the German invaders (1940) against the wishes of the Government and the majority of the population. The Government went into exile in the UK but Leopold chose to remain a prisoner in Laeken Palace. A commission of enquiry (1947) absolved him from the charge of major collaboration with the occupying Germans. Although 58% of the population voted in a referendum (1950) for him to remain the monarch, a dangerous situation arose with street demonstrations and rioting, and he abdicated in favour of his son Baudouin.

liberalism, a loose term for political views favouring progress, reform and individual freedom.

Liberal Party, British, Australian and Canadian political parties.

The **British Liberal Party** is the successor of the 18th and 19th-cent. Whig Party and, until it was overtaken by the Labour Party (1922), was one of the two major political parties, a position it has never been able to regain. Its greatest period in office was 1906–15, when CAMPBELL-BANNERMAN and ASQUITH were PM. During this period the foundations of the WELFARE STATE were laid with the introduction of minimum wages, old-age pensions and national insurance. Trade-union legislation and the PARLIAMENT ACTS were also features of the administrations.

The decline in the Party's popularity started with the WWI split between the Asquith and LLOYD GEORGE factions, the abandonment of FREE TRADE policies, and the rise of the Labour Party. Since WWII it has campaigned, with minimal success, for the decentralization of government from London to the N and W of England and to Scotland and Wales, for the prevention of the growth of monopolies, for individual liberties, civil rights and racial and religious tolerance, and for employees to be awarded shares in the decision-making and profits of the firms where they are employed.

In 1977 the so-called 'Lib-Lab Pact' was concluded with the Labour Party which helped to sustain in office the minority Labour Government in return for prior consultation over aspects of government policy. This effectively split the Liberal Party and the arrangement was abandoned at the time of the 1979 election. In 1981 the Liberals joined the SOCIAL DEMOCRATIC PARTY in a political alliance, fighting the 1983 and 1987 elections on this basis.

The **Australian Liberal Party** was founded (1944) by MENZIES out of the United Australia Party which evolved (1931) from the Nationalist Party established in 1917. In coalition with the COUNTRY PARTY it was in power (1949–72 and 1975–83), its policies in many ways resembling those of the British Conservative Party.

The **Canadian Liberal Party** has held power for much of this century (1896–1911, 1935–57,

1963—79, and 1980—84). In coalition with the Progressive Party it was also in office from 1921 to 1930. Its policies are in line in many ways with those of the British Party. It split into two factions due to policy disagreements in the period from 1911 through WWI. It also campaigns on Commonwealth interdependence and minority rights, esp. those affecting the French-speaking population of the country.

Libya, Socialist People's republic of N Africa. Area: 1,759,540 sq km. Pop: 3,100,000 (est. 1981). Language: Arabic. Religion: Islam. Cap: Tripoli.

Formerly an Italian colony, it became a battleground during WWII and gained independence in 1951. From then until 1969 the country was ruled by King Idris I (1890—1983). He was overthrown by a coup led by GADDAFI, who formed a Revolutionary Command Council which declared the country a republic with Gaddafi as Head of State.

At first the republic relied on the UK and the USA for financial assistance in return for the use of military bases, but the agreements were terminated by Libya because it considered the UK and the USA to have shown a pro-Israeli bias during the 1967 Arab-Israeli War. The Anglo-Libyan Treaty of Friendship negotiated during the monarchy (1953) was abrogated (1972) and UK oil interests were nationalized.

Since then Libya has developed cordial relationships with WARSAW PACT countries, but because of its fundamentalist Islamic outlook it has alienated itself from all but a few Arab states. Egypt in particular has attracted considerable threatening abuse following the CAMP DAVID AGREEMENT, and other Arab states have also been targets of vilification and attempts at internal interference. Libya has actively supported the PLO, and has provided money, arms and refuge for various terrorist organizations. In addition assassination squads have been sent to Europe to eliminate Libyans opposed to the present regime.

Lie, Trygve (1896–1968), Norwegian socialist politician, first Secretary-General of the UN (1946–53). His period as Secretary-General was notable for his unsuccessful advocacy of the admission of China to the UN and his organization of UN forces to stem North Korea's attack on South Korea (1950–53).

Liebknecht, Karl see SPARTACIST RISING.

Lin Biao or **Lin Piao** (1908–71), Chinese Communist soldier, politician. He was appointed Minister of Defence (1959), setting himself the task of politicizing the army, incl. the unusual step of abolishing ranks. During the CULTURAL REVOLUTION he emerged as Mao Zedong's principal supporter and was designated his successor (1969). He disappeared in unusual circumstances, supposedly dying in an air crash while fleeing to the USSR after organizing an unsuccessful coup against Mao Zedong in Peking.

Lithuania, see BALTIC STATES.

Little Entente (1921), an alliance formed under French patronage by Czechoslovakia, Romania and Yugoslavia to resist any attempt by Hungary to recover territory. In the same year France itself concluded an alliance of mutual guarantee with

Poland. The alliances were intended to maintain the status quo in Central Europe and to prevent a restoration of the AUSTRO-HUNGARIAN EMPIRE or any change in the frontiers. In 1933 the Little Entente was converted into an international community with a Permanent Council and Secretariat. It was dissolved in 1939.

Litvinov, Maxim (1876–1951), Soviet diplomat, politican. In the 1930s he was an ardent advocate of Soviet support for the League of Nations, rapprochement with the West, and collective security against the rising tide of Fascism. During this period he was Commissar for Foreign Affairs (1930–39), negotiated the Franco-Soviet Pact (1935) and generally worked for the acceptance of his country abroad. He was Ambassador to the US (1941–43) and Vice-Minister of Foreign Affairs (1943–46).

Liu Shaoqui or **Liu Shao-chi** (1898–1974), Chinese Communist politician. The Party's principal theoretician, he became Chairman of the People's Republic and Head of State (1959), but during the CULTURAL REVOLUTION he was deposed and denounced for opposing Mao Zedong's belief in the importance of the peasantry over industrial workers, for 'taking the capitalist road', and being an advocate of 'Soviet revisionism'.

Lloyd George, David, Earl of Dwyfor (1863–1945), British Liberal statesman, PM of coalition governments (1916–22). He was President of the Board of Trade (1905–08) and Chancellor of the Exchequer (1908–15). On the radical wing of his party, he advocated social reforms such as old-age pensions and national health insurance. He introduced the 'People's Budget' by which such social reforms, and a large defence programme, were to be financed by higher death duties, an extra tax on high incomes and a land tax. The Budget's rejection by the House of Lords led to the 1911 PARLIAMENT ACT.

As PM from 1916 he proved an energetic war leader. He modified the harsher proposals of the Treaty of VERSAILLES, but fell from power following his handling of the CHANAK CRISIS.

Locarno, Treaties of (1925), agreements between various groups of nations in an attempt to settle problems stemming from WWI.

The principal Treaty was signed by Belgium, France and Germany, agreeing to the maintenance of their existing frontiers, settlement of disputes by arbitration without resort to force, and acceptance of the demilitarization of the RHINELAND. This Treaty was guaranteed by Italy and the UK, but neither they nor Belgium and France took action, other than by formal protest, when Germany occupied the Rhineland in 1936.

The other Treaties concerned France, which agreed mutual security guarantees with Czechoslovakia and Poland; and Germany, which concluded agreements to settle disputes by arbitration with Belgium, Czechoslovakia, France and Poland.

Lomé Conventions (1975 and 1979), trade agreements, the first of which permitted 46 developing countries (known as the African, Caribbean and Pacific States) free access for their exports into the EEC. Provision was also made for aid and investment to be supplied by the EEC. The second Convention (1979) provided for £3.6 billion aid from the EEC to developing countries in the period 1980—85.

London, Treaty of (1915), secret agreement between Britain, France, Russia and Italy, guaranteeing Italy territorial gains if it entered WWI on the Allied side within a month of signing, which it duly did.

The Treaty's terms were made public by the USSR in 1918 when the Bolsheviks disclaimed all pre-revolutionary international commitments, and the revelation angered the USA to the extent that it rejected them as binding on the grounds that they contravened the principle of each people's right to self-determination — the territories involved incl. many non-Italian-speaking peoples.

At the PARIS PEACE CONFERENCE (1919), Britain and France refused to honour the Treaty, and Italy received considerably less territory than she had been promised. This caused much resentment in Italy and was a factor in the rise of Italian FASCISM.

Long March (1934—35), an epic migration of Chinese Communists in the course of the civil war with the KUOMINTANG. In 1931 the Communists had established a Chinese Soviet Republic in Jiangxi, but the successes of Chiang Kai-shek's armies forced the Communists to evacuate and march 8,000 miles, heading NW for a year to Yanan. Of the 100,000 who set out, less than half survived, but they regrouped in stronger positions against the Kuomintang until 1937, when a truce was declared in order to fight the common enemy, Japan. MAO ZEDONG established himself as the

Communist leader during the march.

Ludendorff, Erich von (1865–1937), German general and politician. He achieved prominence in WWI when he captured Liège and was successful in the Battle of TANNENBERG and the Masurian Lakes (1914), victories on which he subsequently built his political power, claiming that his military responsibilities gave him a legitimate interest in any policy which had a bearing on the prosecution of the War. His military prestige made him something of a national hero and he was able to dictate government policy by threatening to resign from his military command. His power collapsed with the 1918 Allied successes and he resigned and fled to Sweden before Germany capitulated.

Ludendorff was a nationalist and racist, and as such took part in the Munich PUTSCH (1923). He became a Reichstag National Socialist member (1924–28), and unsuccessfully stood as Nazi Presidential candidate (1925). He remained on the fringes of extremist politics, even founding his own right-wing anti-Semitic movement, the Tannenbergerbund.

Luftwaffe, the German air force. Commanded in WWII by Goering, it was defeated by the RAF in the Battle of BRITAIN, and was then used for the air-raids of the BLITZ.

Lusitania, British liner torpedoed and sunk without warning by a U-boat off Ireland in 1915, with the loss of 1200 lives of whom over 100 were US citizens. The sinking caused wisespread anger and resentment in the USA with calls for a declaration of war on Germany, which maintained that the vessel's cargo incl. war material. The incident contributed to the entry of the USA into WWI in 1917.

Luthuli, Albert John (1898—1967), South African political leader, president of the AFRICAN NATIONAL CONGRESS (1952—67). Openly opposed APARTHEID, advocating nonviolent resistance. Kept under restriction after 1952; arrested for treason (1956) but acquitted (1959). Awarded Nobel Peace Prize (1960).

Luxembourg, grand duchy of NW Europe. Area: 2,586 sq km. Pop: 364,000 (1981). Languages: French and Letzeburgesch (German dialect). Religion: RC. Cap: Luxembourg.

A duchy from 1354, it became a grand duchy within the Netherlands in 1815 and an independent country in 1890. Invaded by Germany in both WWs. Formed the Benelux customs union with Belgium and the Netherlands in 1948 and is now a member of the EEC and NATO. It houses the headquarters of the European Court of Justice and the secretariat of the European Parliament.

Luxemburg, Rosa (1871—1919), Polish-born German revolutionary. A Marxist, she founded the Spartacus League (1916) with Karl Liebknecht. Arrested and killed after leading the SPARTICIST RISING.

M

McCarthyism, term used to describe the practice of accusing people of being associated with Communist-oriented organizations with little evidence to substantiate the claim, and named after Joseph McCarthy (1908–67), Republican Senator for Wisconsin.

At the height of the COLD WAR in 1950, McCarthy alleged that the US State Department had on its staff 205 employees known to be Communist sympathizers and 57 who were Party members. This revelation was followed by a campaign to discredit prominent Democrats, incl. such respected figures as Dean Acheson and George Marshall. On becoming Chairman of the Permanent Sub-committee on Investigation (1953) his attacks intensified, involving Robert Stevens, Secretary of the Army, and many intellectuals and officials. His activities led to the establishment of 'black lists', and many people's careers were ruined. Finally, after his activities were condemned by the Senate (1954), McCarthy attacked President Eisenhower and this completed the discrediting of his campaign.

MacDonald, Ramsay (1866–1937), British Labour statesman, PM (1924 and 1929–35). He was Leader of the Labour Party (1911–14), resigning over his opposition to WWI, but became Leader again after the War (1922–31).

He was the first Labour PM and Foreign Minister

(1924), but his government collapsed over the
ZINOVIEV LETTER. He became PM again in 1929,
but his desire for a 'responsible party of
government' led to the 1931 Cabinet split over his
plan to cut unemployment benefit. This in turn led
to his decision to form a NATIONAL GOVERNMENT
and to campaign against the Labour Party, for
which he was expelled from the Party during the pre
1935 election campaign. He served in Baldwin's
government (1935−37).

Macmillan, Harold, 1st Earl of Stockton
(1894−1986), British Conservative statesman, PM
(1957−63). He was successively (1951−57) Minister of Housing and Local Government, Minister of
Defence, Foreign Secretary, and Chancellor of the
Exchequer, before becoming PM.

His administration was marked by stable prices
and economic prosperity (characterized by his
phrase, 'You've never had it so good'), followed by
BALANCE OF PAYMENTS problems and rising
unemployment. In 1961 his administration established the National Economic Development Council
('Neddy').

In foreign affairs, his administration strengthened Anglo-American collaboration, and assumed
a mediating role between the USSR and USA.
The colonial policy of his government, which
involved the dissolution of the Federation of Rhodesia and Nyasaland, the granting of independence to many African states, and opposition to
apartheid, was summed up in his 'Wind of
Change' speech to the South African Parliament
(1960). An attempt to take Britain into the EEC
was vetoed by France (1963), largely because De

Gaulle regarded the NASSAU AGREEMENT (1962) as a sign that the UK was too closely allied to the USA to assume a role in Europe. In 1963 Macmillan was forced to resign because of ill health.

Maginot Line, series of French fortifications built (1929—34) from Longwy (on the Luxembourg border) to the Swiss frontier and named after the Minister of War, André Maginot (1877—1932). Belgian opposition prevented the Line being continued along the Franco-Belgian frontier to the North Sea, and it was this weakness that Germany exploited in WWII by circumnavigating the Line and advancing into France from Belgium (1940). The Line was practically intact when France capitulated.

Makarios III (1913—77), orig. Mikhail Christo-doulou Mouskos, Cypriot archbishop and politi-cian. As head of the Cypriot Orthodox Church from 1950, he became the political and spiritual leader of the Greek Cypriots, leading the movement for union with Greece (Enosis). The British arrested him and deported him to the Seychelles (1956—57) believing he was involved with the EOKA terrorist organization.

Makarios eventually renounced Enosis in favour of British proposals for Cypriot independence, when he realized that the opposition to Enosis by Turkish Cypriots could lead to the partition of the island. On independence (1960), Makarios was elected President, but independence failed to stop intercommunal violence (*See* CYPRUS). In 1974 Makarios was overthrown by a pro-Enosis coup backed by Greece, which led to the invasion and occupation of N Cyprus by Turkey. Makarios resumed the presidency, but was left in control of only about 60% of the island.

Malta, Commonwealth republic of the C Mediterranean, comprising the islands of Comino, Gozo and Malta. Area: 316 sq km. Pop: 341,000 (est. 1981). Languages: Maltese and English. Religion: RC. Cap: Valletta.

The islands became a British colony (1814), internal self-government was granted (1947) and independence (1964). For many years it was a principal Royal Naval base and during WWII was of great strategic importance owing to its position between Italy and the N African coast and about half way between Gibraltar and the Suez Canal. It was heavily bombed and very nearly starved into submission, but convoys always managed to get through, although frequently suffering heavy losses in the process. The bravery and fortitude of its inhabitants was acknowledged by the award of the George Cross (1942).

From independence to 1971 the Nationalist Party of Dr Borg Olivier (1911–) was in power. From 1971 until 1987 the Labour Party, led by Dominic Mintoff, has formed the administration. Immediately after his electoral victory Mintoff terminated the defence agreement made with the UK on independence, forbade US naval vessels from visiting the country, and proved antagonistic to NATO defensive arrangements without financial compensation.

Since the withdrawal of the British garrison and the closure of the Royal Naval Dockyard, unemployment has been a major problem, and to bolster an ailing economy Mintoff turned to China and Libya for support, the important tourist industry not providing sufficient income to sustain prosperity. Another domestic issue which has troubled the islands from time to time is the administration's differences with the RC Church on political and religious issues.

Manchuria, region of NE China. It was developed by Russia, but after the RUSSO-JAPANESE WAR Japan gained concessions with the Treaty of Peking (1905). These incl. the right to maintain troops to guard the South Manchurian Railway which connected Port Arthur with the Trans-Siberian Railway. Japan occupied the whole region in 1932 after accusing the Chinese of destroying part of the line at Mukden.

The area was named Manchukuo and placed under the titular control of a puppet regime headed by Hsuan T'ung (Henry Pu-Yi) (1906–67) who had been deposed as the last Emperor of China (1908–12) whilst still a child. China protested to the League of Nations which responded by sending a 5-man Commission of Inquiry headed by Lord Lytton and representing France, Germany, Italy, the UK and the USA. Its report rejected the pretext made by Japan for its occupation, repudiated the establishment of Manchukuo, and recommended the creation of an autonomous Manchuria under Chinese sovereignty. Japan refused to accept the Commission's report and left the League (1933).

The territory was regained by China at the end of WWII in accordance with the terms of the CAIRO CONFERENCE, but was controlled by the Communists who used it as a base against KUOMINTANG forces.

mandates or **mandated territories,** former German colonies and non-Turkish areas of the OTTOMAN EMPIRE ceded to the Allies after WWI but remaining the ultimate responsibility of the LEAGUE OF NATIONS. The UN took over responsibility from the League (1946) and mandates were renamed 'trust territories'.

Mandated territories incl. such divergent areas as the Cameroons, Iraq, Lebanon, New Guinea, Palestine, Samoa, South West Africa, Syria, Tanganyika, Togoland and Transjordan. The administering countries incl. Australia, Belgium, France, New Zealand, South Africa and the UK.

Mannerheim, Carl Gustav Emil, Freiherr von (1867—1951). Finnish soldier and statesman. After Finland gained independence (1917) there was civil war between the Bolsheviks and the Whites led by Mannerheim. The Bolsheviks were defeated and Mannerheim became supreme commander and regent but was defeated in the 1919 presidential election. He was responsible for the construction of the system of fortification known as the 'Mannerheim Line' close to the Russian frontier near Leningrad, and when the Russians attacked Finland at the beginning of WWII was appointed C-in-C and allied the country with Germany. He was elected President (1944—46) and made peace with the Russians (1944), joining them in the fight against Germany (1945).

Maoism, MARXISM-Leninism as interpreted by MAO ZEDONG, based on the revolutionary potential of the peasantry and guerrilla warfare.

Mao Zedong or **Mao Tse-tung** (1893—1976), Chinese revolutionary and statesman. He was a

founder of the Chinese Communist Party (1921). In
its formative years the Party cooperated with the
KUOMINTANG, but after the break between the
parties Mao Zedong organized the abortive
Autumn Harvest Uprising (1927) and fled to the
mountains where he established a guerrilla base on
the Hunan-Jiangxi border. This became the main
centre of Communist activity until it was disbanded
prior to the LONG MARCH, during which he was
elected Party Chairman by the Politburo.

During the SINO-JAPANESE WAR the Communists once more collaborated with the Kuomintang (1937—45) but then resumed their struggle for
supremacy over CHIANG KAI-SHEK's forces. After
the Communist victory, Mao Zedong became
Chairman of the People's Republic (1949—59), and
remained as Party Chairman until his death. He
developed a personality cult, instigated the GREAT
LEAP FORWARD and the CULTURAL REVOLUTION,
believing as always in peasant supremacy over urban
proletarianism. For the last 5 years of his life ill-
ness intervened to remove him from political activity, and though he remained the figurehead,
ZHOU ENLAI was effectively in control.

Maquis, French underground RESISTANCE MOVE-
MENT which fought against the German occupying
forces in WWII.

March on Rome (1922), a Fascist-inspired legend
of the way in which Mussolini came to power in
Italy. Throughout 1922 there was a danger of civil
war in Italy, with the Fascists seizing control of
several cities. Mussolini demanded a Fascist
government and concentrated his supporters on the
approaches to the capital. King Victor Emmanuel

III gave way before the Fascist threat, dismissed the PM, and invited Mussolini to return from Milan to Rome to form a government.

Marne, Battles of the, 2 engagements fought at the beginning and end of WWI. The first battle (1914) halted Germany's advance into France. The enemy came within a few miles of Paris and the French had to withdraw troops from Lorraine and rush them by train and taxi to the River Marne, such was the extremity in which they were placed. This desperate move was successful and the French supported by the British, were able to force the Germans back behind the Aisne to positions they were to hold until the second battle (1918). This was the last German offensive of the War and brought them again within striking distance of Paris, but French counter-attacks drove them back, the strategic initiative passed to the Allies, and within 4 months the War was over.

Marshall Plan (1947), proposals drawn up by the US Secretary of State, George Marshall (1880–1959), offering US economic and financial help wherever it was needed to fight the hunger, poverty, desperation and chaos that followed WWII. The Plan led to the establishment of the European Recovery Programme by which 16 W European countries (but not the USSR or other Communist states) accepted US aid. $13 billion flowed into W Europe, fostering the recovery of agriculture and industry. The Russians saw the Programme as an attempt at political indoctrination by the USA, rather than as an economic necessity.

Marxism, political theory and doctrine based on the writings of Karl Marx (1818–83).

Marx saw history as a struggle between one CLASS and another to control the means of production (i.e. agriculture, industry, banking, etc.). The old feudal society ruled by the aristocracy had by this time been largely overthrown (e.g. in the French Revolution) by the BOURGEOISIE (the middle class), who controlled the economic system known as CAPITALISM. According to Marx, capitalism, although increasing the sum of human wealth through industrial expansion, relied on the exploitation of the PROLETARIAT (the industrial working class), whose material wealth and social conditions were not improved.

Although Marx believed that capitalism contained the seeds of its own destruction, he saw the inevitability of its revolutionary overthrow by the proletariat (leading to the 'dictatorship of the proletariat') followd by the establishment of COMMUNISM. Under Communism classes would be abolished, the means of production owned in common by all members of society, and humanity would be free to develop its full potential.

Since the 19th cent. the followers of Marx have been divided into social democrats and socialists on the one hand, who believe in the gradual and non-violent transformation of capitalism, and on the other hand Communists (such as LENIN and MAO ZEDONG) who believe in the need for immediate and violent revolution, even before a large industrial proletariat exists.

Many of the specific points that Marx advocated — such as the NATIONALIZATION of industry and transport, a state bank, a graded income-tax system, universal state education, and the abolition of child labour — have been established in various degrees in many democracies without the tight and often repressive controls of many Communist countries. However, the redistribution of land and the abolition of private property, which Marx also advocated, have by and large only taken place in Communist states.

Masaryk *see* CZECHOSLOVAKIA.

Mau Mau, Kenyan secret terrorist society based in Kikuyu tribal area. It considered itself to be a national liberation movement, and was committed to the expulsion from the country of white settlers. The organization was operative 1952—59, but its worst excesses — also committed against Africans who opposed them — were committed in 1952—54. Some 11,000 Mau Mau members were killed against about 2,000 settlers and loyal Africans. After it was eliminated rapid constitutional change took place leading to independence (1963).

means test, practice of checking a person's income to ascertain qualification for financial or social assistance by the state. It was imposed in the UK (1931) as part of government spending cuts arising from the international economic crisis (1929—31) and its resulting long-term unemployment problem, which rendered inadequate the existing national insurance provision. The government refused to meet the deficiency by additional borrowing or increased taxation so applicants for relief had to prove their need. The system was ended in 1948.

Meir, Golda (1898—1978). Russian-born Israeli politician. She settled in Palestine in 1921. A founder member of the Zionist Socialist Party (Mapai), she held various ministerial posts from the

1950s, incl. Foreign Minister (1955–66). She was Secretary-General of Mapai (1966–68), and PM (1969–74) of a series of coalition governments, during which period she successfully led the country during the 1973 ARAB-ISRAELI WAR.

Mendès-France, Pierre (1907–82), French Radical Socialist statesman. He represented France at the BRETTON WOODS CONFERENCE, on the IMF and at the World Bank. He was PM of a coalition government (1954–55) which ended the INDO-CHINA War, but which was dissolved due to internal differences over ALGERIA.

Menshevism, *see* BOLSHEVISM.

Menzies, Sir Robert (1894–1978), Australian Liberal statesman. He entered the Federal Parliament as a United Australian Party (UAP) member (1934), serving as Attorney-General (1935–39) and PM (1939–41 and 1949–66). He reorganized the UAP into the broader-based Liberal Party (1943–45), which became the official Opposition and which he led (1943–49). He was an advocate of close links with the UK and of Commonwealth interests.

In office from 1949, he concluded the ANZUS PACT and participated in the establishment of the SOUTH-EAST ASIA TREATY ORGANIZATION. After WWII he encouraged British and European immigration, university expansion, and large-scale industrial enterprises as part of national development and reconstruction, coupled with an imaginative social-security programme.

mercenary, person hired to fight for a foreign army.

Messina Conference, *see* EUROPEAN ECONOMIC COMMUNITY.

ministerial responsibility, British constitutional principle that government ministers are responsible to Parliament for their actions and those of their departments. If a minister or the department's actions are condemned by Parliament then the minister may have to resign, even though the department may have acted without the minister's knowledge or approval.

Mitterand, Francois (1916–   ), French statesman. As leader of the Socialist Party (1971–   ), he became the first socialist in 35 years to be elected President (1981–   ).

Molotov, Vyacheslav, orig. Skriabin (1890–1986), Soviet politician. He was Foreign Minister (1939–49 and 1953–56). He negotiated the NAZI-SOVIET PACT (1939), the 20-year Treaty of Alliance with the UK (1942), and the Austrian State Treaty (1955). He attended the San Francisco Conference (1945) as USSR representative at the founding of the UNO, but was subsequently an uncompromising protagonist of the Cold War. Having opposed the rise of KRUSHCHEV, Molotov was relieved of his posts.

Monnet, Jean (1888–1979), French economist. He was initiator of the Monnet Plan (1947–53), a programme for the modernization and re-equipment of French industry, based on transport and a few key industries. He became first President of the EUROPEAN COAL AND STEEL COMMUNITY (1952–55) and founded (1956) the Action Committee for the United States of Europe, the ideals of which were counter to those of DE GAULLE. Subsequently Monnet became a severe critic of De Gaulle's foreign policy.

Monroe Doctrine, principle of US foreign policy expounded (1823) by President James Monroe (1758—1831), which stated that 'the American continents . . . are henceforth not to be considered as subjects for future colonization by any European power'.

In 1904 President Theodore Roosevelt extended the principle to justify any future US intervention to stop European interference in the Americas (the 'Roosevelt Corollary'). Eventually this unilateral US policy was adopted by all the republics of the W hemisphere, acting on the theory that aggression against one would be considered an attack against all.

Since WWII Communist penetration of the area has given added significance to the Doctrine, and the USA has supplied vast amounts of economic and military aid to its neighbours to counter what it sees as the Communist threat. In particular, the actions of the USA over Cuba, such as the BAY OF PIGS and the CUBAN MISSILES CRISIS, have been examples of the Doctrine in action.

Montenegro (Serbo-Croat, *Crna Gora*), federated republic of SW Yugoslavia. As a kingdom it fought against Turkey in the BALKAN WARS and joined Serbia against the German alliance (1914). In 1918 it became part of a newly constituted Yugoslavia.

Moslem League, Pakistani political party emanating from a religious organization established to protect Islamic interests in British India. Under JINNAH's leadership the League advocated the partition of India and the foundation of an Islamic state (Pakistan). Since Jinnah's death the League's authority and power have declined, its parliamentary majority has disappeared, and it has fragmented into opposing factions.

Mosley, Sir Oswald (1896−1980), British politician. He was successively a Conservative, Independent, and Labour MP (1918−31). In 1931 he founded the New Party, and in 1932 the BRITISH UNION OF FASCISTS. He was interned (1940−43), and afterwards lived in Paris.

Mountbatten, Louis, Earl Mountbatten of Burma (1900−79), British Admiral of the Fleet and statesman. During WWII he was Supreme Allied Commander, SE Asia (1943−46). He was Viceroy of India (1947) and supervised the granting of independence and the transfer of power. Due to communal strife and mounting disorder he decided on the partition of the sub-continent into India and Pakistan, and was India's first Governor-General (1947−48). He was C-in-C Mediterranean (1952−55), First Sea Lord (1955−59) and Chief of the Defence Staff (1959−65). He was assassinated by the IRA.

Mubarak, Hosni (1929−   ), Egyptian statesman. He succeeded SADAT as President (1981−   ), and has continued his moderate, pro-Western policies.

Mugabe, Robert (1924−   ), Zimbabwean nationalist leader and socialist politician. In 1961 he became Deputy Secretary-General of the Zimbabwe Afican People's Union (ZAPU), but left it to found the Zimbabwe African National Union (ZANU) in 1963. After being a political prisoner (1964−74) he became joint leader with NKOMO of the Patriotic Front and leader of the guerrilla organization, the Zimbabwe African Liberation Army, which fought the illegal regime of Ian SMITH

in what was then Rhodesia. He attended the
London talks (1979) with Nkomo and Smith which
eventually led to the independence (1980). ZANU
won the ensuing election and Mugabe became PM,
subsequently dismissing his old rival Nkomo from
the government (1982).

multiracial, comprising people of many races.

Munich Agreement (1938), settlement agreed
between HITLER, DALADIER, CHAMBERLAIN and
MUSSOLINI on behalf of Germany, France, Britain
and Italy.

The Agreement compelled Czechoslovakia to
cede the SUDETENLAND to Germany, and smaller
amounts of territory to Hungary and Poland. In
return the signatories to the Agreement guaranteed
Czechoslovakia's revised frontiers. France had
previous treaty obligations with Czechoslovakia,
but these were ignored at Munich in the hope that
the Agreement would put an end to Hitler's
territorial demands.

Chamberlain claimed it was 'peace for our time
. . . peace with honour', and at the time it was widely
felt that Britain and France's policy of APPEASE-
MENT had avoided another world war. However,
there were many who saw the Agreement as a
betrayal of democracy and a victory of 'might over
right', Churchill commenting, 'We have sustained a defeat without a war.'

In 1939 Germany occupied the remainder of
Czechoslovakia, ignoring the territorial guarantees
made at Munich, and appeasement was shown to
have failed.

Mussolini, Benito (1883—1945), Italian dictator
and founder of FASCISM (1919).

In his early years he was a revolutionary socialist but after serving in WWI decided to promote his nationalist ambitions by establishing Fascism, the system that was to become synonymous with his name. His socialism withered as he developed the movement into an anti-Communist, conservative, middle-class organization.

In the aftermath of WWI the country was practically in a state of civil war and King Victor Emmanuel III appointed Mussolini as PM in an effort to subdue the rioting that was prevalent in the major cities (see MARCH ON ROME) and to prevent a Communist insurrection. Mussolini assumed the title *Duce* (Leader) and headed a Fascist and nationalist coalition.

Mussolini assumed dictatorial powers in 1925, curtailing civil liberties, intensifying attacks on the opposition and creating a 1-party state which ruled by decree with the aid of the secret police. His sense of grandeur and desire for military glory prompted the conquest of Abyssinia (see ETHIOPIA) and ALBANIA, support for FRANCO in the SPANISH CIVIL WAR, the AXIS ties with Germany and Japan, and entry into WWII (1940).

The disasters of WWII caused his followers to desert him and he resigned (1943), was arrested, rescued by German paratroopers and placed at the head of a puppet regime in German-occupied N Italy where he arranged the execution of some of his principal opponents, including his son-in-law CIANO. He himself was executed by partisans after being captured beside Lake Como (1945).

Muzorewa, *see* ZIMBABWE.

N

Nagasaki, Japanese port on the island of Kyushu destroyed (1945) by the USA by means of an atomic bomb, the second wartime use of a nuclear weapon. This event and the earlier devastation of HIROSHIMA brought about Japan's unconditional surrender to the allies.

Nagy, *see* HUNGARY.

Nassau Agreement (1962), settlement reached at Nassau in the Bahamas, whereby the USA agreed to supply the UK with Polaris missiles for its nuclear submarines. The outcome of this meeting between KENNEDY and MACMILLAN displeased DE GAULLE, who considered Anglo-American nuclear collaboration an indication that the UK was not sufficiently orientated towards Europe to merit admission to the EEC, and accordingly he vetoed the British application (1963).

Nasser, Gamal Abdel (1918–70), Egyptian soldier and politician. After the first ARAB-ISRAELI WAR he and other officers saw a need for radical change and in 1952 mounted a coup d'état. After some political intrigue, Nasser became PM (1954) and President (1956) with virtually dictatorial powers.

His social and economic policies were dominated by the need to improve agriculture, establish industries, and introduce improved social welfare schemes. In 1956 he nationalized the Suez Canal, so precipitating the SUEZ CRISIS. Nasser united Syria and Egypt as the United Arab Republic (1958—61), and he concentrated on cementing relations with the USSR in order to receive aid. His offer to resign after the Egyptian defeat in the 1967 Arab-Israeli War was not accepted, and he remained in office until his death.

National Governments (1931—35 and 1935—45), administrations formed from members of several parties with the objectives of unifying the country in the national interest in times of crisis.

The first of these Governments, initially comprising members of the Conservative, Labour and Liberal parties, was formed by the Labour PM, MACDONALD, to combat the economic crisis of the Depression and the problem of growing unemployment.

The Government was formed when a significant minority of ministers in the previous Labour Government refused to support reductions in unemployment benefit. These reductions were part of heavy expenditure cuts required by the French and US money markets before they would provide financial assistance to counteract the loss of international confidence in London as a reliable financial centre. The Labour Government collapsed and MacDonald thereupon formed a coalition to restore credibility and implement the cuts, which incl. the abandonment of the gold standard for sterling.

The Labour Party went into opposition and MacDonald and other ministers who supported him were expelled from the Party; they subsequently called themselves the National Labour Party. In practical terms the coalition became a Conservative

Government when the Liberal Party split in 1932, some Liberals supporting the Opposition, and others, calling themselves the Liberal National Party, supporting the Government.

The 1935 election resulted in a landslide victory for the National Government, again dominated by the Conservatives. Its PMs were BALDWIN (1935—37), Neville CHAMBERLAIN (1937—40) and CHURCHILL (1940—45). This administration was dominated by the Depression and high unemployment, and by WWII, which resulted in the postponement of the next election to 1945.

nationalism, (a) devotion or loyalty to one's country, patriotism; (b) sentiment founded on common cultural characteristics that unites a population, frequently producing measures towards separatism or national independence. FASCISM contains elements of extreme nationalism (*see also* NATIONAL SOCIALISM).

nationalization, subjection of an industry or resource to state control or ownership, a policy espoused by Communist and socialist doctrine.

Nationalization measures in the UK have been implemented by Labour governments, and incl. the Bank of England, most hospitals, and coal (1946), railways and electricity (1947), gas (1948), iron and steel (1949, denationalized in 1953 by the Conservatives, nationalized again in 1967), and aircraft manufacture and shipbuilding (1977). These measures have been opposed by the Conservative Party, which favours free enterprise; *see* PRIVITIZATION.

National Socialism (Nazism), extreme right-wing political ideology similar to Italian FASCISM,

adopted by the National Socialist German Workers'
Party (NSDAP), successor of the German Workers'
Party of which HITLER was a founder member
(1919). Hitler soon gained control of the German
Workers' Party and renamed it the NSDAP (1920).
Membership grew rapidly and by the time Hitler
achieved power it was some 2 million strong, its
representation in the Reichstag rising from 12
(1928) to 288 (1933).

The Nazi doctrine incl. the principle of the
individual being subservient to the state and the
state being subservient to the Party, which in turn
was controlled by a single leader — Hitler himself. It
also incl. the conviction of Aryan superiority, the
Germans being considered the 'master race'; the
pursuance of a policy of anti-Communism, ANTI-
SEMITISM and racialism; the building up of armed
forces; and a determination to regain territory lost
at the Treaty of VERSAILLES and to create a German
empire in E Europe (*see* LEBENSRAUM).

These were Hitler's own beliefs which he
successfully imposed on the Party by demagogy,
aided by the malaise and frustration which had
befallen the country following the German defeat in
WWI and the unemployment resulting from the
DEPRESSION. After WWII the Party was dissolved
and its re-establishment became an offence.

nation-state, independent sovereign nation
inhabited by people of that state only, as opposed to
several nationalities. The term does not necessarily
imply a racist policy, but indicates opposition to
foreign domination.

NATO, *see* NORTH ATLANTIC TREATY ORGAN-
IZATION.

Nazism, *see* NATIONAL SOCIALISM.

Nazi-Soviet Pact (1939) also known as the Hitler-Stalin Pact or Non-aggression Pact, treaty signed in Moscow by RIBBENTROP and MOLOTOV on behalf of Germany and the USSR.

The published section of the treaty covered a 10-year non-aggression period, and agreement by each party to remain neutral should the other be involved in war. Secret clauses defined spheres of influence in the BALTIC STATES, FINLAND and POLAND. In 1939 Germany invaded W Poland, so precipitating WWII, and 2 weeks later the USSR invaded E Poland, and the country was formally divided between the 2 occupying nations. The Pact was nullified by the German attack on the USSR in 1941.

Nehru, Jawaharlal (1889–1964), Indian Congress Party statesman, PM (1947–64). He became a leader of the nationalist movement and follower of Mahatma GANDHI in the 1920s. For this he was imprisoned several times between 1921 and 1945; his imprisonment during WWII was largely due to his opposition to Indian aid to the UK unless immediate independence was granted. When independence was achieved he became PM and Foreign Minister.

Domestically Nehru attempted to solve the poverty problem by adopting a series of FIVE-YEAR PLANS, accompanied by efforts to secularize the nation and, by equality of educational opportunities, to eliminate restrictions imposed by Hindu religious and social customs, he himself being an agnostic. He committed the country to a process of industrialization and to a reorganization of its states on a linguistic basis, but a population explosion nullified efforts at economic reform.

His foreign policy was one of non-alignment and he became a leader of uncommitted Afro-Asian nations. He cultivated relationships with China and the USSR while maintaining firm Commonwealth connections. He was an anti-colonialist and an opponent of the use of force, although he did not shrink from using it when India annexed Goa from Portugal (1961). However, although unwilling to compromise, he displayed commendable restraint in dealing with Pakistan over the intractable problem of KASHMIR.

NEP, *see* NEW ECONOMIC POLICY.

Neuilly, Treaty of (1919), post-WWI peace settlement between Bulgaria and the Allies, arising out of the Paris Peace Conference. The Treaty restricted the Bulgarian army to 20,000; made the country liable for REPARATIONS; and compelled it to cede territory to Greece and Yugoslavia, the loss of W Thrace to Greece depriving Bulgaria of access to the Aegean Sea.

neutrality, state of being impartial or neutral, esp. in a dispute, war, etc., thereby not getting involved in hostilities, or in diplomatic or political exchanges.

New Deal, economic and social programme launched to help the USA recover from the DEPRESSION. 'A new deal for the American people' was the phrase used by Franklin ROOSEVELT in his Presidential nomination acceptance speech (1932).

There were 2 programmes (1933—35 and 1935—39) and they incl. measures to meet the immediate economic and financial crises; to assist the large numbers of unemployed; to increase economic and social security for the aged and those in ill-health; to provide agricultural and industrial aid; to permit the re-financing of mortgages at low interest rates; and to inaugurate large-scale federal industrial developments which incl. forestation schemes, the construction of hydroelectric power stations, dams and other public-works projects.

New Economic Policy (NEP), a modification in Communist practice instituted in the USSR by Lenin in 1921, following peasant disturbances and riots in Petrograd (now Leningrad) and KRONSTADT. The NEP allowed some freedom of internal trade, re-introducing limited private commerce and re-establishing state banks. It was formally abolished by the Bolshevik Party Congress (1929), which gave full support to the first of the FIVE-YEAR PLANS.

Nicaragua, republic of Central America. Area: 128,000 sq km. Pop: 2,700,000. Language: Spanish. Religion: RC. Cap: Managua.

From the 1930s the government was dominated by the Somoza family, whose corrupt and dictatorial rule was finally ended in 1979 after a civil war with the Sandinista National Liberation Front. The Sandinista government has subsequently pursued socialist policies. The US government has alleged that the Sandinistas are arming the rebels in the neighouring El Salvador, and has supported the army of right wing 'Contra' rebels that is attempting to oust the Sandinistas.

Nicholas II (1868–1918), Tsar of Russia (1894–1917). His reign was marked by the RUSSO-JAPANESE WAR, alliance with Britain and France against the CENTRAL POWERS in WWI, bad harvests, and the RUSSIAN REVOLUTIONS of 1905 and 1917.

He was against badly needed political reforms and was unduly influenced in his choice of ministers by the unscrupulous RASPUTIN. He was forced to abdicate (1917), and was executed in 1918.

Nigeria, Commonwealth republic of W Africa. Area: 923,773 sq km. Pop: 55,654,000 (1983). Official language: English. Religion: Islam, Christian. Cap: Lagos.

Formerly a British colony, Nigeria achieved independence (1960) and was declared a republic in 1963. A federal structure of 12 states was created in 1967, and 7 new states were added in 1976. Its recent history has been one of regional and tribal rivalry, of civil war (*see* BIAFRAN WAR), and a succession of military coups. In spite of its great natural wealth, incl. oil, the country has never exploited its economic potential to the full, owing to its succession of corrupt and unstable regimes.

Night of the Long Knives, *see* SA.

Nixon, Richard (1913–), US Republican statesman, Vice-President (1953–60), and President (1969–74). Domestically he introduced his 'new economic policy' (1971), designed to reduce unemployment, stimulate the economy, contain inflation, and correct the BALANCE OF PAYMENTS deficit.

In foreign affairs he followed a policy of DÉTENTE with Communist states. He gradually reduced US commitments in the Vietnam War; sought normalization of relations with China, in the course of which he paid the first ever visit there of a US President (1972); reached an agreement at the STRATEGIC ARMS LIMITATION TALKS with the

USSR (1972); and initiated peace moves in the Middle East which proved to be unsuccessful.

Nixon became the first US President to resign from office when he was in danger of impeachment for his involvement in the WATERGATE AFFAIR.

Nkomo, Joshua (1917–), Zimbabwean nationalist leader. He founded the Zimbabwe African People's Union (ZAPU) in 1961, which was banned in 1962. Nkomo spent 10 years in detention as a political prisoner and then joined MUGABE as joint-leader of the Patriotic Front, promoting guerrilla activities to achieve independence and black majority rule. With Ian SMITH and Mugabe, he participated in the London talks (1979) which eventually led to independence (1980). Nkomo lost the ensuing election to Mugabe, in whose government he served until his dismissal in 1982.

Nkrumah, Kwame (1909–72), Ghanian politician. In 1949 he founded the Convention People's Party with the slogan 'self-government now'. When Ghana gained independence (1957) he became PM after the Party's election victory. In foreign affairs he pursued a non-aligned policy in the Cold War but was pro-Arab, Pan-African, and opposed to South Africa. Domestically, his drastic economic reforms, interference with the judiciary and the introduction of a 1-party state aroused considerable opposition. He was overthrown by a military coup and went into exile (1966).

NKVD, see SOVIET SECURITY SERVICE.

Non-aggression Pact, see NAZI-SOVIET PACT.

Non-aligned Movement, grouping of nations established at the Belgrade Conference (1961) and consisting for the most part of African and Asian states. The Movement is pledged to fostering and maintaining foreign policies independent of the East and West superpower blocs, and to use its good offices to mitigate antagonism between the USSR and the USA and their respective allies. India and Yugoslavia may be considered the principal members of the Movement, which holds regular meetings in the capitals of the associated states.

nonviolence, (a) passive resistance or peaceful demonstration for political attainments, (b) refraining from violence on moral grounds to achieve objectives; pacifism.

Normandy Landings (1944), start of the Allied invasion of Europe in WWII when British, Canadian and US troops stormed the French beaches between the River Orne and St Marcouf after being transported from S England by an armada of ships, heavily protected by air and naval forces. D-Day was 6 June and the operation was code-named 'Overlord'. After heavy fighting, breaches were made in the German positions and the drive across W Europe commenced, rolling back the enemy, freeing occupied territory, and finally advancing into Germany itself.

North African Campaigns or **Desert Campaigns** (1940–43), series of defensive and offensive operations in WWII, in which Allied forces fought those of Germany and Italy in efforts to control the S coast of the Mediterranean. The AXIS objective was to capture Alexandria, Cairo and the Suez Canal, and ultimately to advance into the Middle East and secure the oilfields. The Allied purpose was to wage a campaign which would secure the area from Egypt through Libya to Tunisia as a springboard for the invasion of S Europe, and which would also relieve pressure on MALTA.

Major engagements incl. those fought at El Alamein (in 1942 — the first major Allied victory of WWII), Tobruk, Benghazi and Tripoli, attack and counter-attack resulting in frequent changes in occupation of many places. Finally the Allied forces advancing from the E joined those which had landed in Algeria. The meeting took place in Tunisia where the Axis forces finally surrendered.

North Atlantic Treaty Organization (NATO), military alliance established by the North Atlantic Treaty (1949). The original members were Belgium, Canada, Denmark, France, Iceland, Italy, Luxembourg, the Netherlands, Norway, Portugal, the UK and the USA. Greece and Turkey joined in 1952, West Germany in 1954, and Spain in 1982. France withdrew from the integrated military command (1966).

The Organization's policy-making body is the Council of Ministers comprising the PMs or departmental ministers of member nations according to the matters under consideration. It normally meets twice yearly, its chief administrative officer being the Secretary-General. There are Defence and Military Committees on which chiefs-of-staff and other high-ranking officers serve, the Supreme Allied Commander Europe being in overall charge of the multinational armed forces.

The Treaty provides that should any of the participating states be subject to armed aggression then such attacks will be considered as being made against them all, and collectively and individually they will provide all possible aid deemed to be necessary to retore and maintain the security of the North Atlantic area. The WARSAW PACT was formed in 1955 by E European Communist states following West Germany's entry into NATO.

Northern Ireland, part of the UK consisting of the northern 6 counties of Ireland, and forming part of the old province of Ulster. Area: 14,146 sq km. Pop: 1,556,000 (1981). Language: English. Religion: Protestant and RC. Cap: Belfast.

The Protestant majority in Northern Ireland results from the fact that the area was heavily settled by Scottish and English Protestants in the early 17th cent. Northern Ireland achieved its own parliament (meeting at Stormont Castle) in 1920, which was dominated throughout its existence by the Ulster Unionist Party, representing Protestant interests (*see* ULSTER LOYALISTS).

In 1968 the RC minority began to demonstrate against discrimination in housing, employment and voting rights in local elections. The demonstrations led to worsening violence between Protestants and Catholics, and in 1969 British troops were sent to Northern Ireland to keep the peace. The RC population, represented politically by the moderate SOCIAL DEMOCRATIC AND LABOUR PARTY and the militant SINN FEIN (the political wing of the IRA), largely wants unification with the Republic, while this aim is vehemently resisted by the Protestants.

The violence, verging on civil war, has continued, with the IRA and similar paramilitary Protestant groups carrying out numerous murders and bomb attacks. In 1972 the UK government suspended the Northern Ireland parliament and implemented

direct rule from Westminster. An attempt by the
UK government to introduce 'power-sharing'
between Catholics and Protestants in 1973—74
broke down in the face of mass strikes by
Protestants, and direct rule was restored. Both the
UK and the Republic of Ireland have agreed that
Northern Ireland should not become part of the
Republic until the majority of its inhabitants
consent to unification. Attempts to find a political
solution, in the face of continuing violence, are still
being made; *see* ANGLO-IRISH AGREEMENT.

Northern Rhodesia, *see* ZAMBIA, and RHODESIA
AND NYASALAND, FEDERATION OF.

Novotný, Antonin (1904—75), Czechoslovak
Communist politician. He became First Secretary of
the Party (1953—68) and President of the Republic
(1957—68). He was a hard-line Stalinist and as such
progressively became more unpopular as the
liberalization processes demanded by intellectuals
and students spread through the civilian population
and armed forces, eventually enforcing his
retirement. His efforts to remain in power incl. a
limited number of political concessions and the
abandonment of the third FIVE-YEAR PLAN, but
these were of no avail against a mounting tide of
opposition. He was succeeded as First Secretary by
DUBČEK.

Nuclear Test Ban Treaty (1963), agreement
between the UK, the USA and USSR whereby
nuclear testing in the atmosphere, outer space or
under water is prohibited. Many other nations have
since subscribed to the Treaty, notable abstainers
being China, France, India and South Africa.

nuclear warfare, potential form of conflict

employing either atomic weapons (based on the
fission of a heavy atomic nucleus), or hydrogen
weapons (based on the fusion of two light nuclei).
The theory behind the possession of such horrific
weapons is that they act as a deterrent, no nation
daring to use them for fear of retaliation. *See also*
DISARMAMENT, DETERRENCE.

Nuremberg Rallies, annual convention of the
Nazi Party held in the 1930s in Nuremberg,
Bavaria. They were characterized by vast open-
air gatherings, impressive marches, torchlight
processions, and oratorical performances by Party
leaders designed to disseminate propaganda and
rouse the assembled multitude to a state bordering
on hysteria. They also served to demonstrate the
Party faithful's devotion to HITLER who used the
occasion to deliver major policy speeches.

Nuremberg Trials, *see* WAR CRIMES.

Nyerere, Julius (1922–   ), Tanzanian politician.
He became President of the Tanganyika African
National Union after completely reorganizing it
(1954–55). He entered the Legislative Council
(1958) and became chief minister (1960) after the
Union's electoral successes. He was PM (1961)
before resigning to establish the Union as a
Christian Socialist movement. He became President of Tanganyika on independence (1962) and
President of Tanzania when Tanganyika and
Zanzibar merged (1964), retiring in 1985. Nyerere
adopted a non-aligned policy in foreign affairs for
his 1-party state but was an ardent exponent of Pan-
Africanism and made his country a leading member
of the ORGANIZATION OF AFRICAN UNITY.

O

OAS, *see* ORGANIZATION OF AMERICAN STATES.

OAU, *see* ORGANIZATION OF AFRICAN UNITY.

Obote, Milton (1924–   ), Ugandan politician. He played a prominent part in the independence negotiations with the UK and was PM (1962–66). The first President of Uganda, the Kabaka (Prince) of Buganda, opposed Obote's desire to establish a 1-party state so Obote deposed him in a coup. Obote assumed the presidency but was overthrown himself by AMIN (1971). He sought refuge in Tanzania and regained the Presidency (1980) following Amin's downfall. He was deposed again in 1985.

Oder-Neisse Line, post-WWII frontier between East Germany and Poland agreed at the POTSDAM CONFERENCE (1945). The line follows the course of the River Oder S to its confluence with the River Neisse, and then along the Neisse to the Czechoslovak border.

OECD, *see* ORGANIZATION FOR ECONOMIC CO-OPERATION AND DEVELOPMENT.

OEEC, *see* ORGANIZATION FOR EUROPEAN ECON-OMIC COOPERATION.

OGPU, *see* SOVIET SECURITY SERVICE.

Oil Crisis, problem arising in the late 1960s and early 1970s caused by a rise in demand and the simultaneous political action by Arab oil-producing nations against Israel and those countries they considered to be aiding or sympathizing with Israel.

The Arab oil-producers imposed price increases of some 70%, and this increased inflation and imposed BALANCE OF PAYMENTS difficulties for the consumer nations of the West. The situation was further aggravated by supplies being cut or interrupted by about 15% owing to the ARAB-ISRAELI WARS, and the closing of the Suez Canal, which obliged tankers to make the long detour around the Cape of Good Hope. The attitude of the Arab producers was criticized by non-Arab members of the ORGANIZATION OF PETROLEUM EXPORTING COUNTRIES and the crisis gradually faded, although not before it had become of such concern to the UK government that it considered introducing a petrol rationing system.

In the UK the Oil Crisis developed into a wider energy crisis with the miners' strikes of 1972 and 1974. In 1974 a state of emergency was declared by HEATH's Conservative Government and a 3-day working week imposed on industry. Heath called a general election and was defeated by Labour.

Ojukwu, see BIAFRAN WAR.

OPEC, see ORGANIZATION OF PETROLEUM-EXPORTING COUNTRIES.

Orange Order, largest Protestant organization in Northern Ireland, founded in 1795. It was named after William II (William of Orange; reigned 1688—1702) who defeated the Catholic ex-King James II (reigned 1685—88) at the Battle of the Boyne (1690). The Order was vehemently opposed to HOME RULE and wishes Ulster to remain part of the UK.

Organization for Economic Cooperation and Development (OECD), international agency

with HQ in Paris which replaced the ORGAN-
IZATION FOR EUROPEAN ECONOMIC COOPERATION
(1961) when Canada and the USA joined the
18 W European members. Japan joined in 1964,
and Finland in 1968, and Australia, New
Zealand and Yugoslavia are associate members.
The Organization comprises the West's leading
industrial states, its objectives being to contribute
to the expansion of world trade, provide aid for
developing countries, achieve financial stability,
and promote economic growth.

**Organization for European Economic
Cooperation (OEEC),** international agency
established (1948) with HQ in Paris. Its members
were Austria, Belgium, France, Greece, Iceland,
Ireland, Italy, Luxembourg, the Netherlands,
Norway, Portugal, Sweden, Switzerland, Turkey
and the UK. West Germany joined in 1955 and
Spain in 1959. Canada and the USA were associate
members, and Yugoslavia was permitted limited
participation. Its objective was to attack collectively
the economic problems resulting from WWII
by maximizing the use of aid supplied through
the MARSHALL PLAN. It was superceded by the
ORGANIZATION OF ECONOMIC COOPERATION AND
DEVELOPMENT in 1961 as a result of US pressure to
broaden its objectives to incl. responsibilities to
developing countries worldwide.

Organization of African Unity (OAU), body of
48 African states established (1963) with HQ in
Addis Ababa, Ethiopia. The founding membership
was 31 nations but 17 more have since joined.

The OAU's objectives are the eradication of
colonialism (now virtually accomplished); the

promotion of solidarity and unity among the
membership; the raising of living standards by
increasing progress in the fields of education, health
and social welfare; the expansion of cultural, economic, scientific and technical affairs; the promotion
of international cooperation; and the defence
of independence, sovereignty and territorial
integrity.

Heads of state meet annually and the Council
of Ministers bi-annually, but the Organization's
purposes are at times frustrated by the different
stages of development of its members, and by their
cultural, economic, political and religious differences.

Organization of American States (OAS), body
of 21 American states established (1948) by the
Ninth International Conference of American States
at Bogota, Colombia. Its HQ is in Washington, D.C.
Cuba was expelled in 1962, Trinidad and Tobago
was admitted in 1967, Barbados in 1968 and
Jamaica in 1969, so present membership totals 23.

The objectives of the OAS incl. promotion of
economic and social development; peaceful
settlement of disputes; strengthening of security,
incl. military aid; and opposition to Communist
subversion. Policy arrangements are made by a
Council on which every state is represented, by
meetings of foreign ministers, and by a 5-yearly
Inter-American Conference.

**Organization of Petroleum-Exporting
Countries (OPEC),** body of 13 states established
(1961) in Caracas, Venezuela, to administer a
common policy for petroleum products and
marketing. The founder-members were Iran, Iraq,

Kuwait, Qatar, Saudi Arabia and Venezuela, but 7 more have joined at various times since: Abu Dhabi, Algeria, Egypt, Indonesia, Libya, Nigeria and Syria. These nations collectively produce about 45% of world output and some 85% of world exports outside the Soviet bloc.

OPEC's aims incl. the maintenance of stable price structures by regulating production, so avoiding fluctuations that might affect the economies of both producing and purchasing nations.

Ostpolitik, term for West Germany's attempt to improve relations with the WARSAW PACT countries, instigated by BRANDT when Foreign Minister (1966–69) in Kiesinger's government and pursued later when he became Chancellor (1969–74). Agreements were reached on posts and telecommunications, traffic, and visits by relatives between East and West BERLIN. West Germany recognized East Germany and the ODER-NEISSE LINE, and peace treaties were signed with Poland and the USSR (1972).

Ottawa Conference (1932), meeting convened to discuss economic problems affecting the UK and the DOMINIONS, India and Southern Rhodesia. It established an IMPERIAL PREFERENCE system based on quotas and TARIFFS, following the introduction by the UK of protective tariffs to combat the effects of the DEPRESSION.

Ottoman Empire, former Turkish empire in Africa, Asia and Europe, dating from c. 1300 to 1922 when the Sultanate was abolished in favour of the Republic of TURKEY.

Overlord, Operation, *see* NORMANDY LANDINGS.

P

Pahlavi, Mohammed Reza (1919–80), Shah of
Iran (1941–79). He was a popular monarch early in
his reign when he instituted a liberal Westernized
system of government, but lost favour when he imposed a series of autocratic reforms incl. the social
emancipation of women. Islamic susceptibilities
were outraged and the most vociferous Moslem
critic, Ayatollah KHOMEINI, was arrested and exiled.

For some time the Shah appeared to have quelled
opposition but eventually high inflation, a series
of repressive measures, displays of outrageous
imperial grandeur, and lack of sympathy with Arab
opposition to Israel, roused uncontrollable
opposition from fundamentalist students and
puritanical religious leaders, leading to massive
street demonstrations and violence. The Shah left
the country in 1979, and 2 months later he was
deposed, dying in exile in Cairo.

Pakistan, republic of SC Asia. Area: 803,943 sq
km. Pop: 83,780,000 (est. 1981). Language: Urdu.
Religion: Islam. Cap: Islamabad.

Pakistan came into existence as a result of
the Indian Independence Act (1947). Following
pressure from JINNAH and the MOSLEM LEAGUE
for an independent state for Moslems, the Act
partitioned Pakistan from INDIA, dividing the new
state into two parts, E and W. Pakistan became a
republic in 1956.

The bloodshed accompanying Partition left a

legacy of hostility between Pakistan and India, and the two countries have fought wars over the disputed territory of KASHMIR (1947—49 and 1965). Tension also developed between the two parts of Pakistan, separated by 1750 km of Indian territory. In 1971 E Pakistan declared itself independent as BANGLADESH. The Pakistan army put down the secession with much boodshed, causing millions of refugees to flee to India. India then intervened militarily in support of Bangladesh and its own claims to Kashmir, defeated the Pakistan army, and ensured Bangladeshi independence. Pakistan left the Commonwealth when Bangladesh applied to join (1972).

Politically, Pakistan has been quite turbulent, with military coups and periods of martial law interrupting democratic rule. The country's leaders have incl. AYUB KHAN (1958—69), YAYHA KHAN (1969—71), BHUTTO (1971—77), and ZIA UL-HAQ (1977—   ). Much remains to be done to achieve economic stability in spite of vast amounts of aid supplied by the USA. Fear of India to the E and the USSR to the N has forced the country to rely on China for support, and to spend money on defence rather than on modernizing agriculture and building up industrial potential.

Palestine, area on the E seaboard of the Mediterranean. It was part of the OTTOMAN EMPIRE until after WWI, and is now occupied by the state of ISRAEL. After the Turks had been expelled (1917—18) and following the BALFOUR DECLARATION, Palestine was a British mandated territory (1922—48), a period marked by mounting hostility between Arabs and Jews, with the British Army trying to maintain peace and stability.

The Arabs resented the huge influx of Jews caused by Nazi persecution in Europe and the Jews resented immigration quotas imposed by the British so that many were assisted to enter the country by illegal means. Jewish opposition to the British grew and extremists launched terrorist attacks which only ceased during WWII. Afterwards these were resumed by IRGUN ZVAI LEUMI and the STERN GANG, and eventually the UK referred the problem (1947) to the UNO which partitioned the land between Jews and Arabs, the UK being relieved of the mandate.

As a result of the ARAB-ISRAELI WARS Israel has occupied the Palestinian lands allocated to the Arabs by the partition settlement, and it is this state of affairs that has been the cause of so much unrest in the Middle East since WWII.

Palestine Liberation Organization (PLO), body formed (1964) in Jordan, uniting various Palestinian Arab factions and representing c. 1½ million Palestinian refugees who lived in PALESTINE until the creation of ISRAEL. Formerly its intention was to destroy the state of Israel, but now it aims to secure a homeland for the Palestinian Arabs on the WEST BANK, occupied by Israel since 1967.

The principal unit is AL FATAH, led by Yasser ARAFAT, who in recent years has moderated the Organization from a terrorist-orientated body to one endeavouring to achieve its objectives by political means. This has resulted in various extremist groups breaking away from Al Fatah and persisting with terrorist operations, now largely carried out in Israel but formerly in various parts of

Europe and the Middle East. These activities incl. the hijacking of aircraft, hostage-taking and assassination. Al Fatah, by pursuing more moderate policies, is gaining sympathetic and considerate understanding of its objectives by large parts of the non-Arab world.

Pankhurst, Emmeline (1857—1928), British campaigner for WOMEN'S SUFFRAGE. She founded the Women's Franchise League (1889) and the more militant Women's Social and Political Union (1903), with its slogan of 'Votes for Women'. Mrs Pankhurst served 8 prison sentences for participating in acts of violence, which she called 'the argument of the stone'. Her objective of women's suffrage on the same terms as that for men was achieved during the month of her death. Her daughters, Christabel (1880—1958) and Estelle Sylvia (1882—1960) were also identified with their mother's cause.

Panmunjom Armistice (1953), peace agreement between North and South Korea ending the KOREAN WAR, signed at the village of Panmunjom in the demilitarized zone separating the 2 states. Talks had been in progress for over 2 years with political rather than military overtones, and it was Stalin's death that finally modified the previously inflexible Communist position, opening the way to agreement and a general relaxation of international tension.

Pan-Slavism, a movement of opinion in E Europe in the 19th cent. which sought to emphasize the brotherhood of Slavonic peoples and to integrate them culturally and linguistically. It was strong in Russia, sustaining and exploiting the country's historic purpose of gaining Constantinople (Istanbul) and freeing the southern Slavs from Austrian and Turkish domination. The movement was at its peak between the 1860s and 1880s, and it was revived during the BALKAN WARS and WWI, albeit in a more moderate form.

Papen, Franz von (1879—1969), German diplomat and politician. He was a Centre Party Deputy (1921—32) and Chancellor (1932). He tried to solve the country's political problems by making concessions to the Nazis, suppressing the Socialist government and calling fresh elections.

However, the elections only strengthened Nazi representation in the Reichstag and increased the violence. HITLER's insistence on being appointed Chancellor frustrated Papen's efforts to form a Centre-Nazi coalition and he resigned under pressure from the Army, which feared a civil war. After Hitler became Chancellor, Papen was appointed Vice-Chancellor (1933—34).

Paris Peace Conference (1919—20), assembly held after WWI during which the LEAGUE OF NATIONS was established and the peace agreements between the Allied and Central Powers were evolved and ultimately concluded by the Treaties of VERSAILLES, SAINT GERMAIN, NEUILLY, TRIANON and SÈVRES. Proceedings were dominated by Britain, France, Italy, Japan and the USA, although 32 nations participated.

Paris Peace Talks (1968—73), series of meetings aimed at terminating the VIETNAM WAR. These protracted negotiations between representatives of North and South Vietnam and the USA concerned political as well as military matters, and much time was wasted in procedural wrangling over such trivialities as the shape of the conference table. Within a fortnight of the cease-fire agreement being signed (1973) the first US troops left Vietnam, which remained partitioned until the North finally overran the South and unified the country (1975).

Paris student demonstrations (1968), massive street disturbances caused by what many considered excessive defence expenditure, esp. on an independent nuclear deterrent, at the expense of the educational and social services.

The demonstrations, organized by a loose alliance of left-wing and anarchist factions, rapidly developed into riots, and the police responded with great severity. The demonstrations and riots were followed by a general strike, workers taking the opportunity to protest at the policies of the Fifth Republic. The government, realizing that its Gaullist practices were unacceptable, granted the workers considerable concessions, including wage increases of $33\frac{1}{3}\%$, and the students were placated with many of the reforms they were seeking.

Parliament, supreme legislative authority in the UK, consisting of the House of Commons, the House of Lords, and the monarch. The Commons is the lower chamber and comprises members elected at general elections or by-elections. The Lords is the upper chamber and comprises the Lords spiritual (2 Archbishops and 24 senior Church of England bishops), and the Lords Temporal (hereditary and life peers and peeresses). The life peers incl. the Lords of Appeal who constitute the highest UK appeal court.

Parliament Acts (1911 and 1949), legislation to

curb the powers of the House of Lords.

The **1911 Act** arose out of the rejection by the Lords of Lloyd George's 1909 Budget and abolished the Lords' delaying powers over money bills. It also restricted its delaying powers over bills passed by the Commons to 3 Parliamentary sessions spread over 2 years. The only exception are bills to extend the maximum duration of a Parliament, which the Act reduced from 7 to 5 years. The Lords only approved these measures, introduced by Asquith's Liberal Government, because of George V's threat to create 250 Liberal peers in order to outnumber the Conservative Party's numerical superiority in the Lords.

The **1949 Act** was introduced by Attlee's Labour Government to reduce the Lords' delaying powers to 2 sessions, i.e. 1 year. The Act arose from Labour's fear that their nationalization programme, esp. of the iron and steel industry, would be frustrated by the delaying power of the Lords, which was dominated by the Conservatives.

partisan, member of an armed resistance group within occupied territory. During WWII such guerrilla groups were Communist-led, Stalin having encouraged their formation. They operated successfully in parts of the USSR, Albania, Czechoslovakia, Greece, Italy and, in particular, Yugoslavia under the leadership of TITO. They lived off the land where possible, but also on supplies dropped by Allied air forces or captured from the enemy. *See also* RESISTANCE MOVEMENTS.

Partition, *see* INDIA, PAKISTAN, IRELAND.

Passchendaele, *see* YPRES, BATTLES OF.

Pearl Harbor, the main US naval base in Hawaii.

Although there had been no declaration of war,
Japanese carrier-borne aircraft attacked Pearl
Harbor early on 7 December 1941, sinking or
disabling 19 ships (incl. 5 battleships), destroying
120 planes and killing 2,400 people. The US
Congress declared war on Japan on 8 December,
and Germany and Italy, Japan's allies, declared war
on the USA. American naval losses at Pearl Harbor
gave an initial advantage to Japanese sea power.

Pentagon, the main offices of the US Department
of Defense and HQ of the US armed forces in
Arlington, Virginia. Hence the term is also used for
the military leadership of the USA.

perestroika, (Russ.) restructuring. The term is
applied to the Soviet policy of economic liberalization embarked upon under GORBACHEV since
1985. *See also* GLASNOST.

Perón, *see* ARGENTINA.

Pétain, Henri Phillipe (1856–1951), French
soldier and statesman. As a WWI general he won
fame by his defence of VERDUN (1916). He was
appointed C-in-C (1917), promoted to marshal
(1918) and was the leading military figure in the
1920s and 1930s.

In WWII he was appointed PM (1940) and
within a week had concluded an armistice with the
Germans. He then assumed the title of Head of
State (1940–42) and adopted a collaborationist
policy with the Germans (*see* VICHY GOVERN-
MENT). His government became a puppet régime
enacting anti-Semitic legislation, conniving in the
transfer of c. $\frac{3}{4}$ million workers to Germany for
forced labour, and doing little to oppose German
demands.

After being replaced by LAVAL, the Germans eventually forced Pétain to retreat with them into Germany. After the War he returned voluntarily to France where he was tried for treason and condemned to death, although this sentence was commuted to life imprisonment.

Phoney War, name given to the inactivity which prevailed between the start of WWII (1939) and the German onslaught in the West (1940). During these months little hostile action occurred, the period being used for the dissemination of propaganda and the mutual probing of enemy positions on land and in the air for strategic purposes. The most serious hostilities occurred at sea.

Pilsudski, Josef (1867–1935), Polish marshal and statesman. After WWI he was made head of state until 1921, and C-in-C of the armed forces fighting the Bolsheviks, a position he retained until 1923. In 1926 he led a military coup, and became virtual dictator of Poland until his death. He was PM (1926–28 and 1930) and Minister of War (1926–35). He signed a non-aggression pact with Germany (1934) in a vain attempt to stave off the rising menace of Nazism against his country.

plebiscite, *see* REFERENDUM.

PLO, *see* PALESTINE LIBERATION ORGANIZATION.

pogrom, (a) organized extinction or persecution of an ethnic group, esp. Jews, (b) anti-Semitic violence and incitement to hatred practised by Communist and Fascist régimes before and during WWII.

Poincaré, Raymond Nicolas Landry (1860–1934), French statesman. He was PM of a coalition government (1912–13), and as President of the Third Republic (1913–20) he was an inspiring leader during WWI. When he again became PM (1922–24), he pursued a severe REPARATIONS policy towards Germany. When payments were in arrears his government, jointly with Belgium, ordered the occupation of the RUHR (1923–25). His conservative and nationalist policies and the decision to occupy the Ruhr brought about his government's downfall (1924), but he became PM again (1926–29).

Poland, Communist republic of E Europe. Area: 312,683 sq km. Pop: 36,400,000 (1982). Language: Polish. Religion: RC. Cap: Warsaw.

Poland became an independent state in 1918, having previously been partitioned between Austria, Prussia and Russia since the 18th cent. In 1919–20 Poland conducted a successful war against the USSR, gaining territory to the E of the CURZON LINE. Between the Wars Poland was largely ruled by right-wing dictatorial governments, notably those of PILSUDSKI.

In 1938 Germany pressed for the return of DANZIG and for extra-territorial routes across the Polish Corridor to East Prussia, demands which were resisted by Poland. Following the NAZI-SOVIET PACT, Germany invaded Poland (1939), bringing the UK and France (which had earlier guaranteed Polish security) into WWII. The USSR invaded at the same time, and occupied E Poland until the German attack on Russia in 1941. Poland became a battleground, leading to the decimation of its population and widespread destruction. It was liberated by Soviet forces (1945).

After WWII Poland lost territory in the E to the USSR, the new frontier following the Curzon Line, but gained territory in the W from Germany, the new frontier being the ODER-NEISSE LINE. The country fell under the political influence of the USSR, became a Communist state, and joined the COUNCIL FOR MUTUAL ECONOMIC ASSISTANCE and the WARSAW PACT.

The curtailment of political liberty, rising food prices and shortage of consumer goods have led to periods of rioting, strikes and demonstrations of anti-Soviet feelings from 1956 onwards. The disturbances, strengthened by nationalist sentiment and the fact that the majority of Poles are devout Catholics, led to the fall of GOMULKA in 1970 and GIERECK in 1980. In 1980 the independent trade union *Solidarity* initiated demands for reform, although these were crushed by the imposition of martial law (1981—83) under JARUZELSKI.

Polish Corridor, *see* DANZIG.

politburo, abbreviation for 'political bureau of the central committee of the Communist party', the executive and policy-making committee of a Communist party, esp. in the USSR, where the name was first used (1917). Stalin replaced the Politburo with the Presidium (1952), but the name was restored in 1966.

Pompidou, Georges (1911—74), French Gaullist statesman. After WWII service with the French resistance he served DE GAULLE as an adminis-trator and advisor, and played an important part in achieving the Evian Agreements which ended the Algerian War (1962). He was PM (1962—68), and succeeded De Gaulle as President, (1969—74), following similar policies.

Popular Front, the name of various coalitions of

centre and left-wing parties opposed to Fascism in
the 1930s, esp. those that formed the governments
in France, Spain and Chile. Social reforms and
economic improvements for the working classes
characterized these governments. In Spain, the
violent reaction of the right resulted in increasing
disturbances and ultimately the outbreak of the
SPANISH CIVIL WAR.

Potsdam Conference (1945), meeting following
Germany's defeat attended by the Allied leaders
Stalin, Truman, Churchill and Attlee to decide the
fate of postwar Germany and to implement the
agreement reached at the YALTA CONFERENCE.

The main decisions were: (1) to partition
Germany into 4 zones occupied by French, US, UK,
and Russian forces, (2) to initiate a programme of
de-Nazification, (3) to appoint local administrations and central authorities run by Germans
in each of the zones under the supervision of an
Allied Control Council, (4) to control German
industry and dismantle certain industrial plants as a
form of reparations to the Allies, (5) to redistribute
certain German territories to Poland and the USSR.

privatization, the policy of transferring industries
and services from public to private ownership; the
opposite of NATIONALIZATION. Since 1979 the UK
Conservative Government has privatized several
industries (incl. British Telecom, Britoil, British
Gas, British Airways and British Petroleum) by
selling its shares to the public.

proletariat, in Marxist philosophy, the class of
wage-earners, esp. industrial workers, in a capitalist
society, whose only possession of significant
material value is their labour and who are exploited

by the ruling class (the BOURGEOUSIE).

propaganda, (a) organized dissemination of allegations, information, etc., to assist or damage the cause of a government, movement, etc., (b) such allegations, information, etc.

The technique was the principal ideological instrument used by Hitler, Mussolini and Stalin to brainwash their own people and to attempt to undermine the resolve of their enemies, using broadcasting, the cinema, and massive stage-managed demonstrations such as the NUREMBURG RALLIES.

protectionism, (a) imposition of duties or quotas on imports, designed for the protection of domestic industries against foreign competition, (b) policy, system or theory of such restrictions.

On occasion most industrialized countries have adopted such practices and since WWII the method has been used by trading blocs, such as the EEC, to protect their members' interests. The opposite of protectionism is FREE TRADE.

purge, elimination of dissidents or opponents from a political party or state, esp. associated with events during Stalin's dictatorship in the USSR. These purges (esp. in the period 1936—38) resulted in the execution, exile or imprisonment of millions of Russians after the charade of show trials, when the accused usually pleaded guilty to the 'crimes', frequently after a period of brainwashing or torture.

putsch, German name for a sudden, violent political uprising. Hilter led an unsuccessful Nazi putsch in Munich (1923), as a result of which he was imprisoned.

Q

Quebec Conferences (1943, 1944), WWII meetings between Churchill and Roosevelt and their respective Chiefs of Staff. The 1943 Conference discussed the implications of Mussolini's overthrow, the invasion of Europe, and operations in the Far East, particularly the Burma campaign. The 1944 Conference discussed the transfer of resources to the Far East after the ending of hostilities in Europe, the Philippines campaign, and the LEND-LEASE ACT, on the assumption it would continue after the War's ending. Henry Morgenthau (1891–1967), US Secretary of the Treasury, put forward a plan for the removal of Germany's means of industrial production. Churchill and Roosevelt agreed to the proposals but they were later rejected by their ministers as being too costly and impracticable.

Quisling, Vidkun (1887–1945), Norwegian politician. He was Minister of Defence (1931–33) but disillusionment with democratic methods led him to form National Unity, a Fascist movement (1933) but it gained little support. On the outbreak of WWII he became involved in German plans for the occupation of Norway, and when the invasion occurred he seized power and administered the country as a puppet of the occupiers. After the War he was executed for treason. The term 'quisling' is now applied to any person who betrays their country to, and collaborates with, an enemy.

R

racialism or **racism,** (a) belief that races possess distinctive cultural characteristics determined by hereditary factors and so endow some races with intrinsic superiority over others, (b) abusive or aggressive behaviour towards members of another race on the basis of such belief.

Racism was a tenet of Nazi philosophy and is still prevalent in many parts of the world, though rarely as government policy (a notable exception being APARTHEID in South Africa). *See also* ANTI-SEMITISM.

radicalism, desires, practices or principles of political radicals, i.e. those favouring extreme or fundamental changes in economic or social conditions, institutions, etc.

Rahman, Sheikh Mujibur (1920–75), Bangladeshi politician. He became leader of the Awami League (1954), the principal objective of which was to secure the independence from West Pakistan of East Pakistan as BANGLADESH. After the war of independence (1971) and the establishment of the new state he declined the Presidency but became PM. His attempt to create parliamentary democracy based on socialist principles failed and he assumed dictatorial powers (1975) which resulted in his assassination when a military coup overthrew his government.

Rahman, Tunku Abdul (1903–), Malaysian statesman. He became PM of Malaya (1957) and of the Federation of Malaysia (1963). Following the breakdown of the harmonious relationships between the country's different races which Rahman had worked hard to achieve, he retired from office (1970).

Rapallo, Treaty of (1922), agreement between Germany and the USSR. Diplomatic relations were renewed after their severance during WWI, financial claims against each other (incurred during the War) were withdrawn, and economic cooperation pledged.

Rasputin, Grigori, orig. Novykh (1871–1916), Russian peasant monk and mystic. He wielded a magnetic power over the Tsarina Alexandra Feodorovna (1872–1918), who believed he could cure her son Alexis of haemophilia. From 1911 he exerted increasing influence over ecclesiastical and political appointments, gaining positions for his nominees and obtaining dismissal of those of whom he disapproved, including PM Kokovtsev. This power, coupled with his alcoholism and depraved private life, earned him the name of 'Rasputin' (debauchee), and made him many enemies. He was assassinated in the Yusupov Palace by a party of noblemen.

reactionary, (a) characterized or relating to reaction, esp. against radical political or social change, (b) anyone opposed to such changes.

Reagan, Ronald (1911–   ), US statesman, Republican President (1981–   ). He has followed generally conservative policies, cutting taxes and welfare expenditure, while massively increasing defence spending, e.g. on the STRATEGIC DEFENSE INITIATIVE. His hard-line attitude towards the

USSR has moderated somewhat since GORBACHEV came to power, and in 1987 he signed the INTERMEDIATE NUCLEAR FORCES TREATY. In Central America he has attempted to topple the left wing regime in NICARAGUA by supporting the Contra rebels, despite the opposition of Congress and condemnation by the UN.

Red Army, armed land forces of the USSR established (1918) by the Bolshevik Government. The word 'Red' was dropped from the title in 1946.

Red Cross Society, international and national humanitarian organization for relief of suffering in time of war and disaster. It was founded (1864) as a result of the inspiration of a Swiss philanthropist, Jean Henri Dunant (1828–1910), who had been overwhelmed by the plight of the wounded at the Battle of Solferino (1859). He was joint winner of the first Nobel Peace Prize (1901). The Society's emblem is a red cross on a white background. The earliest of the agreements comprising the GENEVA CONVENTION was closely connected with the Society's development.

Red Guards, *see* CULTURAL REVOLUTION.

referendum or **plebiscite,** submission of an issue of national or public importance to the vote of the electorate of a state, region, etc. Referenda were held by Norway and the UK on the issue of EEC membership.

Reichstag Fire (1933), conflagration which destroyed the German Reichstag (parliament building) in Berlin for which a Dutchman, Marinus van der Lubbe, was found guilty of arson and executed. The fire occurred a month after Hitler became Chancellor and he put the blame for it on the Communists, 3 of whom, Dmitrov, Popov and Tanev, all Bulgarians, were tried with van der Lubbe but acquitted.

Nevertheless, Hitler took advantage of the incident to have conferred on himself and the Nazi Government totalitarian powers, incl. suspension of basic constitutional freedoms, extension of the concept of treason to cover any opposition to the regime, and an intensified level of penalties for many offences. These measures proved to be forerunners of the abolition of the rule of law and the introduction of a permanent state of emergency.

reparations, compensation exacted as an indemnity from a defeated nation by the victors, esp. that extracted from Germany and its allies after both World Wars.

republic, a country in which the head of state is an elected or nominated president, as opposed to a monarch, and in which the people or their elected representatives possess (at least nominally) supreme power. Examples incl. France, Italy and the USA. The USSR and Yugoslavia are both federations of semi-autonomous republics.

Republican Party, one of the two main political parties in the USA. Founded in 1854, its strength is drawn from the higher-educated, higher-income, business and professional classes based in small towns and suburbs across the country, and the rural areas of the NE and Middle West. It favours economic imperialism, high tariffs, personal savings, private enterprise, balanced budgets, and a reduction in the machinery of central government. Internationally it once favoured isolationist policy but since WWII has followed the principle of

COLLECTIVE SECURITY to combat Communist expansionism.

resistance movements, underground organizations engaging in sabotage and secret operations against collaborators and enemy occupying forces, esp. in France, Norway, etc., during WWII. *See also* PARTISAN, MAQUIS.

revisionism, Marxist movement developed in Germany about 1900, favouring evolutionary rather than revolutionary transition to socialism; considered by Marxist-Leninist ideologists as a dangerous departure from Marx's precepts.

revolution, (a) fundamental political change, esp. activity supporting the overthrow or repudiation of a government, ruler or system, and the substitution of another by the governed, (b) in Marxist theory, historically necessary, violent transition from one system of production in a society to another, as from feudalism to capitalism, and from capitalism to socialism.

Reynaud, Paul (1878–1966), French Radical Party politician. He held several ministerial offices during the 1930s before becoming PM (1940). He was in power only 3 months during WWII before having to resign when the Assembly decided to sue for peace and dissolve the Third Republic. He was subsequently imprisoned by the Vichy Government and later sent to concentration camps by the Germans. After the War he became Finance Minister (1948) and Deputy PM (1953–54), campaigning for European integration.

Rhineland, area of West Germany on both banks of the Rhine bordering France and the Low Countries. After WWI the Treaty of VERSAILLES provided for

the demilitarization of the region and its occupation
for 15 years by Allied troops. The Treaties of
LOCARNO reaffirmed the demilitarization of the
Rhineland but the British and French occupation
forces were withdrawn (1926 and 1930 respectively).

Germany occupied the Rhineland (1936) — so
breaking the terms of the Treaties — declaring that it
was required as a fortified security zone against
possible French aggression. The British and French
response was muted owing to their policy of
APPEASEMENT towards Germany and the crisis
caused by Italian aggression against Abyssinia.

Rhodesia, *see* ZIMBABWE.

Rhodesia and Nyasaland, Federation of, union
(1953–63) of Northern and Southern Rhodesia
(now Zambia and Zimbabwe) and Nyasaland (now
Malawi), championed by Sir Godfrey HUGGINS and
Sir Roy WELENSKY. They considered that the
copperbelt industries of Northern Rhodesia, the
sophisticated economy of Southern Rhodesia and
the agriculture of Nyasaland could be profitably
integrated within a single political entity.

The union failed largely because African
nationalists saw it as hindering moves towards
independence, and because right-wing whites in
Southern Rhodesia objected to the Federation's
policies of improving the status of black Africans.

Ribbentrop, Joachim von (1893–1946),
German Nazi politician. He was ambassador to
the UK (1936–38) and was Foreign Minister
(1938–45). He negotiated the ANGLO-GERMAN
NAVAL AGREEMENT, the NAZI-SOVIET PACT, and
the Tripartite Pact (1940) which allied Germany,

Italy and Japan. He was executed as a war criminal.

Rio Treaty (1947), formally known as the Inter-American Treaty of Reciprocal Assistance, signed at Rio de Janeiro, Brazil, by 21 American states, the only non-participating nations being Canada, Ecuador and Nicaragua. The Treaty, entirely military in character and operative only in the Americas security zone, provides for aid to be given by all member states to any of their number subjected to aggression, an armed attack against any being considered an attack against all.

Romania, a republic of SE Europe. Area: 237,500 sq km. Pop: 22,480,000 (1982). Language: Romanian. Religion: Romanian Orthodox, RC, Calvinist and Lutheran. Cap: Bucharest.

Until the end of WWII the country was a kingdom, ruled successively by Carol I, Ferdinand, Carol II and Michael. It was involved in the BALKAN WARS and during WWI fought on the Allied side, more than doubling its territory as a result of these involvements.

Between the World Wars political corruption was widespread and anti-Semitic in character, under the malign influence of a Fascist organization called the 'Iron Guard' led by ANTONESCU. During WWII Romania joined the Axis powers and participated in the invasion of the USSR. After being forced to retreat during the Russian counter-offensive the Romanians made peace with the Allies and declared war on Germany.

Because it had changed sides Romania received favourable treatment when the peace treaties were agreed, although it soon fell under Russian influence, King Michael abdicated (1947) and a

People's Republic was declared, dominated by the Communist-inspired Democratic Front. The state was redesignated a Socialist Republic (1965) but has in recent years followed an independent course under the successive leadership of Gheorghe Gheorghu-Dej (1901–1965) and Nicolae Ceausescu (1918–   ), at the same time remaining a member of the COUNCIL FOR MUTUAL ECONOMIC ASSISTANCE and the WARSAW PACT.

Rome, Treaties of (1957), agreements establishing the EUROPEAN ECONOMIC COMMUNITY and the EUROPEAN ATOMIC ENERGY COMMUNITY, effective from 1958. They were signed by Belgium, France, West Germany, Italy, Luxembourg and the Netherlands.

The Treaties aimed to establish: a closer and enduring union between European peoples; FREE TRADE between the members and common external tariffs for all goods; common policies for agriculture, transport, labour mobility and important sectors of the economy; and common institutions for economic development. Overseas territories and possessions of member states were to be associated with the new Community. The essential aim was to improve the life and work of the peoples of the member countries.

Roosevelt, Franklin Delano (1882–1945), US statesman, Democratic President (1933–45). He was elected President 4 times, an achievement unique in US history. Stricken by poliomyelitis in the early 1920s he nevertheless fought against the crippling disability and was Governor of New York (1928–32) before defeating Herbert Hoover, the incumbent President.

The USA was in the grip of the Depression when Roosevelt took office and his NEW DEAL programme did much to alleviate the crisis. However, the progress of the programme was retarded by the Supreme Court which ruled against certain aspects of the New Deal legislation, and when Roosevelt attempted to reorganize the Court to secure a compliant judiciary, he met with vehement and successful opposition.

In foreign affairs Roosevelt strove to overcome the country's traditional isolationism, and although the USA was formally neutral until the end of 1941, he supported the European Allies during the early period of WWII with such measures as the LEND-LEASE ACT and the ATLANTIC CHARTER. After the US entry into WWII he attended the CASABLANCA, QUEBEC, CAIRO, TEHERAN and YALTA CONFERENCES. He has been criticized for his distrust of De Gaulle, a naive indulgence of Stalin, a misjudgement of CHAING KAI-SHEK's authority and control over China, and failure to press on in the drive across Europe to occupy Berlin, Prague and Vienna before the Russians. He was a strong supporter of the concept of the United Nations and died only 3 weeks before it was founded.

Roosevelt, Theodore (1858–1919), US statesman, Republican President (1901–1909). He became Vice-President to McKinley (1901), becoming President after McKinley's assassination. He was expansionist both in terms of US influence abroad and in terms of industry and commerce at home, and he insisted on a strong navy, the regulation of monopolies and trusts, and the eradication of corruption in the civil service. In

foreign affairs he successfully mediated in the
RUSSO-JAPANESE WAR, for which he received the
Nobel Prize (1906).

After 3 years away from politics he failed to
win the 1912 Republican Presidential nomination
from TAFT whom he then opposed in the election, standing as an Independent Progressive. His
intervention allowed Wilson, the Democratic
candidate, to win, and caused the withdrawal of
Roosevelt's followers from the Republican Party,
which took several years to recover from the schism.
Roosevelt deplored US neutrality in the early years
of WWI, strongly opposing Wilson's isolationist
policy.

Roumania, *see* ROMANIA.

Ruhr, principal manufacturing and mining area of
NW West Germany. It was occupied by the French
(1923—25) because Germany did not pay her
REPARATION dues imposed by the Treaty of
VERSAILLES. During WWII the region suffered
severely from Allied bombing raids.

Rumania, *see* ROMANIA.

Rusk, Dean (1909—   ), US diplomat. He was
Secretary of State (1961—69) serving the KENNEDY
and JOHNSON administrations. He was particularly
involved with the CUBAN MISSILES CRISIS and the
VIETNAM WAR.

Russia, *see* UNION OF SOVIET SOCIALIST REPUBLICS.

Russian Revolutions (1905, 1917), internal
upheavals which radically changed the political
system of Russia, ultimately replacing the autocratic monarchy of the Tsars with a Communist
dictatorship.

The **1905 Revolution** started when a peaceful workers' demonstration was fired on while petitioning the Tsar, resulting in widespread demonstrations and strikes throughout the country. These developed into a general strike, peasant uprisings, and a terrorist campaign by socialist revolutionaries. To placate the people, limited trade-union activity was permitted together with freedom of association, of the press and of speech. These concessions, combined with the conclusion of the RUSSO-JAPANESE WAR which freed troops to crush the Revolution, brought the voilence to an end. The Revolution did, however, lead to land reforms and a period of semi-constitutional government.

The **February 1917 Revolution** arose from the military disasters of WWI, which had eroded the authority of the monarchy. Widespread opposition to the War was aggravated by the bitter winter and the breakdown of the transport system, which resulted in soaring food prices and severe fuel shortages. Strikes and bread riots broke out and the working-class populace crossed the frozen River Neva and advanced on the administrative and fashionable quarter of Petrograd (now Leningrad). The police called on the army for assistance but the troops, in sympathy with the workers, mutinied and soon took control of the city.

Similar unrest occurred in other parts of the country and reached such a peak that the DUMA elected a provisional government which forced the Tsar's abdication, but continued the War. Meanwhile, the socialists established a SOVIET which challenged the authority of the provisional government.

The **October 1917 Revolution** arose from continued opposition to the War, and the determination of LENIN and the Bolsheviks to seize power. Lenin had little difficulty in winning over the masses, already short of food and dreading what another severe winter might entail. Lenin's promises of peace, land and bread met with popular support, and his well-organized revolutionaries overthrew the provisional government in Petrograd and quickly established Bolshevik authority.

Private trading was abolished, factories were handed over to workers' control, property of counter-revolutionaries and the Church was confiscated, a cease-fire was arranged with the Germans, and Bolshevik administrations established in all the principal cities, with a Council of People's Commissars as the country's executive authority. However, counter-revolutionary ('White') forces continued to fight the Bolsheviks, and a civil war followed until the Bolshevik victory in 1920. In 1923 the UNION OF SOVIET SOCIALIST REPUBLICS was established.

Russo-Japanese War (1904–05), conflict caused by attempts by both countries to gain ascendency in MANCHURIA for purposes of economic and territorial expansionism.

The War was precipitated by a Japanese naval attack on the Russian fleet at Port Arthur without a declaration of war, and ended by the overwhelming victory of the Japanese in a naval engagement in the Straits of Tsushima. On land the Russians also suffered considerable losses before managing, in Manchuria and along the Yalu River, to stem Japanese incursions.

The War was terminated by the signing of the Treaty of Portsmouth (1905), with President Theodore Roosevelt of the USA acting as mediator. Russia lost the South Manchurian Railway, S Sakhalin, the Liaodong Peninsula, and considerable prestige at home and abroad.

S

SA (Sturmabteilung), German organization founded in 1921, and also known as the Brown Shirts, Storm Division or Storm Troopers. It was a paramilitary organization, eventually becoming a political arm of the Nazi Party. Under Ernst Röhm's leadership (1931–34) it came more and more into conflict with the SS and the army, inducing Hitler to put an end to its activities and have it absorbed by the SS. He did this by liquidating Röhm and the rest of the SA leadership in what came to be known as 'The Night of the Long Knives' (1934).

Saarland, area of West Germany bordering France and Luxembourg with important mining and iron and steel industries. It was placed under League of Nations control (1919), France being granted permission to exploit the coalmines for 15 years as part of its REPARATION claim against Germany. As the result of a plebiscite it was returned to Germany (1935). After WWII it was in the French occupation zone until being integrated with West Germany (1957).

Sadat, Anwar El (1918–81), Egyptian statesman. He succeeded Nasser as President (1970–81), and continued Egypt's confrontation with Israel, culminating in the 1973 ARAB-ISRAELI WAR. After the failure to overcome the Israelis, Sadat began a policy of rapproachement with the West and ended the country's military dependence on the USSR. The Suez Canal, blocked during the War, was reopened (1975), and then Sadat, in a bold initiative, went to Jerusalem (1977) for talks with Israeli ministers and to address the Knesset (Parliament). This remarkably courageous act led to the CAMP DAVID AGREEMENT and a peace treaty with Israel (1979), which ultimately restored to Egypt territory previously occupied by Israel. However, scorn and vilification was heaped on Sadat by radical Arab states and the PLO, and he was assassinated in 1981. He was awarded the 1978 Nobel Peace Prize jointly with BEGIN.

Saint Germain, Treaty of (1919), WWI peace settlement between the Allies and Austria. It limited the Austrian Army to 30,000 men, forbade Austria to unite with Germany, dismembered the Austro-Hungarian Navy, and provided for the payment of REPARATIONS. Austria's territorial and population losses were enormous: Bohemia and Moravia were transferred to Czechoslovakia; the Trentino and South Tyrol to Italy; Galicia to Poland; Bukovina to Romania; and Bosnia-Herzegovina, Dalmatia and Slovenia to Yugoslavia.

Salazar, António de Oliveira (1889–1970), Portuguese dictator, PM (1932–68). Although Fascist in character, his administration carried out many beneficial reforms, incl. improvements in education, industrial development, living conditions and public works. However, independence movements in the Portuguese colonies and political opposition at home were suppressed, the only permitted party being Salazar's own, the Portuguese National Union.

SALT, *see* STRATEGIC ARMS LIMITATION TALKS.

sanctions, coercive measures (usually in the form of

trade bans) taken by one or more states against another guilty of violating international law. As there are always methods of circumveɪ.ting such measures, sanctions have proved ineffective when they have been attempted, notably by the League of Nations on Italy when it invaded Ethiopia (1935), and by the UN on Rhodesia to counter its policy of unilateral independence and white-minority rule (1966—80).

Sandanistas, *see* NICARAGUA.

Sarajevo, capital of the Yugoslav province of BOSNIA-HERZEGOVINA. In 1914 it was the scene of the assassination of Archduke Franz Ferdinand (1863—1914), heir to the AUSTRO-HUNGARIAN EMPIRE, and his wife. The assassin was a Serbian student, Gavrilo Princip (1894—1918), a member of the Young Bosnia secret nationalist movement committed to the liberation of the province from the Empire.

Austria-Hungary immediately sent an ultimatum to SERBIA. Although most of its terms were accepted, Austria-Hungary was not prepared to negotiate the remainder and declared war, backed by its alliance with Germany. As Russia supported Serbia it was only a matter of days before the remaining European powers were involved (through their various alliances) and WWI commenced.

satellite state, a country economically, militarily and politically controlled or dominated by another more powerful state. The Warsaw Pact countries are often regarded as satellite states of the USSR.

saturation bombing, heavy and sustained air attack with the objective of obliterating the target in a single decisive operation; frequently practised during WWII by the Luftwaffe, RAF and USAAF.

Scapa Flow, large natural anchorage in the Orkney Islands, used as a British naval base in both World Wars. A large part of the German fleet was impounded there at the end of WWI and scuttled (1919) on the orders of Admiral von Reuter. During WWII The battleship HMS *Royal Oak* was torpedoed and sunk there by a German U-boat (1939). The base was closed in 1956.

Schlieffen Plan (1905), detailed scheme prepared by General Count Alfred von Schlieffen (1833–1913) who was German Chief of General Staff (1891–1905). It was intended to ensure a German victory over a Franco-Russian alliance by stemming any Russian advance westwards with minimal strength while speedily defeating France by a massive flanking movement through the Low Countries, then southwards to cut off Paris from the sea.

At the outbreak of WWI, von Moltke, Schlieffen's successor as Chief of General Staff (1906–14), put into effect a modified form of the Plan which nearly succeeded. It was defeated by an Allied counter-offensive on the MARNE (1914), poor liaison between the German HQ and the field commanders, the withdrawal of forces to stem the rapid Russian drive through East Prussia, unexpected Belgian resistance, and the rapid reinforcement of their forces by the French. In WWII the Plan was again put into operation in the West (1940) with considerably more success.

Schmidt, Helmut (1918–), West German Social Democratic statesman. He was Federal

Defence Minister (1969—72), Finance Minister (1972—74) and Chancellor (1974—82). Schmidt followed the policy of OSTPOLITIK initiated by his predecessor, Brandt, and coupled it with full commitment to the EEC and NATO. He was succeeded by KOHL.

Schuman Plan (1950), proposal submitted by the French Foreign Minister, Robert Schuman (1886—1963), for pooling the coal and steel resources of Western Europe. It was implemented when the EUROPEAN COAL AND STEEL COMMUNITY was established.

Schuschnigg, Kurt von (1897—1977), Austrian Christian Socialist Chancellor (1934—38). He followed a moderate middle-of-the-road policy based on an external reliance on Italy against German threats of ANSCHLUSS. Italian support ceased with the signing of the Rome-Berlin Axis, and Schuschnigg, from a much weakened position, vainly sought to appease Germany, which isolated Austria diplomatically and forced Nazi sympathizers into the government. Hitler then delivered an ultimatum (1938) instructing Schuschnigg to form a completely Nazified government, but when Schuschnigg attempted to let the people give their opinion by means of a plebiscite, public disorder was provoked and the Chancellor was pressurized by Hitler to resign in favour of SEYSS-INQUART. Schuschnigg was imprisoned until the end of WWII.

SDI, see STRATEGIC DEFENCE INITIATIVE.

SDLP, see SOCIAL DEMOCRATIC AND LABOUR PARTY.

SDP, see SOCIAL DEMOCRATIC PARTY.

SEATO, *see* SOUTHEAST ASIA TREATY ORGANIZATION.

Second World War, *see* WORLD WAR TWO.

Secretary of State, (a) in the UK the minister heading a senior government department; (b) in the US the head of the government department in charge of foreign affairs (the State Department).

self-determination, the right of a nation or territorial unit to determine the form of government or political status it desires without external coercion or influence.

Senate, *see* CONGRESS.

separation of powers, the constitutional principle (effective in most democracies) that the 3 branches of government — legislative, executive and judicial — should be independent of each other.

Serbia, region of SE Yugoslavia. Area: 88,361 sq km. Pop: 5,687,000 (1978). Cap: Belgrade.

Previously part of the OTTOMAN EMPIRE, Serbia became an independent state in 1878, and a kingdom in 1882. Serbia was involved in both BALKAN WARS, and its desire to 'liberate' Serbians still under Austro-Hungarian rule led to the confrontation (*see* SARAJEVO) that precipitated WWI, in which Serbia fought on the Allied side. In 1918 it became one of the federal units of Yugoslavia.

Sèvres, Treaty of (1920), post-WWI settlement following the Paris Peace Conference. Turkey was to give Greece extensive rights on the E side of the DARDANELLES, and to cede most of European Turkey and most of the Aegean Islands to Greece. The waterway connecting the Aegean and Black Seas was to be demilitarized and internationalized under a 10-power League of Nations commission, and to be opened to merchant vessels and warships of all nations in times of peace and war. Armenia was granted independence, Kurdistan was permitted autonomy, and the Arabian peninsula achieved independence as the Kingdom of Hejaz. Mesopotamia and Palestine were to become MANDATES of Britain, and Syria a mandate of France. Turkish finances were placed under British, French and Italian supervision.

These arrangements were rejected by the Turkish republican movement and ultimately led to the CHANAK CRISIS, the rebellions against the Sultan by Mustapha Kemal (ATATÜRK), and the downfall of Lloyd George's coalition government in the UK. The settlement was later revised by the Treaty of LAUSANNE.

Seyss-Inquart, Artur von (1892–1946), Austrian politician. His friendship with Chancellor SCHUSCHNIGG enabled him to keep Hitler informed of the Chancellor's every move to retain the country's independence, Seyss-Inquart hoping that he would be appointed Chancellor after the ANSCHLUSS. To further his aim he used his influence as a Counsellor of State (1937) to encourage public disorder among Nazi elements. Hitler pressurized Schuschnigg into making Seyss-Inquart Chancellor (1938), an office he only held for 2 days but which gave him time to invite Germany to occupy the country to suppress the disorders. After the Anschluss he was appointed Governor of Austria. During WWII he was appointed Commissioner for the Netherlands (1940) where he ruthlessly recruited slave labour and authorized the deportation of Jews to concentration camps. After WWII he was tried for war crimes and executed.

Shah, see PAHLAVI.

Sharpeville, South African town in the Transvaal where in 1960 a massive demonstration against the Pass Laws (a feature of the country's APARTHEID policy) was organized by the Pan-African Congress. Police opened fire with automatic weapons and 67 blacks were killed and 186 wounded. The episode aroused worldwide condemnation and was a factor in South Africa withdrawing from the Commonwealth to become an independent republic (1961) rather than risk being expelled.

Shastri, Lal Bahadur (1904–66), Indian Congress Party politician, PM (1964–66). He was responsible for the introduction of the law against caste and separatism, and language and religious discrimination, and refused to commit the country to the development of nuclear weapons.

After the outbreak of hostilities between India and Pakistan over KASHMIR (1965), Shastri attended the TASHKENT CONFERENCE (1966). Agreement was reached on a truce but at the end of the conference Shastri died of a heart attack.

Shevardnadze, Eduard (1928–), Soviet statesman. As foreign minister under GORBACHEV (1985–) he has been involved in the thawing of East-West relations.

Show Trials, see PURGE.

Siegfried Line, series of German fortifications built (1936–44) from N of the Ruhr, up the Rhine to the Swiss frontier and named after the mythical German hero. It seriously delayed the Allied advance into Germany from the W in 1944.

Sinai, peninsula of NE Egypt at the N end of the Red Sea between the Gulfs of Aqaba and Suez.

In 1955–56 Egyptian and Israeli animosity intensified because of a series of terrorist raids launched across the frontier into Israel and the closure of the Strait of Tiran by Egypt, effectively preventing access to the Israeli port of Eilat at the head of the Gulf of Aqaba. These actions helped to precipitate the 1956 ARAB-ISRAELI WAR, in which Israel seized a large part of the peninsula, incl. the area around Sharm el-Sheikh, the base at the S end of the peninsula from which the Strait had been closed. Israel withdrew after a UN force had been stationed at Sharm el-Sheikh with the duty of keeping open the Strait.

A similar operation occurred when Nasser obtained the withdrawal of the UN force and again closed the Strait, precipitating the 1967 ARAB-ISRAELI WAR in which Israel seized the whole of Sinai. Following the CAMP DAVID AGREEMENT (1978). Israel returned Sinai to Egypt in stages, completing its withdrawal in 1982.

Sinn Fein (Gaelic, 'we ourselves', or 'ourselves alone'), Irish political party founded (1905) by Arthur Griffith (1872–1922), and closely associated with the socialist leader James Connolly (1870–1916) and other leaders of the EASTER RISING.

DE VALÉRA became leader (1917) and, when a split occurred in the movement (1922), he led the faction following traditional IRA ideals. This faction was opposed to the acceptance by Griffith's group of the formation of the Irish Free State, separating NORTHERN IRELAND from the rest of IRELAND. The movement had won an overwhelming victory in the 1918 elections but members refused to take their seats at Westminster, setting up instead their own republican parliament (Dáil) in Dublin. In 1926 De Valéra founded FIANNA FÁIL, which largely absorbed the old Sinn Fein.

Since 1969 Sinn Fein has been the political wing of the IRA, split like it into 'Official' and 'Provisional' wings.

Sino-Japanese War (1937—45), conflict developing from Japan's seizure of Mukden (1931) and its annexation of MANCHURIA (1932). In 1935 the Japanese began a further advance into N China and full-scale hostilities developed. Japanese progress was rapid, Shanghai, Nanjing, Guangzhou (Canton) and Hankou all being captured in quick succession. Eventually Japan's entry into WWII absorbed the conflict with the Chinese into a wider sphere, China becoming a valued ally in the fight against the AXIS powers, with the UK and the US transporting supplies along the Burma Road to the wartime capital of Chongqing.

Sino-Soviet Split, schism which developed between Communist China and the USSR (1956) and which is still causing friction between them. When Khrushchev denounced Stalin at the 20th Soviet Communist Party Congress, China complained that it and other Communist states should have been consulted beforehand. From this apparently innocuous lack of prior consultation there developed conflicts over domestic, foreign and defence policies, economic relationships, and ideological differences.

The Russians opposed China's GREAT LEAP FORWARD, the revival of its campaign against Taiwan, and its frontier problems with India. China was alarmed by the Russians' efforts at DÉTENTE with the USA and annoyed that technical information on atomic weapons was withheld (1959). There were frontier clashes along the Amur and Ussuri Rivers, and at international Communist Party conferences angry words and denunciations were exchanged.

World Communism was split, all European national parties except that of Albania taking the Soviet side (Yugoslavia remained neutral), and all Asian parties except those of India and Mongolia (and later Vietnam) siding with China. The CULTURAL REVOLUTION signalled further bitterness, and diplomatic relations were severed (1967–70). In recent years there has been a shift by both countries towards a modification of confrontation and hostility.

Six-Day War, *see* ARAB-ISRAELI WARS.

slump, *see* DEPRESSION.

Smith, Ian (1919–   ), Rhodesian politician. With the break-up of the Federation of Rhodesia and Nyasaland he became a founder of the Rhodesia Front Party (1962) and PM (1964–78). Dedicated to immediate independence without African majority rule in Southern Rhodesia, his government made a unilateral declaration of independence (UDI) in 1965 in defiance of the UK decision to forestall independence until there was black majority rule. *See* ZIMBABWE.

Smuts, Jan (1870–1950), South African soldier and statesman. He was a Boer general in the BOER

WAR, entered the House of Assembly (1907), and held several ministerial offices while helping towards reconciliation with Britain. That this was achieved by 1914 was largely due to his efforts and it ensured that South Africa joined the UK against Germany in WWI.

He was a member of the Imperial War Cabinet (1917—18), PM of South Africa (1919—24 and 1939—48), and Deputy PM (1933—39) in HERTZOG'S coalition government comprising the National Party and Smuts' United Party. Smuts was made a Field Marshal (1941), became a close adviser of Churchill and other Allied leaders during WWII, attended the CAIRO CONFERENCE, and was treated as an elder statesman.

In South Africa, however, Smuts was regarded as a traitor by Afrikaans Nationalists for his pro-British attitude, and was disliked by the left and opponents of segregation because of his active support of white supremacy.

Social Democratic and Labour Party (SDLP), Northern Ireland (mostly Catholic) political party founded (1970) with a radical left-of-centre policy campaigning for a just distribution of wealth, civil rights, friendship and understanding between Eire and Ulster, and the eventual unification of Ireland with the consent of the majority of the people.

Social Democratic Party (SDP), British political party of the centre. It was founded in 1981 by four former Labour ministers: Roy Jenkins (leader 1981—83), David Owen (leader 1983—87), Shirley Williams and William Rodgers. In the same year it joined the Liberal Party in a political alliance, fighting the 1983 and 1987 elections on this basis. In

1987 the Party voted to negotiate a merger with the Liberal Party.

social democracy, beliefs, practices, principles or programme of social democrats or a social democratic party, based on the transformation of capitalism into socialism by gradual reform within a parliamentary system.

socialism, (a) an economic and political theory advocating collective or government control over the means of distribution, exchange and production, distinguished by equality of wealth, the absence of competitive economic activity, production for use rather than profit, and frequently by government determination of investment, prices and production norms; (b) in Marxist theory, a transitional period in society's development from CAPITALISM to COMMUNISM, based on income distribution according to work done as opposed to need.

Solidarity, an independent Polish trade union founded in 1980. Led by Lech Walesa (1943–), Solidarity received widespread popular support for its demands for wage increases and political liberalization. It was banned following the imposition of martial law in 1981, but has continued its activities underground. Walesa was awarded the 1983 Nobel Peace Prize.

Somme, Battle of the (1916), a 20-week engagement of WWI fought along a 32 km front N of the River Somme in N France. Well over a million men perished, and the Allied territorial gain was a mere 16 km. The combined British and French objective was to relieve pressure on the French at VERDUN and the 2 battles so weakened the German

Army that it was not able to rebuild its fighting strength even though the War lasted a further 2 years. Despite the appalling losses the Somme is now considered in retrospect to have been the turning point of the War in France.

South Africa, republic of S Africa. Area: 1,140,519 sq km. Pop: 29,290,000 (est.). Languages: Afrikaans and English. Religion: Christianity. Cap: Pretoria.

Following the BOER WAR, the Union of South Africa was formed (1910) from the former self-governing British colonies of the Cape of Good Hope, Natal, the Orange Free State and the Transvaal, and remained a Commonwealth member until becoming a republic (1961).

Although South African forces fought loyally on the Allied side in both World Wars there was an underlying nationalist element which became particularly apparent in WWII when leading National Party members openly declared themselves to have Fascist sympathies.

When the National Party achieved power (1948) these sympathies were put into practice amongst their own people with the adoption of a strict system of racial segregation (*see* APARTHEID), which alienated the country from most of the rest of the world in cultural, political and sporting activities — but not economically. Such antagonism had little affect on South Africa, which continued to get its own way, conscious that its strategic position guaranteed its military importance to the West against Communist expansion, particularly in the event of the closure of the Suez Canal, as happened during the Arab-Israeli Wars.

In the 1960s the clandestine AFRICAN NATIONAL CONGRESS (ANC) started to launch sabotage attacks on industrial targets from within the country and from neighbouring black African states. However, some of the black states rely on the South African transport system for their exports and imports and dare not permit the ANC to become too militant for fear of South African reprisals, which have occurred when its forces have crossed frontiers to destroy ANC bases.

From the 1976 riots in the black township of SOWETO there has been an escalation of violent unrest among the black and coloured population. This, combined with increasing international pressure, has brought about some limited reforms of apartheid, incl. the granting in 1984 of a degree of parliamentary representation for coloureds. However, the majority black population is still without a vote, and there have been widespread calls for economic sanctions against South Africa, although these have been resisted by the UK, South Africa's principle trading partner.

Southeast Asia Treaty Organization (SEATO), defensive alliance established (1954) in Manila by Australia, France, New Zealand, Pakistan, the Philippines, Thailand, the UK and the USA. Pakistan withdrew (1973) and France (1974) and the remaining members resolved (1975) to phase out the Organization because of changing circumstances in the area.

Southern Rhodesia, *see* ZIMBABWE, and RHODESIA AND NYASALAND, FEDERATION OF.

sovereignty, (a) absolute unlimited political power by a state; (b) political AUTONOMY; (c) a sovereign's authority or status.

soviet, elected administrative or governmental council in the USSR at either local, regional or national level, culminating in the Supreme Soviet.

Soviet Security Service, organization which incl. the secret police. It has had several bewildering name changes since it was established by the Bolshevik Government. Known as the Cheka (1917–22), it was reorganized as the GPU (1922–23). It was the OGPU (1923–34) and the NKVD (1934–41). The NKVD was split (1941–46) into the NKVD and NKGB, and these were renamed MVD and MGB (1946–54). The MGB became the KGB in 1954.

The heads of all these departments have been cunning and ruthless men responsible for PURGES (most notoriously in the 1930s), political trials, banishment to forced labour camps, executions, censorship, investigations and searches. The Gulag (that part of the Service which administers corrective labour camps) uses forced labour for such activities as forestry, mining and canal, railway and road construction.

Soweto, black township in the Transvaal, South Africa, where rioting occurred (1976) after it had been announced that Afrikaans would be the compulsory language of instruction in schools. The trouble lasted 3 days and a further 3 days elsewhere in the Transvaal, 236 blacks being killed and over 1,100 wounded when the police opened fire. The proposed compulsory teaching of Afrikaans was abandoned a few weeks later.

Spain, kingdom of SW Europe. Area: 504,879 sq km. Pop: 37,682,000 (1981). Language: Spanish.

Religion: RC. Cap: Madrid.

Until 1931 Spain was a kingdom subject to political strife and violent demonstrations. The last monarch of this early period of the century was Alfonso XIII (1886—1941) who tried to remedy the situation by encouraging General Miguel Primo de Rivera (1870—1930) to stage a coup and establish a right-wing dictatorship (1923). For a time this expedient was successful but opposition to his authoritarian regime gradually grew and he resigned in 1930.

In 1931 the King abdicated and a republic was proclaimed but this did little to solve the country's problems since the left-wing government, although it had received a substantial mandate in the 1936 elections, was hampered in its reforming zeal by strong right-wing opposition led by the FALANGE and an assortment of aristocracy, the military, monarchists and politically motivated members of the RC church. These groups supported the rebellion organized in Spanish Morocco by FRANCO (1936). It spread to the mainland and, rapidly gathering momentum, developed in to the SPANISH CIVIL WAR.

Following the rebel victory in 1939 Franco became Head of State, a position he held until his death in 1975. One of the important achievements of his regime in foreign policy was the conclusion of an agreement whereby air and naval bases were granted to the USA in exchange for economic and military assistance (1953). He was succeeded by King Juan Carlos de Bourbon (1938—   ), grandson of Alfonso XIII. Juan Carlos had been nominated by Franco as his successor in 1969,

Franco having pledged himself in 1947 to a restoration of the monarchy after his death.

With the return of the monarchy came the re-establishment of political parties, thereby relaxing the 1-party system of the Franco regime. There had not been a general election for 21 years until 1977 when the Democratic Centre Party was elected to power. In 1982 a moderate socialist government was elected. Spain joined NATO in 1982 and the EEC in 1986.

One of the problems facing the new democracy is the question of provincial autonomy. A step in this direction occurred when Basque and Catalan parliaments were established (1980) although even this move has not satisfied extreme Basque separatists who continue to maintain terrorist activities through the ETA organization.

Spanish Civil War (1936–39), conflict between the Republican Spanish Government and rebel forces. Alarmed by the land reforms and anti-clerical and left-wing tendencies of the POPULAR FRONT Government of the Republic, a group of high-ranking army officers started a rebellion, launched from Spanish Morocco and the Canary Islands. The rebels were supported by the land-owning aristocracy, big industrialists, the RC Church, nationalists, monarchists and the FALANGE (Fascist party), while the Republican Government drew support from socialists, Communists, anarchists, and those seeking regional autonomy, esp. in the Basque country, Catalonia and Galicia.

Command of the rebels soon fell to General FRANCO, who declared that he would establish a Fascist state on the Italian model. The rebels received increasing amounts of military aid from Italy and Germany, and the German bombing of the Basque town of Guernica (1937) caused an international outcry. However, the European democracies maintained a policy of non-intervention, refusing to help the Republican Government, and the USSR sent only a limited amount of aid, although European and US Communists organized volunteers into the INTERNATIONAL BRIGADES. Internal dissensions among the Republicans, combined with their inability to obtain essential supplies, contributed to Franco's eventual victory in 1939.

Spartacist Rising (1919), name given to a week of street violence in Berlin organized by radical socialists of the Spartacus League, which was named after the leader of a slave revolt against Rome (73–71 BC). The movement was founded in 1916 and was reconstituted as the German Communist Party in 1918. All its leaders were arrested or killed in the rioting, incl. the founders Karl Liebknecht and Rosa Luxemburg. The Spartacists' objective was the overthrow of capitalism, and they believed this could only be achieved by a revolutionary rising of German workers throughout the country. In the same year, SOVIETS of revolutionary workers, soldiers and sailors were established in several major German cities, but these were similarly suppressed.

Sri Lanka, island republic off the SE coast of India; known as Ceylon until 1972. Area: 66,000 sq km. Pop: 14,800,000 (1981). Languages: Sinhalese, Tamil. Religions: Buddhism, Hinduism. Cap: Colombo.

Annexed from the Dutch by the British (1815),
the country became independent in 1948. In recent
years the main problem has been increasingly
violent civil strife between the majority Sinhalese
and the minority Tamils, many of whom want to set
up a separate state in the N and E of the Island.
India, which has a large Tamil population in the SE,
has tried to play a mediating role, but with little
success.

SS (Schutzstaffel), German organization (literally
meaning 'protection squad') founded in 1925
as Hitler's bodyguard, but when HIMMLER took
command (1929) he transformed the black-
uniformed troopers into a militarily trained and
ideologically indoctrinated Nazi elite. It was used to
suppress the larger rival SA (1934), absorbed the
police force (1936) and became the most feared and
powerful movement in the country. It embodied
racialism at its worst, and carried out the Nazi policy
of exterminating all opposition, esp. in the
CONCENTRATION CAMPS which it controlled.

Stalin, Josef, orig. Dzhugashvili (1879—1953),
Soviet Communist statesman and dictator. He spent
some years in exile before the Revolution, and
formed close ties with Lenin and the Bolsheviks.
From 1919 he contrived to gain control over the
principal levers of power in party and state,
culminating in his election as First Secretary of the
Communist Party (1922), a post he held until his
death.

In a few years in the 1920s he ruthlessly disposed
of all his rivals, and with the exile of Trotsky in 1929
his ruling position was unchallenged. He then set
about reorganizing the economy by instituting

FIVE-YEAR PLANS, but they suffered many set-backs and were far less successful than he had hoped. Agriculture was the worst sufferer, COLLECTIVIZATION proving highly unpopular with the wealthier peasants (kulaks). After dealing ruthlessly with the peasantry Stalin turned on the officer corps. Many thousands of them perished on the grounds that they were guilty of pro-German sympathies, the result being a grave shortage of experienced men when the Germans invaded the USSR in WWII. In all, several million people are believed to have died in the PURGES of the 1930s.

During the War Stalin directed the campaigns against the invaders and wielded immense political power over the Allied leaders, which resulted in far from satisfactory outcomes to postwar problems as far as the West was concerned. These incl. the dropping of the IRON CURTAIN and the opening of the COLD WAR. One of history's greatest tyrants, Stalin was denounced publicly by KHRUSHCHEV at the 20th Party Congress (1956).

Stalingrad, city of the USSR, renamed Volgograd in 1961. It was the scene of a massive Soviet victory after the Germans besieged the city (1942–43). The battle was the decisive turning point on the Eastern Front in WWII.

Star Wars, *see* STRATEGIC DEFENCE INITIATIVE.

Statute of Westminster (1931), Act of Parliament by which the self-governing DOMINIONS (Canada, Newfoundland, the Irish Free State, South Africa, Australia and New Zealand) gained legislative independence from the UK, confirming resolutions approved at the 1926 and 1930 IMPERIAL CONFERENCES.

Stern Gang, Zionist underground movement, founded (1940), by Abraham Stern (1907−42) when he left IRGUN ZVAI LEUMI because of its decision to suspend anti-British activities in PALESTINE during WWII. The Gang was responsible for various acts of terrorism incl. the assassination of the UN mediator in the first Arab-Israeli War, Count Folk Bernadotte (1948). The movement was dissolved in 1948.

Strategic Arms Limitation Talks (SALT), succession of meetings (1969−72 and 1974−79) between Soviet and US respreseratives, with the objective of curtailing the arms race. In 1972 a treaty (SALT I) was signed limiting anti-ballistic missiles defensive systems. The second round of talks (SALT II) concentrated on types and numbers of nuclear missiles possessed by the 2 states and, though agreement was reached, the US Senate refused to ratify the proposals.

Strategic Defence Initiative (SDI) (popularly known as 'Star Wars'), a proposed US system of artificial satellites armed with lasers to destroy enemy missiles in space. The USSR is conducting research into a similar system.

Stresemann, Gustav (1878−1929), German statesman. He became leader of the National Liberal Party (1917), which was re-formed as the German People's Party (1919). During WWI he was a hard-line nationalist but moderated his views under the WEIMAR REPUBLIC, of which he was Chancellor for 3 months (1923). He was Foreign Minister (1923−29), pursuing a conciliation policy towards Germany's former enemies. He negotiated the DAWES PLAN, the Treaties of LOCARNO, and

Germany's admission to the League of Nations (1926). He was awarded the Nobel Peace Prize jointly with BRIAND (1926).

Sudetenland, area of N and NW Bohemia. It was ceded by the Austro-Hungarian Empire to the newly formed state of Czechoslovakia by the Treaty of SAINT GERMAIN. A large part of the population was German-speaking, and this prompted Hitler to demand that the territory be absorbed into Germany. To this end the German-Sudeten Party, financed by Germany, began a campaign of agitation and civil disturbances. By the MUNICH AGREEMENT (1938), Germany was allowed to annex the area, which it retained until 1945. It was then returned to Czechoslovakia, which deported the German-speaking population.

Suez Crisis (1956), international tension aroused when Israel invaded Egypt, closely supported a few days later by an Anglo-French force. The Israeli move was to halt Egyptian raids across the frontier and the Anglo-French sortie was in retaliation for the nationalization by Egypt of the Suez Canal Company, the shares of which were held by the British Government and French investment interests. President NASSER argued that Egypt required the Canal dues to pay for the construction of the Aswan High Dam which the UK and the US had refused to finance.

The Anglo-French invasion, concentrated around Port Said, met with initial success but aroused world-wide condemnation incl. threats of Soviet intervention, as well as much home-based opposition. The most virulent opponent of the action was the USA (represented by President

Eisenhower and Secretary of State Dulles), which exerted diplomatic and economic pressures. This, coupled with the condemnations of other Western states, resulted in the action being stopped and the ultimate withdrawal of all forces.

Israel, which withdrew its forces from Sinai (1957), probably gained most from the incident: a UN force was sent to act as a buffer against Egyptian incursions; the Straits of Tiran, which the Egyptians had closed, were opened to give access to the port of Eilat; and the defeat of the Egyptians in the field, although limited, acted as a morale booster. Egypt, having suffered a military setback, nevertheless strengthened its claims to leadership of the Arab world by its defiance of 2 strong Western powers, but it became much more dependent on the USSR for financial and military aid (e.g. for the construction of the Aswan High Dam). UK and US relations became very strained, and the British PM, EDEN, had his reputation as a statesman destroyed, and resigned (1957). *See also* ARAB-ISRAELI WARS.

suffrage, *see* FRANCHISE, WOMEN'S SUFFRAGE.

suffragettes, *see* WOMEN'S SUFFRAGE.

Suharto, General T.N.I. (1921–) Indonesian army officer and politician. He played a leading part in the indpendence war against the Dutch. After the army seized effective power from SUKARNO (1967), Suharto became Acting President. As full President from 1968 he has concentrated on economic development, suppression of the Communist Party (c. 80,000 members were killed in the coup), encouragement of foreign investment, and a non-aligned foreign policy.

Sukarno, Achmed (1902–70), Indonesian

politician. He founded the Indonesian National Party (PNI) in 1927, and was imprisoned and subsequently exiled by the Dutch for independence and revolutionary activities (1929—42). During WWII he led the nationalists in cooperating with Japan (1942—45) and proclaimed an independent republic with himself as President (1945), fighting off all attempts by the Dutch to reassert their authority. His authoritarianism coupled with economic stagnation and a readiness to follow a pro-Chinese Communist policy eventually alarmed the army and other right-wing circles which seized power in 1967 and finally removed him from office in 1968. He was succeeded by SUHARTO.

Sun Yat-sen (1866—1925), Chinese politician. He was educated in the West and became a Christian. Because of revolutionary activities against the Manchu Dynasty he had to flee the country in the 19th cent. The early years of the 20th cent. were spent in organizing revolution from outside China. His growing support as leader of the KUOMINTANG within the country eventually led to the uprisings which overthrew the Dynasty (1911).

Sun Yat-sen was briefly President (1912), but handed over to a military regime, with Yüan Shihkai as President (1912—16), which was later opposed by Sun Yat-sen. After Yüan's death the country collapsed into civil strife between rival warlords. Sun Yat-sen attempted to unify the country by establishing a military government in 1923, but this goal was not achieved until after his death. Meanwhile he led a series of governments in S China, but they only controlled a small area. Becoming disenchanted with Western policies he turned to the USSR for aid and cooperated with the Chinese Communists.

Although little respected during his lifetime he later became acclaimed by both left and right — as the 'father of the country' by the Nationalists and as the 'pioneer of the revolution' by the Communists.
Syria, republic of the Middle East. Area: 185,680 sq km. Pop: 10,400,000 (est. 1981). Language: Arabic. Religion: Islam. Cap: Damascus.

Until 1918 the country was part of the OTTOMAN EMPIRE, afterwards becoming a French MANDATE. It was invaded by the British and Free French contingents to prevent the establishment of German air bases during WWII and to remove Vichy French government followers (1941), before achieving independence in 1944.

Politically Syria has been dominated by the Pan-Arab BA'TH SOCIALIST PARTY which aspired to enhance its philosophy by uniting the country with Egypt as the United Arab Republic (1958—61). Economic and political antagonisms soon developed between the two countries and the union was terminated by a military seizure of power in Syria. The current President is Lieutenant General Hafiz al-Assad (1930—   ) who seized power in 1970.

Syria is a member of the ARAB LEAGUE and has never acknowledged the existence of Israel. This led to involvement in the ARAB-ISRAELI WARS, the giving of support to guerrilla activities against Israel, and opposition to SADAT's attempts at détente. Syria invaded LEBANON (1976) ostensibly to check the civil war there by backing the PLO and Lebanese Moslems in their struggle against the

Lebanese Christians (Phalangists). This move provoked the Israelis to invade Lebanon to protect their country against PLO guerrilla attacks and possible encroachment by the Syrians. Syrian forces remain in control of large parts of Lebanon. Syria has close ties with the USSR and is generally ill-disposed towards the West, especially the USA.

T

Taff Vale Case (1901), legal action arising when
the Amalgamated Society of Railway Workers
was sued for damage by the Taff Vale Railway
Company to compensate for losses sustained during
a strike. £23,000 compensation was awarded to the
Company, the Society being considered responsible
for its members' actions. Union anger at the
judgement was a factor in the early development of
the Labour Party, and unions were given immunity
from similar actions by the passing of the Trade
Disputes Act (1906).

Taft, William Howard (1875–1930), US
Republican President (1909–13). Although an
able administrator he was a conservative and
cautious politician, having uneasy relations with
Congress even though both Houses had Republican
majorities. This led to a Party split resulting in Taft's
overwhelming defeat by the Democratic candidate,
Woodrow Wilson, in the 1912 Presidential election.
Taft became Chief Justice of the Supreme Court
(1921), an office he held until his death.

Taiwan, *see* CHINA.

Tannenburg, Battle of (1914), engagement
between German and Russian armies in East
Prussia during WWI when a Russian force was
routed to such an extent that a second Russian army
was easily defeated a fortnight later near the
Masurian Lakes. The Russians retreated in good
order from the Masurian Lakes and the pursuing

German forces were in their turn thrown back by the Russians so that on balance the two encounters resulted in stalemate, although Russian forces never again entered Germany in WWI.

tariffs, government taxes levied on imports (and occasionally on exports), for the purpose of protecting domestic industry (*see* PROTECTIONISM), strengthening the BALANCE OF PAYMENTS, or raising revenue.

Tashkent Conference (1966), meeting between President Ayub Khan of Pakistan and PM Shastri of India, convened by the Soviet PM Kosygin following the 1965 Indo-Pakistan War. The War had arisen over the disputed territory of KASHMIR, where border incidents and disturbances led to full-scale conflict. At the Conference both countries renounced the use of force in the settlement of the Kashmir dispute, and agreed to withdraw their respective armed forces to the original frontier.

Teheran Conference (1943), first meeting during WWII between Churchill, Roosevelt and Stalin. Agreement was reached to coordinate a Russian offensive with the opening of a second front in W Europe; on a declaration of war at a convenient time by the USSR on Japan; on the postwar extension of the USSR frontier to the CURZON LINE, with a compensatory acquisition of German territory by Poland along the ODER-NEISSE LINE; and on the establishment of a postwar peace-keeping organization.

Teng Hsiao-ping, *see* DENG XIAOPING.

terrorism, systematic use of terror, manifesting itself in violence and intimidation. Terrorism has been used by groups wishing to coerce a government in order to achieve political or other objectives, and also by dictatorships or other autocratic governments in order to overcome opposition to their policies.

Teschen (Ger.; Polish, *Cieszyn*; Czech, *Tešin*), small industrial town of SW Poland which was part of the Hapsburg Empire (1772—1918). After the Empire's dispersal the town and surrounding area were claimed by Czechoslovakia and Poland. These countries resorted to a week's fighting over the problem (1919) before a Conference of Ambassadors in Paris (1920) awarded the town to Poland and the surrounding area to Czechoslovakia. Both countries remained in disupte over the settlement and it was not until 1945 that the matter was finally resolved with Poland retaining the town and acquiring the surroundings from Czechoslovakia.

Test Ban Treaty, *see* NUCLEAR TEST BAN TREATY.

Thant, U (1909—74), Burmese diplomat, Secretary-General of the UN (1961—71). He played a leading role in resolving the CUBAN MISSILES CRISIS; formulated a plan for the ending of the Congolese civil war (1962); initiated the establishment of a peace-keeping force in CYPRUS (1964) and the cease-fire arrangements after the 1967 ARAB-ISRAELI WAR; and obtained the acceptance of Communist China as a member of the UN with a seat in the Security Council.

Thatcher, Margaret (1925—), British Conservative stateswoman, PM (1979—). She was Secretary of State for Education and Science (1970—74), and was elected Leader of the Conservative Party in 1975. She is the first woman in the UK to lead a political party and to hold the post of PM.

Her government's economic policies have generally favoured unfettered free enterprise, which has involved cutting taxes and public expenditure, extensive PRIVATIZATION, and legislation to reduce the power of the trade unions. Her government has also had to deal with high levels of unemployment. She has favoured a hard line in relations with the Soviet Bloc, and a strengthening of the UK's nuclear forces. She was re-elected in 1983 and 1987; her 1983 success has been partially attributed to the UK victory in the Falkland's War.

Third Reich, the name given by the Nazis to their regime in Germany (1933–45), which Hitler boasted would last for a thousand years. According to the Nazis the First Reich was the Holy Roman Empire (962–1806) and the Second Reich the German Empire (1871–1918).

Third World, term which became current in the 1960s to distinguish the rest of the world from the 2 blocs of the USA and USSR. It is now loosely applied to the developing countries, esp. those of Africa, Asia and Latin America, which are largely non-industrialized and therefore poor. Such countries are generally considered neutral in the East-West alignment (*see* NON-ALIGNED MOVEMENT), frequently suffer from mass illiteracy, have political systems dominated by small, often Western-educated elites, and bear considerable resentment of IMPERIALISM stemming from their past colonial status.

Tibet, autonomous region of W China. Area: 1,221,600 sq km. Pop: 1,273,000. Language:

Tibetan. Religion: Buddhism. Cap: Lhasa.

On suspicion that Russia was gaining a foothold in the country, and that such a presence would be a danger to India, a British expeditionary force under the command of Colonel Francis Younghusband was despatched to Lhasa (1904). Many of the inhabitants were killed by the invading force and no evidence was found of Russian penetration. However, a trade treaty was negotiated providing a commercial relationship between India and Tibet.

China occupied the country (1910—13), forcing Tibet's spiritual ruler, the Dalai Lama, to seek refuge in India. He returned when the Chinese left and the country practically vanished behind a screen of self-imposed isolation from the rest of the world.

China reoccupied Tibet (1951) and for 8 years held the country in subjection. Then in 1959 a serious rebellion occurred, involving heavy fighting and the flight of the new Dalai Lama to India, accompanied by many thousands of his subjects. At first Chinese rule was harsh and illiberal but in recent years there has been considerable relaxation of oppression, hospitals and schools have been opened, highways constructed, air links inaugurated with China, frontiers opened for trade, agriculture expanded and reformed, irrigation, mining, forestry and industrial projects instituted, and closed monasteries reopened.

Tindemans Report (1976), investigation on European union prepared by the Belgian PM, Leo Tindemans (1922—) at the request of the Council of Europe. The Report proposed a common foreign policy; progress towards economic and monetary union; a directly elected European Parliament; and the granting of greater powers to the EUROPEAN COMMISSION. Some of these proposals have already been accepted and put into operation.

Tirpitz, Álfred Friedrich von (1849—1930), German grand admiral. He was Minister of Marine (1897—1916) and instrumental in building-up the strength of the Navy, incl. the construction of large capital ships to rival the British DREADNOUGHTS. He was naval C-in-C (1914—16) but resigned when Kaiser Wilhelm II opposed his advocacy of unrestricted U-BOAT warfare and prevented the fleet's deployment in offensive operations in European waters. He turned to politics and was a Nationalist Deputy in the Reichstag (1924—28).

Tito, Josip Broz (1892—1980), Yugoslav marshal and statesman. He became a Communist after being captured by the Russians while serving in the Austro-Hungarian Army during WWI. He fought in the Russian Revolution and on returning to Yugoslavia spent 6 years in prison as a political undesirable and enemy of the monarchist regime.

During WWII Tito organized the National Liberation Front of PARTISANS to fight the invading German forces (1941). He headed a provisional government from 1943, and had managed to liberate much of the country before the arrival of Soviet forces. He was such a prestigious and successful leader that he was a popular choice as PM (1945—53). He led Yugoslavia in its break with the Soviet bloc (1948) and became President in 1953. He denounced the Soviet invasion of Hungary (1956) and the Warsaw Pact invasion of Czechoslovakia (1968), and by developing independent and moderate policies raised

Yugoslavia to a prominent position in the NON-ALIGNED MOVEMENT. He was himself considered a world statesman of considerable prominence.

Tobruk, *see* NORTH AFRICA CAMPAIGNS.

Todd, Garfield (1908–   ), Rhodesian politician. He was President of the United Rhodesia Party and PM (1953–58). His administration was notable for the legalizing of trade unions and the extension of the franchise to an increasing number of black citizens. He co-founded the Central Africa Party (1959) and founded the New African Party (1961). After the Unilateral Declaration of Independence (1965) he spent many months in prison or under house arrest because of opposition to Ian Smith's illegal regime.

Tojo, Hideki (1884–1948), Japanese general and politician. He was leader of the militarist party from 1931 and Chief of Staff of the Kwantung Army (1938–40). His appointment as Minister of War (1940–41) and PM (1941–44) marked the final control of the military over the country's political affairs and transformed the state into a dictatorship. US successes in WWII eventually persuaded Emperor HIROHITO that Tojo was leading Japan to disaster and Tojo ultimately resigned. He was executed as a war criminal by the Americans.

totalitarianism, centralized control by an authoritarian, autocratic, single-party regime. Examples incl. the USSR, Nazi Germany and Fascist Italy.

total warfare, waging of comprehensive and unrestricted hostilities against an enemy, incl. the civilian non-combatant population. Such warfare was not conducted on a large scale until WWII, when c. 14 million civilians are thought to have died.

Trades Union Congress (TUC), central organization of UK trade unions founded in 1868. Policy is formulated by the General Council which is in contact with government departments and takes an interest in proposed legislation affecting organized labour. It holds an annual conference which enables union representatives to consider matters of mutual concern to members. It has close ties with the LABOUR PARTY which it helped to establish and for which it is the principal source of funds.

trade union, association of employees, formed for the purpose of progressing and safeguarding its members' interests in connection with benefits, wages and working conditions, by collective bargaining with an employer.

Transkei, *see* APARTHEID.

trench warfare, military action in which opposing armies face each other in entrenched positions. In WWI, soon after the outbreak of war, both sides dug themselves into massive lines of trenches stretching along the whole of the Western Front. So strongly were these trenches defended (esp. by machine guns) that attacking infantry could generally only capture them after enormous loss of life, which meant that much of the fighting on the Western Front resulted in a stalemate.

Trianon, Treaty of (1920), Allied peace settlement with Hungary after WWI which resulted in the transfer of two-thirds of Hungary's prewar population and territory to Austria, Czechoslovakia, Italy, Poland, Romania and Yugoslavia. The Treaty also provided for REPARATIONS to be made and the army to be limited to 35,000 men.

Trieste, a port in NE Italy on the Gulf of Trieste at the head of the Adriatic Sea. Under Austrian rule (1382—1918) it became Italian after WWI despite Yugoslavian claims. At the end of WWII it was seized by TITO but this action was disputed by Allied troops. It was established as the Free Territory of Trieste (1947—54). In 1954 the city passed to Italy and its environs to Yugoslavia.

Triple Alliance, *see* CENTRAL POWERS.

Triple Entente (1914—17), alliance in WWI between Britain, France and Russia arising from 3 separate understandings developed in the period 1894—1907 to counterbalance the Triple Alliance (*see* CENTRAL POWERS). These were the Franco-Russian Alliance (1894), the ENTENTE CORDIALE between the UK and France (1904), and the ANGLO-RUSSIAN ENTENTE (1907). The first of these agreements was for joint mobilization if the Triple Alliance mobilized, and that if either state was attacked by Germany alone or with an ally then the other would provide all possible military aid. The second and third agreements coupled to the first ensured collective response by the signatories should there be trouble with the Triple Alliance. Russia left the Alliance in 1917 following the Bolshevik Revolution.

Trotsky, Leon, orig. Lev Davidovich Bronstein (1879—1940), Russian politician and revolutionary. He spent many years in exile, returning to take part in the unsuccessful 1905 Russian Revolution. After another period in exile he returned to Russia (1917), joined the Bolsheviks, and played a leading role in their seizure of power.

He became Commissar for Foreign Affairs (1917—18), and as Commissar for War (1918—25), he raised the Red Army and was largely responsible for its success in the civil war (1918—20).

After Lenin's death, STALIN undermined Trotsky's authority and gained control of Party administration. Trotsky was deprived of all his offices, expelled from the Communist Party (1927) and exiled (1929), but continued to agitate, intrigue and condemn Stalin's autocratic ambitions. He was credited with organizing, in conjunction with foreign powers, a vast plot to overthrow the Soviet regime, was sentenced to death in his absence (1937), and assassinated by a Soviet agent in Mexico City (1940).

Trudeau, Pierre (1919—), Canadian Liberal statesman. He was Minister of Justice and Attorney General (1967—68) and PM (1968—79, and 1980—84).

Truman, Harry S. (1884—1972), US Democratic Vice-President (1945), who became President (1945—53) following the death of President Roosevelt. He attended the POTSDAM CONFERENCE with Churchill and Stalin, and his decision to drop atomic bombs on Japan ended WWII. He played a leading role in the establishment of the UN and of NATO. He was responsible for the implementation of the MARSHALL PLAN, and altered US policy towards the USSR (see TRUMAN DOCTRINE) following the WWII alliance. In the KOREAN WAR he despatched troops to aid South Korea as part of the UN contingent, and after public disagreement he dismissed General MacArthur from command of the UN forces in Korea. Having served for 2 terms, he did not seek re-election in 1952.

Truman Doctrine, policy expounded by President TRUMAN in a message to Congress in 1947 stating that the USA should be committed 'to support free peoples who are resisting attempted subjugation by armed minorities or by outside pressures'. The message was in support of his request for economic and military aid to Greece and Turkey to help them withstand Communist subversive pressures, and signalled a change to all-out anti-Communism by the Truman Administration with the onset of the COLD WAR. The MARSHALL PLAN (proposed in 1947) put into practice the Doctrine's objectives.

TUC, *see* TRADES UNION CONGRESS.

Tunisia, republic of N Africa, on the Mediterranean. Area: 164,150 sq km. Pop: 6,513,000 (1981). Languages: Arabic and French. Religion: mostly Islam. Cap: Tunis.

Ruled by Carthage until 2nd cent., it became a Roman province before passing to the Berbers then Turkey. Occupied by France (1881) it gained independence in 1955 under BOURGUIBA. Economic restraint in the 1970s led to political unrest and an attempt, aided by Libya, to destabilize the country. Tunisia concluded special treaties with the EEC in 1969 and 1976, and the latter was renegotiated in 1982.

Turkey, republic of SE Europe and W Asia. Area: 779,452 sq km. Pop: 45,218,000. Language: Turkish. Religion: officially a secular state, but most of the population follow Islam. Cap: Ankara.

From the 14th cent. Turkey had ruled the extensive OTTOMAN EMPIRE. In 1914 Turkey joined the CENTRAL POWERS and after its defeat in WWI, the Empire disintegrated (*see* SÈVRES, TREATY OF).

A war of independence (1919—22) was fought in which ATATÜRK was successful in repelling a Greek invasion and in overthrowing the Sultanate, and in 1923 he proclaimed the country a republic. At the Treaty of LAUSANNE, the new republic succeeded in revising the terms dictated at Sèvres. After Atatürk's death, his former PM, Ismet Inönü (1884—1974) became President (1938—50), continuing Atatürk's transformation of Turkey into a modern state, and introducing beneficial political reforms.

Subsequently Turkey joined NATO but has undergone a succession of civil and military governments, coups and periods of martial law, and even the widely supported invasion of CYPRUS (1974) failed to overcome this instability. There has been political and religious turmoil with left and right erupting into violence. Shiites endeavouring to impose their fundamentalist Islamic doctrine, Armenians and Kurds trying to achieve autonomy, and economic problems compounded by severe inflationary pressures. Turkey has applied to join the EEC.

U

U-2 Incident (1960), name given to the shooting down by the Russians of a US Lockheed U-2 high-altitude photographic reconnaissance aircraft over the Soviet city of Sverdlovsk. The pilot, Francis Gary Powers, was captured and confessed to being on an espionage operation. Similar missions had been going on for several years without Soviet protest, but this time Khrushchev demanded an apology from President Eisenhower at the Paris summit conference a fortnight later, and when it was not forthcoming withdrew from the meeting. Thereafter such flights ceased and Powers was exchanged for a Soviet spy (1962).

UAR, *see* EGYPT.

U-boats, German submarines, used effectively in WWI and WWII to put economic pressure on Britain by sinking large numbers of merchant ships carrying vital food and other supplies. *See* ATLANTIC, BATTLE OF THE.

UDI, *see* ZIMBABWE.

UK, *see* UNITED KINGDOM.

Ulbricht, Walter (1893–1973), East German Communist politician. He went into exile (1933–45) on Hitler's rise to power, spending most of it in the USSR. On returning to Germany he had by 1950 become deputy PM of the GDR and Party Secretary-General. He was chairman of the Council of State (1960–71) and the country's virtual dictator, believing in Stalinist repressive measures without resorting to the drastic enforcement practices of the USSR. He was responsible for the building of the Berlin Wall (1961), and influential in urging the Warsaw Pact invasion of Czechoslovakia (1968).

Ulster, *see* NORTHERN IRELAND.

Ulster Loyalists, those Protestants who desire to maintain Northern Ireland's link with the British Isles. Many Loyalists are members of the ORANGE ORDER and the majority are represented by the Ulster Unionist Party, the largest political entity in the province.

The Party was the ruling body of Stormont, the Northern Ireland parliament (1921–72), until direct rule was imposed by the UK government. This, together with demands for reform and tensions caused by the violence, were factors in the Party splitting into differing groups operating under various new party labels.

Although the Party has been weakened by the schism, all the splinter factions retain the basic desire of maintaining union with the UK, in opposition to such Catholic nationalist movements as the Social Democratic and Labour Party and Sinn Fein, which desire a united Ireland.

UN, *see* UNITED NATIONS ORGANIZATION.

UNCTAD, *see* UNITED NATIONS COMMISSION FOR TRADE AND DEVELOPMENT.

underground movements, *see* RESISTANCE MOVEMENTS, MAQUIS, PARTISAN.

unemployment, (a) condition of being out of work or unemployed; (b) the fluctuating number of an area's or country's working population unemployed at a specific time.

UNESCO, *see* UNITED NATIONS EDUCATIONAL, SCIENTIFIC AND CULTURAL ORGANIZATION.

UNHCR, *see* UNITED NATIONS HIGH COMMISSIONER FOR REFUGEES.

UNICEF, *see* UNITED NATIONS INTERNATIONAL CHILDREN'S EMERGENCY FUND.

unification, process of uniting or joining together by states or parts of divided nations, usually for mutual defence, economic or political benefit, and arising out of nationalist sentiments.

unilateral declaration of independence, *see* ZIMBABWE.

unilateralism, *see* DISARMAMENT, and CAMPAIGN FOR NUCLEAR DISARMAMENT.

Unionist Party, *see* ULSTER LOYALISTS.

Union of Soviet Socialist Republics (USSR), Communist federal republic of E Europe and N Asia. Area: 22,400,000 sq km. Pop: 273,843,000 (1984). Languages: Russian and many national minority languages. Religion: Eastern Orthodox and many minority religions, but the major part of the population is atheist. Cap: Moscow.

The Union comprises 15 republics and is governed by the Supreme Soviet consisting of 2 chambers (the Soviet of the Union and the Soviet of Nationalities) with equal legislative rights and elected for a 5-year term. The highest executive and administrative body is the Council of Ministers, appointed by the Supreme Soviet. Between sessions of the Supreme Soviet the state authority is the Presidium, accountable for all its activities to the Supreme Soviet, which elects its membership. In reality, considerable power is vested in the leadership of the Communist Party.

Prior to 1917 Russia was ruled by the autocratic Tsar NICHOLAS II. He failed to implement political reforms, and did little either to remedy the terrible poverty resulting from poor harvests and industrial unrest, or to revitalize the state after the humiliating defeat inflicted in the RUSSO-JAPANESE WAR. Widespread unrest with his rule led to the RUSSIAN REVOLUTIONS, the first of which was suppressed in 1905.

Russia's alliance with SERBIA took it into WWI following the SARAJEVO incident (1914), and it was immediately joined by France and Britain (*see* TRIPLE ENTENTE and ANGLO-RUSSIAN ENTENTE). Military defeat and worsening conditions at home led to the Revolutions of 1917. After the February Revolution the Tsar abdicated, and following the Bolshevik October Revolution led by LENIN, the Communists came to power, making peace with Germany at BREST-LITOVSK. Civil war broke out, but in 1920 the Communist forces under TROTSKY were victorious. The USSR was established in 1923.

Following disturbances and riots Lenin introduced the NEW ECONOMIC POLICY (NEP) in 1921, modifying Communist practice. Lenin began the process of turning the USSR into a totalitarian dictatorship, ruthlessly eliminating all opposition, a process continued after his death (1924) by STALIN (*see* PURGE). In 1928 Stalin initiated the first of the FIVE-YEAR PLANS, which introduced rapid industrialization and the COLLECTIVIZATION of agriculture.

Following the signing of the NAZI-SOVIET PACT (1939), the USSR and Germany invaded Poland, so precipitating WWII. In 1941 Germany attacked the USSR, but at the cost of millions of lives the Germans were eventually driven back across E Europe and defeated.

In the countries of E Europe liberated by the Red Army, the Soviets set up Communist governments and have subsequently maintained these as satellite states, allied militarily in the WARSAW PACT and economically in the COUNCIL FOR MUTUAL ECONOMIC ASSISTANCE. Attempts to break away from the Soviet bloc have led to Soviet military intervention, as in HUNGARY (1956) and CZECHOSLOVAKIA (1968).

WWII was followed by the COLD WAR between the Soviet bloc and the West, arising out of ideological differences and mutual suspicion, and coming to a climax in the KOREAN WAR (1950–53). The Cold War abated somewhat following Stalin's death and KHRUSHCHEV'S denunciation of Stalin in 1956, but has flared up again from time to time, notably with the CUBAN MISSILES CRISIS (1962). Khrushchev was deposed in 1964 by BREZHNEV and KOSYGIN. The 1970s were marked by attempts at DÉTENTE between East and West, culminating in the STRATEGIC ARMS LIMITATION TALKS, but following the Soviet invasion of AFGHANISTAN (1979) a Cold War atmosphere returned, along with a resumption of the arms race. The USSR's relations with Communist China also deteriorated, a process starting in the 1950s (*see* SINO-SOVIET SPLIT).

Domestically, since Stalin's death the repressive nature of the state apparatus has become less harsh, but the country is still lacking in basic freedoms and life remains shadowed by secret police activities (*see* SOVIET SECURITY SERVICE). Shortages of food, housing and consumer goods are largely due to the inefficiencies of a centrally controlled economy encumbered by a vast and often corrupt bureaucracy. The advent of GORBACHEV (1985) has seen unprecedented (though still cautious) moves towards social, political and economic reform. (*see* GLASNOST and PERESTROIKA), together with improved relations with the West.

United Arab Republic, *see* EGYPT.

United Kingdom of Great Britain and Northern Ireland (UK), monarchy of W Europe. Area: 244,027 sq km. Pop: 55,776,000 (1981). Language: English. Religion: Protestant, RC. Cap: London. The UK incl. England, Scotland, Wales and Northern Ireland but excludes the Channel Islands and the Isle of Man which are Crown dependencies with their own legislative and taxation systems.

Legislative power is vested in PARLIAMENT, but the Sovereign has to give royal assent to bills before they become Acts of Parliament and law. The House of Commons is elected by universal suffrage for a 5-year term and can only be convened and dissolved by the Sovereign.

Much information on the UK's history will be found under the entries for individual PMs, a list of whom is given below. This is followed by a brief survey of the main currents of British history in the 20th cent.

British Prime Ministers 1902–80
Balfour (Con.) 1902
Campbell-Bannerman (Lib.) 1905

Asquith (Lib.) 1908
Asquith (Coalition) 1915
Lloyd George (Coalition) 1916
Law (Con.) 1922
Baldwin (Con.) 1923
MacDonald (Lab.) 1924
Baldwin (Con.) 1924
MacDonald (Lab.) 1929
MacDonald (National) 1931
Baldwin (National) 1935
Chamberlain (National) 1937
Churchill (Coalition) 1940
Attlee (Lab.) 1945
Churchill (Con.) 1951
Eden (Con.) 1955
Macmillan (Con.) 1957
Douglas-Home (Con.) 1963
Wilson (Lab.) 1964
Heath (Con.) 1970
Wilson (Lab.) 1974
Callaghan (Lab.) 1976
Thatcher (Con.) 1979

1900—18 At the beginning of the 20th cent. the UK was at the height of its power, governing the biggest empire the world has ever seen, and leading the world in trade and industry. Domestically, conditions were still very bad for the working classes, a situation that gave rise to the foundation of the LABOUR PARTY, which was to challenge the traditional pre-eminence of the LIBERAL and CONSERVATIVE PARTIES.

The pre-WWI years were marked at home by the reforms of Asquith's Liberal government, incl. old-age pensions, national insurance, and the

PARLIAMENT ACT. Agitation for WOMEN'S SUFFRAGE increased, and some women were eventually given the vote in 1918. Tensions in the Empire incl. the BOER WAR and pressure for Home Rule in IRELAND. In foreign affairs, the period saw the establishment of alliances in Europe (*see* ENTENTE CORDIALE and ANGLO-RUSSIAN ENTENTE) and the growth of imperial, economic and military rivalry with Germany that came to a head in WWI.

1918–45 The post-WWI years were marked at home by the first Labour government (1924), the GENERAL STRIKE (1926), and the Depression and mass unemployment of the 1930s. All adults over the age of 21 were given the vote by 1928. Southern Ireland was granted independence, and agitation for independence in INDIA grew throughout this period. The STATUTE OF WESTMINSTER (1931) gave legal authority to the legislative independence of Canada, Newfoundland, the Irish Free State, South Africa, Australia and New Zealand. The UK was founder-member of the LEAGUE OF NATIONS, but in the 1930s followed a policy of APPEASEMENT towards Italian and German aggression, which culminated in WWII.

1945–85 The successful conclusion of WWII was hastened by the involvement of the USA and the USSR, which in the postwar years established themselves as the world's 2 superpowers, eclipsing the UK's world position. As the developed world split between East and West powerblocs, the UK aligned itself with the USA, becoming a founder-member of NATO and the UN. The UK's decline in the international sphere has not been without its traumas, such as the SUEZ CRISIS (1956).

The process of DECOLONIZATION began in 1947 with the granting of independence to India and Pakistan, and by the mid-1960s the UK had granted independence to most of its larger colonies (*see also* COMMONWEALTH). The UK now looked more towards Europe, and after 2 unsuccessful attempts, eventually joined the EEC in 1973. In NORTHERN IRELAND, sectarian violence erupted in the late 1960s, and as yet no political solution has been found.

At home, the postwar Labour government extended the WELFARE STATE along the lines suggested in the BEVERIDGE REPORT, and began the NATIONALIZATION of many industries. The Conservative Party has opposed nationalization, believing in free enterprise, and when in government has denationalized several industries. The result has been a mixed economy (with both publicly owned and privately owned sectors), akin to that of most other Western nations. Arguments between the Parties also continue over private healthcare and private education, which are supported by the Conservatives and opposed by Labour.

The UK's possession of nuclear weapons has provided another major area of debate. The Conservatives have consistently supported their possession by the UK, arguing that to fall again into the appeasement policies of the 1930s could well lead the country into another war, and that the nuclear deterrent has maintained peace in Europe since WWII. Labour has varied in its attitude, sometimes agreeing with the Conservatives (it was a Labour government that ordered the development of the UK's first atomic bombs), and at other times holding a unilateral stance, believing that nuclear weapons should be banned from the country because they increase the risk of the UK's involvement in a nuclear war. *See also* DISARMAMENT.

One of the major problems the UK has faced over the last 30 years is racial integration, with the immigration from the Commonwealth turning the UK into a multiracial society with the problems inherent in a variety of different cultures.

United Nations, *see* UNITED NATIONS ORGANIZATION.

United Nations Conference on Trade Development (UNCTAD), organization with HQ in Geneva, established (1964) and comprising the Trade and Development Board and 4 committees responsible for matters relative to their titles. The Board meets biannually and its committees on Commodities, Manufacturing, Shipping, and Invisibles and Finances Related to Trade meet annually. The Conference convenes every 4 years to consider and pass judgement on the Board's activities.

United Nations Educational, Scientific and Cultural Organization (UNESCO), agency with HQ in Paris, established (1945) to promote collaboration in the spheres of communications, culture, education and science, and to develop universal respect for justice, the rule of law and human rights without distinction of language, race, religion or sex.

United Nations High Commissioner for Refugees (UNHCR), agency with HQ in

Geneva, established (1951) to provide international protection for refugees, and to seek permanent solutions to their problems through voluntary repatriation, resettlement in other countries or integration into the country of present residence. It was awarded the Nobel Peace Prize (1955).

United Nations International Children's Emergency Fund (UNICEF), organization with HQ in New York established (1946) to aid child health and welfare projects in countries afflicted by the ravages of WWII. Since 1950 its functions have been extended to assist the expansion of maternal and child health services and educational and vocational training schemes in developing countries. The Fund relies for financial assistance on voluntary contributions from individuals and UN member governments. It was awarded the Nobel Peace Prize (1965).

United Nations Organization (UNO), association of states with HQ in New York, established (1945) as successor to the LEAGUE OF NATIONS and arising out of conferences held during WWII at Moscow, DUMBARTON OAKS, YALTA and San Francisco. It's objectives are the maintenance of peace and security and the promotion of international welfare by economic, political and social means. Membership totals 157.

There are 6 principal organs: the General Assembly, the Security Council, the Economic and Social Council, the Trusteeship Council (*see* MANDATES), the INTERNATIONAL COURT OF JUSTICE, and the Secretariat. The Assembly consists of all members, and its work is divided between several committees. The Security Council is the executive organ of the UN and has 15 members, 10 of which are elected for a 2-year term, and 5 of which are permanent – the People's Republic of China, France, the UK, the USA and the USSR, each of which has the right to veto any resolution of which it disapproves. The chief administrative officer is the Secretary-General who is appointed for 5 years by the Assembly on the recommendation of the Council. The Secretary-Generals have incl. LIE (1945–52), HAMMARSKJÖLD (1953–61), THANT (1961–72), WALDHEIM (1972–82), and Javier Perez de Cuellar (1982–   ).

Unlike the League of Nations, the UN has the power to call for military action by its members, as well as the power to impose SANCTIONS. As an arbiter of international disputes, the UN has had a limited success, e.g. in the ARAB-ISRAELI WARS, the KOREAN WAR, in the Congo Crisis, and in Cyprus.

The UN has a large number of specialized agencies, incl. GENERAL AGREEMENT ON TARIFFS AND TRADE, INTERNATIONAL BANK FOR RECONSTRUCTION AND DEVELOPMENT, INTERNATIONAL LABOUR ORGANIZATION, INTERNATIONAL MONETARY FUND, UNITED NATIONS CONFERENCE ON TRADE AND DEVELOPMENT, UNITED NATIONS EDUCATIONAL, SCIENTIFIC AND CULTURAL ORGANIZATION, UNITED NATIONS HIGH COMMISSIONER FOR REFUGEES, UNITED NATIONS INTERNATIONAL CHILDREN'S EMERGENCY FUND, UNITED NATIONS RELIEF AND REHABILITATION ADMINISTRATION, UNITED NATIONS RELIEF AND WORKS AGENCY, WORLD HEALTH ORGANIZATION.

United Nations Relief and Works Agency (UNRWA), organization with HQ in Vienna, established (1950) for the resettlement of Palestinian Arab refugees and the provision of relief services and work opportunities for them. The refugees mostly live in camps in the Gaza Strip, Jordan, Lebanon and Syria and funds are primarily provided by Canada, Sweden, West Germany, the UK and the USA.

United States of America (USA), federal republic of N America. Area: 3,543,883 sq km. Pop: 231,107,000. Language: English. Religion: Protestant and RC. Cap: Washington DC.

The Union of 50 states and the District of Columbia is governed by CONGRESS, the legislative body. The President and Vice-President are elected in the November of every leap year and take power the following January. Executive power is vested in the President who is also C-in-C of the armed forces. The DEMOCRATIC and REPUBLICAN PARTIES are the main political organizations from which the President, Vice-President and Congressional members are elected.

Much information on the USA's history will be found under entries for individual presidents, a list of whom is given below. This is followed by a brief survey of the main currents in US history in the 20th cent.

American Presidents 1901–80

T. Roosevelt (Rep.) 1901
Taft (Rep.) 1909
Wilson (Dem.) 1913
Harding (Rep.) 1921
Coolidge (Rep.) 1923

Hoover (Rep.) 1929
F.D. Roosevelt (Dem.) 1933
Truman (Dem.) 1945
Eisenhower (Rep.) 1953
Kennedy (Dem.) 1961
Johnson (Dem.) 1963
Nixon (Rep.) 1969
Ford (Rep.) 1974
Carter (Dem.) 1977
Reagan (Rep.) 1981

1900—45 By the turn of the century the USA was beginning to establish itself as one of the world's leading industrial nations, but in world affairs it followed a policy of ISOLATIONISM which kept it out of WWI until 1917, when it was prompted to declare war on Germany by the ZIMMERMAN TELEGRAM and the unrestricted U-boat campaign (*see* LUSITANIA). After WWI the USA reverted to an isolationist policy, refusing to join the LEAGUE OF NATIONS and failing to ratify the Treaty of VERSAILLES.

The War was followed by an economic boom but this collapsed with the WALL STREET CRASH (1929). President Roosevelt's NEW DEAL did much to alleviate the problems of the Depression and mass unemployment that followed in the 1930s.

The USA did little to deter the growth of Fascism in Europe and only entered WWII because of the Japanese attacks on PEARL HARBOUR (1941). However, US involvement ensured the eventual Allied victory, after which the USA and the USSR became established as the world's superpowers.

1945—85 Since 1945 the USA has abandoned isolationism in favour of militant opposition to

Communist expansion, enshrined in the TRUMAN DOCTRINE. WWII was followed by the COLD WAR between the West and the Soviet bloc, leading to US involvement in the BERLIN airlift, the KOREAN and VIETNAM WARS, the CUBAN MISSILES CRISIS, and the growth of military alliances such as NATO. A period of DÉTENTE with the USSR began in the late 1960s, marked by the STRATEGIC ARMS LIMITATION TALKS, but following the Soviet invasion of AFGHANISTAN (1979), a Cold War atmosphere returned. Since 1985, relations with the USSR have improved again to a limited degree.

At home, the early 1950s saw anti-Communist feelings at their height in McCARTHYISM. The 1960s were marked by a series of CIVIL RIGHTS ACTS aimed at eliminating racial discrimination, and also social reforms intended to alleviate domestic poverty. The US economy is largely free enterprise, and there is a strong tradition of opposition to government interference, combined with a belief in self-help that tends to oppose government welfare provisions.

UNO, *see* UNITED NATIONS ORGANIZATION.

UNRWA, *see* UNITED NATIONS RELIEF AND WORKS AGENCY.

USA, *see* UNITED STATES OF AMERICA.

USSR, *see* UNION OF SOVIET SOCIALIST REPUBLICS.

U Thant, *see* THANT, U.

V

Verdun, Battle of (1916), WWI engagement which raged for most of the year around the fortress town of Verdun in NE France. Enormous casualties were suffered by both sides but after initial German gains, the French under Pétan recaptured most of the lost ground, assisted by diversionary attacks launched by the British on the SOMME and the Russians on the Eastern Front.

Versailles, Treaty of (1919), settlement concluded at the end of WWI between the Allied powers and Germany at the Paris Peace Conference.

Germany lost some 10% of its population with 12½% of its territory, incl. ALSACE-LORRAINE to France, and parts of East Prussia and Upper Silesia to Poland (*see also* DANZIG). Germany's overseas possessions became MANDATES of the LEAGUE OF NATIONS, whose covenant was incl. in the Treaty. The union of Austria and Germany (ANSCHLUSS) was prohibited, the SAARLAND was to be occupied by French troops and the RHINELAND was to be demilitarized and occupied by Allied forces. Germany was prohibited from manufacturing heavy armaments, military service was abolished, and the armed forces were to be limited in equipment and manpower. Provisions was made for the trial of German war leaders incl. Kaiser Wilhelm II (though these never took place), and Germany was obliged to accept guilt for causing the war. German waterways were to be internationalized, and severe REPARATIONS were imposed.

The loss of territory, manpower and control of waterways restricted Germany's ability to pay the reparations, and means were found of circumventing the disarmament clauses. The bitterness and frustration caused by the imposition of the Treaty helped to foster a resurgence of NATIONALISM and the ultimate rise to power of HITLER. Hitler repudiated the terms of the Treaty, and his attempt to recover the territory lost to Poland was a direct cause of WWII.

Verwoerd, Hendrik Frensch (1901–66), South African politician. A member of the Nationalist Party, he opposed South Africa's entry into WWII. As Minister of Native Affairs (1950–58) he was able to put into practice his uncompromising belief in the principles of APARTHEID. He was elected leader of the Party and PM (1958–66), devoting himself to making the country a republic, which he succeeded in doing when South Africa left the Commonwealth (1961). He was assassinated in the House of Assembly by a Portuguese East African.

Vichy Government (1940–44), French semi-Fascist administration set up after the fall of France in WWII. It took its name from the town in the unoccupied centre of the country where it was established by PÉTAIN, its other prominent leaders being DARLAN and LAVAL. After the armistice with Germany, it terminated the Third Republic, introduced anti-Semitic legislation, banned strikes, dissolved trade unions, and introduced regimented organization of agricultural and industrial workers. When Germany occupied the whole country

(1942) the Government became openly collaborationist, connived in the despatch of forced labour to Germany and acquiesced in the plunder of the nation's resources. It was opposed by the FREE FRENCH and by underground resistence movements.

Victor Emmanuel III (1869–1947), King of Italy (1900–46). In defiance of the wishes of Parliament he took Italy into WWI on the Allied side (1915), and appointed MUSSOLINI as PM (1922). Mussolini made him Emperor of Abyssinia (1936) and King of Albania (1939), but during the Fascist regime he was little more than a constitutional puppet, although he was assertive enough to dismiss Mussolini when the Allied victory in WWII became obvious (1943). He abdicated in 1946 and died in exile in Egypt.

Viet Cong, name given in the 1960s and 1970s to the Communist-led armed forces of the Front for the Liberation of South Vietnam. In the VIETNAM WAR they waged a guerrilla campaign against the South Vietnamese regime and US forces, and were supported and increasingly controlled by the Communist regime in North Vietnam.

Viet Minh, the Revolutionary League for the Independence of Vietnam, a political movement founded (1941) by the Indo-Chinese Communist Party in North VIETNAM to resist the Japanese attack on Indo-China in WWII. It operated with the Workers' Party and the army in expelling the French from the country and its authority N of the 17th parallel of longitude (i.e. in North Vietnam) was recognized by the 1954 Geneva Agreements. The movement's leading members were HO CHI

MINH, Pham Van Dong and Vo Nguyen Giap.
Vietnam, republic of SE Asia. Area: 329,566
sq km. Pop: 60,000,000 (est. 1984). Language:
Vietnamese. Religion: Taoism and Buddhism. Cap:
Hanoi.

The country was established (1949) by the
merger of Annam, Cochin China and Tonkin,
formerly parts of INDO-CHINA. After a war of
independence led by HO CHI MINH the French were
finally defeated at DIEN BIEN PHU, and Vietnam
became independent from France (1954) although
divided at the 17th parallel of latitude into North
and South as a result of agreements reached at
Geneva.

The country remained divided until 1975 when
the Communist North prevailed over the South
(backed by the USA) after US forces withdrew from
the VIETNAM WAR. The unified country has been a
Communist state since 1976, has joined the
COUNCIL FOR MUTUAL ECONOMIC ASSISTANCE and
signed a 25-year treaty of friendship and cooperation with the USSR. These moves, coupled with
the Vietnamese invasion and military domination
of KAMPUCHEA (Cambodia), have exacerbated
relations with China and tension remains high
with border clashes involving minor invasions and
counter-invasions.

Vietnam War, conflict in SE Asia fought between
the US-backed anti-Communist forces of South
Vietnam and the VIET CONG, who were supported
by North Vietnam's Communist forces and Soviet
armaments.

Since the partition of VIETNAM in 1954,
Communists in the South had waged a guerrilla

campaign to reunify the country, and in 1961 the USA began economic and military aid to the South to frustrate the spread of Communism in the region. An attack on the US destroyer *Maddox* in the Gulf of Tonkin by North Vietnamese torpedo boats (1964) prompted the USA to launch retaliatory air raids on naval bases and oil refineries in the North. Following increased Viet Cong activity, President Johnson ordered a huge build-up of US forces in South Vietnam (from 1965), which in turn led to more direct involvement by North Vietnamese forces. Australia, the Philippines, South Korea and Thailand also sent troop contingents to aid the South.

North Vietnamese successes in the Tet Offensive (1968), together with cessation of US bombing of the North and growing opposition to the war in the USA, encouraged both sides to begin negotiations at the PARIS PEACE TALKS. However, bitter fighting continued, spreading to neighbouring Laos and Cambodia (KAMPUCHEA), and US bombing of the North was resumed. Eventually in 1973 a peace agreement was made in Paris. All US forces were withdrawn by 1975, resulting in the occupation of the South by the Communists and the reunification of Vietnam. The USA thus experienced the ignominy of a disastrous and expensive military defeat, and witnessed the failure of its Communist containment policy.

Vishinsky, see VYSHINSKI.

Vorster, Balthazar Johannes (1915–83), South African politician. He was interned (1942–43) during WWII because of his involvement in a Fascist Afrikaner movement. He joined the

Nationalist Party and became Minister of Justice (1961−66), Party Leader and PM (1966−78), and President (1978−79). He subscribed to APARTHEID policies, intensifying repressive measures against blacks and coloureds, but received overwhelming support for his actions from the white electorate.

Vyshinski or **Vishinsky, Andrei** (1883−1954), Soviet politician. He was the hard-line prosecutor of the show trials of the 1930s (*see* PURGE). He became Deputy Foreign Minister (1940−49 and 1953−55), permanent delegate to the UN (1945−49 and 1953−54), and Foreign Minister (1949−53), in which roles he played a prominent part in the policies of the COLD WAR.

W

Waldheim, Kurt (1918–   ), Austrian diplomat. He was Foreign Minister (1968–70), and UN Secretary-General (1972–82). He was elected to the Austrian presidency (1986).

Walesa, Lech, *see* SOLIDARITY.

Wall Street Crash (1929), financial collapse of the US economy, which experienced an artificial BOOM in the 1920s caused by wild speculation on the stock market. Doubt about the security of certain major business enterprises caused panic selling to develop on the New York Stock Exchange (sited in Wall Street), and millions of shares changed hands in 4 days. Banks and businesses failed, unemployment rose rapidly to c. 17 million, and there was commercial recession throughout the country which eventually spread to Europe, causing the DEPRESSION of the early 1930s. This in turn contributed to the rise of FASCISM, and eventually to WWII.

war crimes, acts committed in wartime by civilians or members of the armed services in violation of the accepted customs and rules of war, e.g. as set out in the GENEVA CONVENTION. After WWII many German Nazi leaders were convicted of war crimes and 'crimes against peace and humanity' at the Nuremberg Trials (1945–46) by an Allied military tribunal, several being sentenced to death. Japan's war leaders were also convicted in similar trials in Tokyo.

Warsaw Pact, technically the Eastern European
Mutual Assistance Treaty (1955), signed in Warsaw by Albania, Bulgaria, Czechoslovakia, East
Germany, Hungary, Poland, Romania and the
USSR. The Pact was signed following West
Germany's entry into NATO. It established a
unified military command with each country
undertaking to refrain from using, or threatening to
use, force in its international relationships, and to
give immediate assistance by all means it might
consider necessary to any member subject to attack
in Europe. It also pledged its members to work for a
general reduction in armaments and the outlawing
of nuclear weapons, and to respect each other's
independence and sovereignty by non-intervention
in internal affairs. Albania was excluded from the
Pact's activities in 1961, and withdrew in 1968
following the invasion of Czechoslovakia.

Washington Conference (1921–22), international assembly held with the objective of
arranging reductions in naval armaments and the
relaxation of tension in the Far East. The participating countries were Belgium, China, France,
Italy, Japan, the Netherlands, Portugal, the UK
and the USA.

A complex set of agreements was reached incl. a
collective guarantee of China's independence; the
continuance of the 1899 Open-Door Policy, a
system for China's economic development whereby
the political unity and independence of the country
were assured and all nations guaranteed equal
commercial and tariff rights there; a Japanese
pledge for the eventual return to China of the bay of
Jiaozhou taken by them from Germany (1914)

which had leased it from China (1897); the resolve by the UK and the USA not to strengthen naval bases between, and incl., Hawaii and Singapore; a guarantee by France, Japan, the UK and the USA of each other's existing Pacific possessions; and a naval convention of which all the states undertook to refrain from building capital ships for 10 years, coupled with the establishment of capital ship ratios between France, Italy, Japan, the UK and the USA.

Watergate Affair, incident during the US 1972 presidential election campaign when agents employed by President Nixon's re-election organization were caught breaking into the Democratic Party's HQ in the Watergate Building, Washington, DC. The subsequent scandal was exacerbated by attempts to conceal the fact that senior White House officials had approved the burglary. Eventually the President was implicated in the cover-up and was forced to resign (1974).

Wehrmacht, the armed services of the German Third Reich (1935–45).

Weimar Republic (1919–33), name given to the post-WWI German republic from the town where the National Constituent Assembly met after Kaiser Wilhelm II's abdication. Its constitution, characterized by centralized and socialist tendencies, provided for bicameral government, proportional representation, a 7-year presidential term of office, and federal rights.

The Republic suffered from economic problems caused by the aftermath of WWI and REPARATIONS. The DAWES PLAN was a temporary palliative, but the DEPRESSION after 1929 led to mass unemployment and a worsening of the economic

situation, and paved the way for the advance of the
Nazi Party, which came to power in 1933 and
introduced a new constitution.

Weizmann, Chaim (1874–1952), Israeli
statesman. He played a major part in securing the
BALFOUR DECLARATION. The plight of East
European Jewry determined him to fight for a
Jewish homeland in PALESTINE, using the Declaration as a springboard. He was President of the
World Zionist Organization (1920–30 and
1935–46) and of the Jewish Agency in Palestine
from 1929. On the formation of the state of Israel
(1948) he became its first President, an office he
held until his death.

Welensky, Sir Roy (1907–   ), Rhodesian
statesman. He founded the Northern Rhodesia
Labour Party (1938), and on the formation of the
Federation of RHODESIA AND NYASALAND, towards
which he played a leading part, he became Minister
of Transport and Communications (1953–56)
and PM (1956–63). When the Federation was
dissolved, white Rhodesians forsook his Party in
favour of Ian Smith's Rhodesian Front, and
although he supported the Front's opposition to a
trade boycott, he was against the Unilateral Declaration of Independence (1965).

welfare state, system by which a government
undertakes prime responsibility for the economic
and social wellbeing of the population by such
means as unemployment insurance, pensions of
various kinds, health services, and housing. *See also*
BEVERIDGE REPORT.

West Bank, that part of Jordan to the W of the
River Jordan occupied by Israel since the 1967

ARAB-ISRAELI WAR. The provision of the CAMP DAVID AGREEMENT (1978) that Israel should grant a degree of Palestinian autonomy in the West Bank has not been carried out, and instead the area has been increasingly settled by Israelis, who have also developed agricultural and industrial enterprises. This has led to acts of civil disobedience, rioting and guerrilla activities by the PLO and the indigenous Arab population.

Western European Union (WEU), organization established (1955) to supercede the Brussels Treaty Organization, a military alliance formed in 1948 with the same membership as the WEU apart from Italy and West Germany. Its members are Belgium, France, Italy, Luxembourg, the Netherlands, the UK and West Germany. The foreign ministers form a Council, and there is an Assembly of representatives of the WEU in the Consultative Assembly of the COUNCIL OF EUROPE, and an Armaments Control Agency which operates in conjunction with NATO. The Union's objectives are cooperation on cultural, economic, military and social matters.

West Germany, *see* GERMANY.

Westminster, Statute of, *see* STATUTE OF WESTMINSTER.

WEU, *see* WESTERN EUROPEAN UNION.

White House, the official Washington residence of the US President. The term is also used for the President and his executive.

white supremacy, theory based on the supposition that white races are inherently superior to other races, esp. negroes, a view inherent in the APARTHEID policies of South Africa.

WHO, *see* WORLD HEALTH ORGANIZATION.

Wilhelm II (1859–1941) Emperor (*Kaiser*) of Germany (1888–1918). An arrogant and self-opinionated man, he had visions of German world domination and set out to strengthen the country's military and naval forces at the expense of trying to achieve harmonious relationships with Britain, France and Russia. Despite being a grandson of Queen Victoria, a personal hostility existed between him and his uncle, Edward VII. His actions and personality were contributory factors leading to WWI, in which, however, he was largely dominated by his military leaders. He abdicated 2 days before the armistice (1918) and went into exile in Holland.

Wilson, Sir Harold, Lord Wilson of Rievaulx and Emley (1916–   ), British Labour statesman, PM (1964–70 and 1974–76). In 1963 he was elected Leader of the Labour Party, and became PM in 1964, increasing Labour's majority in the 1966 election. His first premiership was marked by Rhodesian UDI and the rejection of the UK's second application to join the EEC. Both of his terms of office were marked by a difficult BALANCE OF PAYMENTS situation and by high inflation. From 1966 he attempted to deal with inflation by statutory restraints on prices and incomes, and from 1974 by the 'Social Contract' with the trade unions, aimed at a voluntary limitation on wage increases. He resigned in 1976 and was succeeded as PM by CALLAGHAN.

Wilson, Woodrow (1856–1924), US Democratic President (1913–21). He kept the US out of WWI until 1917 when the revelations of the ZIMMERMANN TELEGRAM and the unrestricted U-

BOAT campaign (*see* LUSITANIA), coupled with aroused public indignation, forced him to realize he could no longer keep the country out of hostilities.

His famous FOURTEEN POINTS were a peace programme for a new world order after WWI, but apart from the establishment of the LEAGUE OF NATIONS his ideas did not come to fruition. Isolationist sentiments returned in the USA, and Congress rejected the terms of the Treaty of VERSAILLES and refused membership of the League against Wilson's advice.

His administration introduced Prohibition (ban on alcoholic drink) and WOMEN'S SUFFRAGE in 1920, reorganized the federal banking system, and initiated anti-trust measures. He suffered a stroke (1919) which left him incapacitated for the rest of his life.

women's suffrage, the right of women to the franchise, i.e. to vote in public elections.

The chief British movement in support of this cause was the radical Women's Social and Political Union (WSPU) founded (1903) by Emmeline PANKHURST; its members became known as 'suffragettes'. As it grew rapidly in numbers and wealth so its members increasingly were imprisoned for attacks on property, refusal to pay taxes, and demonstrations. Many went on hunger strikes in prison and were forcibly fed. In a dramatic demonstration on behalf of 'votes for women', Emily Davidson threw herself in front of the King's horse running in the Derby and was killed (1913).

The fact that women took over what had been considered as 'men's work' during WWI, combined with intensifying political pressure, resulted in those over 30 being given the vote subject to educational and property qualifications (1918), and all women were granted the vote in 1928.

A moderate, non-violent, movement with the same objectives as the WSPU was the National Union of Women's Suffrage Societies (NUWSS) founded (1897) by Millicent Fawcett (1847–1929).

Emancipation of women in other parts of the world has had a varied progression spread over many decades, some countries granting women voting rights before Britain but most later, while some still withhold the franchise.

Wood, Edward Frederick Lindley, Baron Irwin and Earl of Halifax (1881–1959), British Conservative politician. He was appointed Viceroy of India (1926–31) at a time of unrest on the North-West Frontier. As Foreign Secretary (1938–40), he at first supported APPEASEMENT, but he played an important part in inducing Chamberlain to take a stronger line with the Germans after 1939. He was Ambassador to the USA (1941–46).

World Bank, *see* INTERNATIONAL BANK FOR RECONSTRUCTION AND DEVELOPMENT.

World Health Organization (WHO), UN agency with HQ in Geneva, established (1948) to develop international cooperation in the following areas: the control of diseases and drug addiction; medical research and drug evaluation; and environmental and family health resources, incl. education, nutrition, family planning, housing, sanitation and working conditions.

World War One (1914–18), conflict in which the Allied Powers, principally Britain, France, Russsia, (*see* TRIPLE ENTENTE), Serbia, Belgium, Japan, Italy (from 1915), Romania (from 1916) and the USA (from 1917) were engaged against the CENTRAL POWERS, principally Austria-Hungary, Germany, Turkey and Bulgaria (from 1915).

The causes leading to hostilities incl. economic and naval rivalry between the power blocs; the division of Europe into groups of alliances; the rivalry in the Balkans between Austro-Hungary and Russia culminating in the assassination of Archduke Franz Ferdinand at SARAJEVO and the subsequent Austro-Hungarian attack on Serbia; and German attacks on Russia and France and then Belgium, whose frontiers had been guaranteed by Britain.

The Western Front On land, the rapid German advance in the W was thwarted near Paris at the MARNE (1914) and was followed by prolonged stalemate with concentrated TRENCH WARFARE. Attempts to break the stalemate, e.g. at YPRES, VERDUN and the SOMME, only resulted in enormous loss of life and little territorial gain, despite the introduction of poison gas, tanks, and the development of aerial warfare, incl. the bombing of military and civilian targets. In the spring of 1918 the Germans launched a massive offensive which again took them close to Paris, but an Allied counter-offensive drove them back again.

Other European Fronts In the E, after the Germans stemmed the Russian advance at TANNENBERG (1914) no spectacular break-throughs were made by either side. Russia was less able to endure the exhaustion of men and materials, and opposition to the war contributed to the outbreak of the October Revolution (1917) after which the Bolsheviks arranged an armistice with Germany.

Fierce fighting also occurred in the Balkans, where Serbia was overrun until the Allied breakthrough of 1918, and on the Austro-Italian border, where there was largely stalemate until the Austrian victory at CAPORETTO (1917) and the successful Italian counter-offensive of 1918.

The Middle East In the Middle East, British and Imperial forces were eventually successful against the Turks in Palestine and Mesopotamia, and in Arabia T.E. LAWRENCE organized a revolt against the Turks. In 1915 the Allies launched the DARDANELLES Campaign to open the straits to Russia, but after prolonged fighting were repulsed by the Turks.

Naval Operations The war at sea was marked by large-scale naval battles (e.g. JUTLAND) and unrestricted German U-BOAT attacks against merchant shipping, which led to the introduction of the convoy system, and contributed to the USA's entry into the War in 1917 (*see* LUSITANIA). Eventually the Allies gained command of the seas and so were able to gain control of the German colonies in Africa and the Pacific.

The European land hostilities finally wore down German resistance, but at an enormous cost to both sides in men and materials, and it was these attritional battles rather than territorial advancement that enforced German capitulation. An armistice was signed in Nov. 1918, and at the PARIS PEACE CONFERENCE (1919), harsh terms were imposed on the defeated powers.

World War Two (1939—45), worldwide conflict between the Allied powers, principally the British Commonwealth, the USSR (from 1941), the USA (from 1941) and several European nations overrun by enemy forces, and the Axis powers of Germany, Italy (from 1940) and Japan (from 1941), supported by Bulgaria, Finland, Hungary and Romania.

The causes leading to hostilities incl. the failure of the WWI peace settlements; the aggressive expansionist policies of HITLER's Nazi Germany and Japan; the APPEASEMENT policies of France and the UK (*see* MUNICH AGREEMENT); and the isolationism pursued by the USA.

The Occupation of W Europe The NAZI-SOVIET PACT opened the way for Germany's invasion of Poland (1939) which prompted Britain and France to declare war on Germany. After a few months of PHONEY WAR, Germany's BLITZKREIG tactics rapidly overran Denmark, Norway, the Low Countries and France. The British Expeditionary Force was evacuated from France at DUNKIRK (1940), and Hitler stood poised to invade the UK, but was foiled by the defeat of his air force by the RAF in the Battle of BRITAIN. His use of massive aerial bombing of civilian and industrial targets (*see* BLITZ) failed to break British morale, and similar raids were carried out by the Allies with increasing intensity against Germany (and later Japan).

The Balkans, the Middle East and N Africa Italy invaded Greece in 1940 but was repulsed. In 1941 Germany overran Yugoslavia, Greece and Crete, and British troops took control in the Middle East to forestall attempts to capture the oilfields. In the

NORTH AFRICA CAMPAIGNS the fighting moved backwards and forwards across the deserts, but eventually Allied forces pushing W from Egypt joined US forces advancing E from Algeria (1943).

The Invasion of Italy In 1943 Allied forces invaded Italy from N Africa. Mussolini was overthrown and Italy joined the Allies. However, German forces entered the country and were only forced northwards after heavy fighting, eventually surrendering in 1945.

The Russian Campaign Hitler's invasion of the USSR in 1941 took German forces close to Moscow and LENINGRAD, and into the Caucasus and the Ukraine. The tide was turned with the Soviet victory at STALINGRAD (1942—43), after which Soviet forces forced the Germans back across E Europe, entering Germany in 1945.

The Liberation of W Europe British, Commonwealth and US forces invaded W Europe at the NORMANDY LANDINGS (1944). Progress was temporarily halted by the German ARDENNES OFFENSIVE (1944—45), but Allied troops advanced into Germany in 1945, linking up with Soviet forces. After the Russians entered Berlin, Hitler committed suicide and Germany surrendered unconditionally.

Naval Operations German U-BOATS, surface raiders and aircraft inflicted huge loses on Allied shipping. The convoy system was utilized in the Atlantic, the Mediterranean and the North Sea, and on the Arctic route to the USSR, and eventually growing Allied air and naval superiority was successful (*see* ATLANTIC, BATTLE OF THE).

The War with Japan Japan entered the war in

Dec. 1941 by attacking the US Navy at PEARL
HARBOR in Hawaii, and then occupied Hong Kong,
Thailand, Malaya, Singapore, Indo-China, the
Philippines, the East Indies and many of the Pacific
islands. Although notable victories were won by the
Allies in Burma and in naval and air engagements in
the Pacific, large areas still remained in Japanese
hands until after the dropping of 2 atomic bombs
on Japan (*see* HIROSHIMA and NAGASAKI) which
forced unconditional Japanese surrender (1945).

Y

Yahya Khan, Agha Mohammed (1917–80), Pakistani soldier and statesman. He was commanding general of the Army (1966) and replaced AYUB KHAN as president (1969–71), imposing martial law. He resolved to settle political problems by allowing the first 'one man, one vote' elections in the country (1970–71). Civil war broke out as a result of his refusal to accept the verdict in favour of the Awami League independence movement in East Pakistan (BANGLADESH). India's military intervention on behalf of Bangladeshi independence (1971) led to Pakistan's defeat and Yahya Khan's enforced resignation. He was replaced by BHUTTO.

Yalta Conference (1945), second and more important of the WWII meetings between Churchill, Roosevelt and Stalin (the first was the TEHERAN CONFERENCE).

Principal agreements reached incl. (1) Germany's division into 4 occupation zones and the establishment of an Allied Control Commission in Berlin following the expected Allied victory; (2) Germany's disarmament and obligation to pay REPARATIONS, coupled with the trial and punishment of war criminals; (3) Poland's re-establishment within new frontiers, the E part of the country to be ceded to the USSR along the CURZON LINE, with the W part extended into German territory along the ODER-NEISSE LINE as compensation; (4) the establishment of democratic governments in liberated countries on the basis of free elections; (5) the declaration of war on Japan by the USSR; (6) the establishment of KOREA's independence after a period of American and Soviet occupation; (7) endorsement of the ATLANTIC CHARTER as the basis of Allied postwar policy; (8) and the convening of a conference for the purpose of founding a UNITED NATIONS ORGANIZATION.

Several of these points were restated at the POTSDAM CONFERENCE after the Allied victory in Europe.

Yaoundé Agreements (1963 and 1969), conventions signed in the Cameroons capital between the EEC and former Belgian, Dutch, French and Italian colonies which wanted to continue their association with the EEC after independence.

Provision was made for duty-free entry into the EEC of certain exports from the former colonies, with a similar arrangement for exports from the EEC into most of the countries. A European Development Fund was also established to assist the associated countries.

Following the enlargement of the EEC (1973), former British colonies entered the Agreements, which were superseded by the LOMÉ CONVENTION in 1975.

Yom Kippur War, *see* ARAB-ISRAELI WARS.

Young Plan (1929), scheme for the settlement of Germany's WWI REPARATIONS proposed by a committee chaired by a US businessman, Owen D. Young (1874–1962).

It superseded the DAWES PLAN and reduced

Germany's payments by some 75%, the remaining debt to be redeemed in the form of annuities to an international bank until 1988. It terminated foreign control over Germany's finances; returned Germany's securities which had been held by the Allies; transferred responsibility for converting reparations payments into foreign currencies from the Allies to Germany; abolished the Reparations Commission; and ended Allied rights to apply sanctions should payments be in default.

After 1935 Hitler blocked further payments which had been suspended for 3 years in 1932 owing to the DEPRESSION. The Plan was, therefore, of little value since only one payment was made under its terms.

Young Turks, Turkish reform movement (1903—09) in the Ottoman Empire instrumental in masterminding a rebellion by liberal army officers in Salonika (1908), followed by the founding of a Committee of Union and Progress in Constantinople (now Istanbul).

The revolt was in support of a demand for the restoration of the 1876 Constitution, and the Committee was headed by 3 officers who had been urging the country's modernization for several years. A parliament was summoned, the Constitution restored, Sultan Abdul Hamid deposed, and a policy of radical reform of government and society was instituted. The movement broke up because of internal disagreements.

Ypres, Battles of, 4 conflicts of WWI centred around the Belgian town of Ypres, which was completely destroyed but never captured by the ...ns. The first battle (1914), resulted in the

Germans capturing the Messines Ridge. The
second battle (1915) was the first occasion when
gas was used in warfare. The third battle (1917)
involved a combined Australian, British and
Canadian offensive against the Messines Ridge and
the village of Passchendaele. The fourth battle
(1918), also known as the Battle of the River Lys,
occurred when the Germans attempted to encircle
Ypres. In total the Germans suffered some quarter
of a million casualties while the Allied losses
amounted to about twice that figure.

Yugoslavia, socialist federal republic of SE
Europe. Area: 255,804 sq km. Pop: 22,420,000
(est. 1981). Languages: Macedonian, Serbo-Croat
and Slovene. Religions: Orthodox, RC and Islam.
Cap: Belgrade.

The federated states of the Republic are BOSNIA and
Herzegovina, Croatia, Macedonia, MONTENEGRO
(Serbo-Croat, *Crna Gora*), SERBIA, and Slovenia;
there are also 2 autonomous provinces — KOSOVO
and Vojvodina.

The kingdom of Yugoslavia was established
(1918) under the terms of the Corfu Pact (1917),
concluded by leaders of Serbia and South Slav
(Yugoslav) refugees from Austria-Hungary. The
diversity of religious beliefs embodied in the various
republics caused considerable political difficulties
in the unification of the new state, reaching a climax
with the assassination of a Croat agrarian leader,
Stefan Radić, in the Constitutional Assembly
(1928). This resulted in King Alexander (1888–
1934) repealing the Constitution and assuming
dictatorial powers (1929). Alexander was a Serb
and his actions aggravated the divisions withi

the country. Croats and Slovenes in particular alleged that the state was too Serbian-orientated, and in 1934 Alexander was assassinated by Croatian extremists.

Alexander was succeeded by his son, Peter II, but as he was a minor, Alexander's cousin, Prince Paul (1896—1976) acted as Regent until 1941 when he was dismissed in a military coup for being too subservient to German and Italian influence. Ten days later Germany invaded Yugoslavia, and King and government went into exile in the UK. Resistance movements fought on and eventually TITO and his followers deposed the King (1944) and established the Republic (1945).

Under Tito, Yugoslavia became a leader of the non-aligned nations. Although a Communist state, it has followed an independent course from that approved by the USSR and its allies, having broken with them in 1948. It condemned the invasions of HUNGARY and CZECHOSLOVAKIA and is not a member of the COMINFORM, COMECON or WARSAW PACT. Foreign investment is encouraged, the tourist industry is being expanded, land reforms without collectivization have occurred, and industrial development covers a wide range of manufacturing processes.

Z

Zhivkov, Todor (1911–), Bulgarian Communist politician. He joined the Party in 1932, and became a partisan resistance leader during WWII. After the Communists seized power (1944) he advanced steadily in the Party's hierarchy, becoming First Secretary in 1954. Following a succession of purges he emerged in a position of dominance (1962) when he became PM, an office he exchanged for the new one of Chairman of the State Council (1971) while retaining the First Secretaryship.

Zhou Enlai or **Chou En-lai** (1898–1976), Chinese Communist statesman. He was a founder member of the French Communist Party when he lived in Paris (1920–24). On returning to China he organized revolts against the war lords in Shanghai, Nanjing and Canton, spent 2 years in the USSR, and then became Mao Zedong's urban revolutionary affairs adviser. During WWII he was the Communists' liaison officer in the capital, Chongqing. He was PM (1949–76) from the time of the Republic's establishment, also holding the office of Foreign Minister until 1958. Pragmatic and urbane, he became the best known of China's leaders on the international scene, travelling widely on diplomatic missions, and as leader of DÉTENTE with the USA (1972–73).

Zhukov, Georgi (1896–1976), Soviet marshal and politician. The outstanding commander of

WWII, he was prominent in the siege of LENINGRAD, the defence of Moscow (1941), the victory at STALINGRAD (1943), the capture of Berlin (1945). He was Minister of Defence (1955—57). Shortly after achieving membership of the Presidium (1957) he was dismissed from government and party posts on the grounds of encouraging his own personality cult, and of undermining the Party's position within the armed forces.

Zia ul-Haq, Mohammad (1924—   ), Pakistani general and politician. After WWII he rose rapidly through the ranks to become Chief of Staff (1976). He led the coup deposing BHUTTO (1977) and succeeded him as President (1978). Martial law was in force and political parties banned (1977—78). Partial democracy was restored after a general election in 1985, but the country remains under Zia's military-backed rule. He has introduced certain elements of Islamic fundamentalism while relying on the USA for defensive requirements and the West in general for economic and financial support.

Zimbabwe, Commonwealth republic of SC Africa. Area: 390,308 sq km. Pop: 7,539,000 (est. 1982). Official language: English. Religions: animist, Christian. Cap: Harare (formerly Salisbury).

Administered by the British South Africa Company from 1893, the country became the British colony of Southern Rhodesia in 1923, and part of the Federation of RHODESIA AND ᴚASALAND (1953—63). In 1965 the Rhodesian government of PM Ian SMITH sought to ᴚhe continuation of white minority rule by making a unilateral declaration of independence (UDI) from the UK, which wished to forestall independence until black majority rule was achieved. Talks with Britain broke down, the UN applied SANCTIONS, and in 1970 Rhodesia was declared a republic.

Rhodesia's international isolation, combined with increasing guerrilla activities by the African liberation movements of MUGABE and NKOMO, forced Smith to form a joint black and white government in 1978, with Bishop Abel Muzorewa (1925–   ) becoming PM in 1979. Meanwhile, the guerrilla war continued and in 1979 talks in London led to independence and the establishment of black majority rule in 1980. The Zimbabwe African National Union (ZANU) won the ensuing election, and Mugabe became PM.

Zimmermann Telegram (1917), coded message from the German Foreign Minister, Arthur Zimmermann (1864–1940), to the German minister in Mexico. It was intercepted by British naval intelligence which disclosed its contents to the US Government.

The message's import was that if the USA declared war on Germany, Mexico should attack the USA with German and Japanese assistance in return for the American states of Arizona, New Mexico and Texas. Japan had entered WWI on the Allied side in 1914, and Germany was seeking (unsuccessfully) to induce it to change sides.

In the event neither Japan nor Mexico collaborated with Germany, but the outrage aroused by the telegram in the USA played a major part in the country's decision 3 months later to enter WWI.

Zinoviev Letter (1924), communication which was allegedly responsible for the Labour Party's defeat in the 1924 UK general election.

The letter purported to be from the Chairman of the COMINTERN, Grigori Zinoviev (1883–1936). It was addressed to the British Communist Party and called for an insurrection against capitalism and the spreading of seditious propaganda among the armed services. The letter was published by the *Daily Mail* 4 days before the election, together with a Foreign Office protest to the USSR.

Proof of the letter's authenticity was never established and many believe it was forged in Berlin by White Russians, as many such documents were being circulated by émigré organizationis at the time. The Labour Party considered that many marginal voters swung to the Conservatives because they had been led to believe, quite erroneously, that the Communist and Labour Parties held similar views to those expressed in the letter.

Zionism, a political movement (founded 1897) for the establishment and maintenance of a national homeland for Jews in what was PALESTINE, and now concerned with the development and prosperity of ISRAEL.